RAISED IN RUINS

A Memoir

TARA NEILSON

ALASKA
NORTHWEST
BOOKS®

Library of Congress Cataloging-in-Publication Data

Names: Neilson, Tara, author.
Title: Raised in ruins: a memoir / Tara Neilson.
Description: Berkeley, CA: West Margin Press, [2020] | Summary: "A personal memoir of Tara Neilson's unconventional childhood growing up in the burnt remains of an old cannery in remote Southeast Alaska"—Provided by publisher.
Identifiers: LCCN 2019047777 (print) | LCCN 2019047778 (ebook) | ISBN 9781513262635 (paperback) | ISBN 9781513262864 (hardback) | ISBN 9781513262871 (ebook)
Subjects: LCSH: Neilson, Tara—Childhood and youth. | Frontier and pioneer life—Alaska, Southeast. | Union Bay Cannery. | Houseboats—Alaska, Southeast. | Alaska, Southeast—Biography.
Classification: LCC F910.7.N45 A3 2020 (print) | LCC F910.7.N45 (ebook) | DDC 979/3.8—dc23
LC record available at https://lccn.loc.gov/2019047777
LC ebook record available at https://lccn.loc.gov/2019047778

Published by Alaska Northwest Books®
an imprint of

WEST
MARGIN
PRESS

WestMarginPress.com

WEST MARGIN PRESS
Publishing Director: Jennifer Newens
Marketing Manager: Angela Zbornik
Editor: Olivia Ngai
Design & Production: Rachel Lopez Metzger

For the Neilsons of Cannery Creek:
Gary, Romi, Jamie, Tara, Megan, Robin, and Chris.
And the cannery workers who went before us.

INTRODUCTION

ONE DAY when it was just my mom and us kids alone in the New House we'd built in the wilderness with our own labor, with lumber our dad milled himself, a huge brown bear paced back and forth in front of the wall of floor-to-ceiling windows in our game room where we spent most of our time.

Back and forth, back and forth, it paced agitatedly, disturbed by our presence next to the salmon-choked creek. Our mom was terrified of guns, but she got down the .22-250, which she probably couldn't have shot if she tried, and told us kids to go upstairs. We ignored her.

We figured if the bear broke in we'd all scatter and the bear might get one or two of us, but he wouldn't get us all. Our tension escalated as the huge mound of fur, teeth, and claws continued its angry pacing. Finally he rounded the house, going around the kitchen to the front where our temporary door was made of thin pieces of wood and plastic. If it just sneezed, the bear could break through it.

We followed it from room to room, our hearts beating uncomfortably hard. Finally, we saw it head down to the creek. With the gun in hand, Mom stepped outside to make sure it kept going. She told us to stay inside, but, again, we ignored her.

Suddenly my youngest brother, Chris, took off after the bear.

"What are you doing? Get back here!" Mom whisper-yelled,

afraid of alerting the bear. She gripped the gun helplessly. "Christopher Michael! Get back here, right now!"

Chris kept running, gaining on the bear.

The rest of kids stared after him, shocked. When no one moved, I sprinted after him. In front of us the huge bear lumbered toward the shining creek filled with salmon fins and sea gulls. This is crazy, this is crazy, I thought as I ran toward the bear.

I collared Chris, and dragged him back. He fought me every inch of the way. I cast glances over my shoulder, sure the bear would come after us and shred us to pieces in front of our family. The bear turned at the noise and raised itself onto its hind legs, sniffing the air and peering at us.

Fortunately, we all escaped a mauling that day.

• • •

There are many, many more stories like this that I couldn't include in this memoir due to lack of space. I had to leave out almost all of our adventures we had with the kids in the village of Meyers Chuck, and at the all-grades bush school we attended there for several years. (Note: some of the names have been changed of the people I do write about.)

I wish I could have spent more time on one of my favorite people in the entire world, my Grandma Pat who lived in the village, a woman who had lived a life of constant adventure, who had a wonderful sense of the absurd and chuckled when we dubbed her "Grambo." I wish I could tell you more about my Uncle Rory and Aunt Marion, who were an influential, wonderful part of my childhood. Or Steve and Cassie Peavey, Alaskans to their core, and owners of the floathouse before my grandparents had it and sold it to us. There are so many important and beloved family members and friends I couldn't include.

The only way I could let those essential people and stories go was to promise myself I'd write a second book, which I hope to do.

• • •

To this day I don't know why Chris ran after the bear. I haven't had a chance to ask him. I think I've worn out my family asking them to comment on cannery experiences for this memoir. You will find that family members sometimes comment in the present tense in these pages, because our experiences in the ruins imprinted so deeply on us that they are still a part of our present and continue to shape who we are.

The past felt just a step away for us as my brothers and sister and I played on the scorched, rusting remains of machinery that had operated in a different era, a different world. The former workers always seemed to be present in a benign, welcoming way that made me want to cross over between my time and theirs so I could get to know them.

Because the past and present were melded together it was easy for me to include the future as well, and acknowledge the moment-by-moment passage of time that created my personal experience of life and shaped my personality.

Ever since I was young I have visualized my personal time as flowing from the future to my Moving Now, like the snow-fed headwaters of cannery creek rushing down to meet me as I played in it and as the salmon, according to their own inexorable sense of time, swam beside me, pointed toward their ancient spawning beds.

Whatever the current brought I needed to decide how to react to it, and when I did there were consequences that became my present and then my past, creating who I was and who I would become.

When friend and author Bjorn Dihle suggested I write a memoir, I hesitated. I didn't think I could capture what it felt like to grow up in the ruins, what it had been like to experience and be shaped by the mystery and richness of Time. But I decided to attempt it.

I soon realized that I couldn't write my memoir in the linear, chronological way most of the memoirs I'd read were written, so I decided that I'd show as well as tell my personal experience of time. This meant structuring it in a way that might be alien to others who were shaped by an urban view of time, but felt organic to me.

It has given me a sense of closure, because at the age of seventeen I went to live for a year in the world and was shocked and alienated by how time was viewed and used in the city. Writing this memoir and reading theoretical physicist Lee Smolin's 2006 book *The Trouble with Physics* has helped me to reconcile and understand my reaction.

Smolin wrote that one of the fundamental problems with physics today that was preventing forward progress to be made was scientists' understanding of time. He traced the problem back to the beginning of the seventeenth century when Descartes and Galileo graphed space and time, making time a single dimension of space. Essentially spatializing time, stopping its motion and freezing its elusiveness, so that scientists could to some extent comfortably regulate and measure it like they did space.

But when time is spatialized, it becomes static and unchanging. This, of course, doesn't reflect our lived experience of ever-changing, ever-flowing time. Smolin called this "the scene of the crime." He believed it was imperative that science find a way to unfreeze time.

Straight out of the ruins, during my year in the city, I saw the spatialization of time firsthand, the frozen quality that Smolin would later point to as a crime. Clocks were everywhere: in school, the library, restaurants, and stores. Time was expected to behave itself so that people could use it to schedule and organize every moment of their lives. With chaotic elements frequently dominating every other aspect of their lives, they wanted no part of time that wasn't straightjacketed and fixed in place.

I felt smothered and took long walks into whatever part of the wilderness the town hadn't covered with asphalt, trying to coax the real, wild and unrestricted time out of wherever it was hiding. Later I would return to the wilderness and embrace time in all of its fullness with a sense of relief.

I realize that the way this book is written might feel jarring at times, and uncomfortable for readers who expect a memoir to be linear rather than having the future making unexpected appearances to comment on the present action of the past.

I do apologize. I know how hard it was for me to accept the way most people have lived time: neatly ordered and well behaved, trained to subjugate itself to society's needs in order to make stressed people feel comfortable and in control.

But in an era that celebrates diversity and encourages all of us to expand and free ourselves from our frozen biases, maybe it's time to unfreeze society's interpretation of Time and allow it to be all that it can be.

Please come with me on a temporal adventure as I show you what it was like to be raised in ruins.

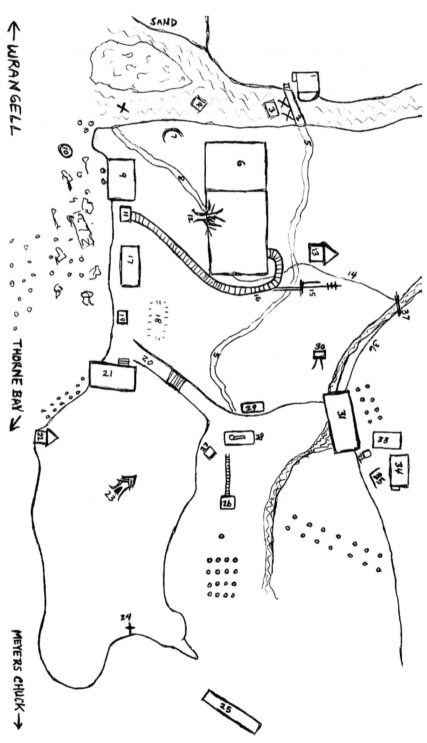

MAP OF UNION BAY

1. Small red cannery cabin
2. Bridge
3. Concrete block in creek
4. Concrete block in creek
5. Trail connecting floathouse side to red cabin
6. New House
7. Japanese garden
8. Path to beach from New House
9. Workshop
10. Cannery retort door
11. Generator shed
12. Duke the alder tree
13. Huge cannery fuel drum
14. Waterline to New House
15. Antenna platform
16. Boardwalk
17. Woodshed
18. Remains of cannery cookshack
19. Sauna
20. Sawdust trail
21. Foundation of a burned building with steps
22. Huge cannery fuel drum
23. Fire tree
24. Gravemarker
25. Dock
26. Wanigan
27. Core shack
28. Sawmill deck
29. Garden
30. Jamie's fort on a stump
31. Floathouse
32. Generator shed
33. Garden
34. School
35. Swing set
36. Waterline to floathouse
37. Dam

The small circles are cannery pilings. The wavy lines are the creek and stream. The scribbles on the New House side are the rusted and scorched cannery machinery. The X at the mouth of the creek is where the photo for the cover of *Raised in Ruins* was taken.

"It's not the end of the world, but you can see it from here."
—slogan on T-shirts sold at the Meyers Chuck store

CHAPTER ONE

EVERY DAY as a child was an adventure for me and my four siblings as we lived in the burned ruins of a remote Alaskan cannery. Some days had more adventure in them than others. Mail day was a day that promised parent-free adventure.

Our mail arrived at a nearby fishing village by floatplane once a week, weather permitting. We lived only seven miles of water away from the village—there were no roads, or trails—but the route was hazardous, even deadly, because of the mercurial nature of our weather. What had been glassy water an hour before as we made the trip in a thirteen-foot open Boston Whaler could turn into a maelstrom of seething white water an hour later to catch us on the return trip.

Tides, weather forecasts, and local signs had to be carefully calculated before the trip could be made. So it sometimes happened that we would miss several mail days in a row and get three weeks' worth of mail at once. My parents usually made the trip by themselves, since freight and groceries would fill the skiff, leaving us kids behind in our floathouse home.

Our sense of adventure, always present since our family comprised the entire population of humans for miles in any direction, quadrupled as we waved goodbye to them. We watched them turn into a speck out on the broad bay with the mountain ranges of vast Prince of Wales Island providing a breathtaking backdrop for them.

Then we cut loose. We ran around the beaches, jumping into piles of salt-sticky seaweed and yelling at the top of our lungs, the dogs chasing us and barking joyously. We tended to do this every day, but it was different on mail days. We lived in an untamed wilderness that could kill full-grown adults in a multitude of ways, and we children had it all to ourselves.

At our backs was the mysterious forest that climbed to a 3,000-foot-high mountain that looked like a man lying on his back staring up at the sky. We called it "The Old Man." In front of us was the expanse of unpredictable water with no traffic on it, except for the humpback whales, sea lions, and water fowl.

As we scattered, my littlest brother, Chris, wound up with me in our twelve-foot aluminum rowing skiff. I was twelve and he was seven, and we were buckled up in our protective bright-orange lifejackets that we never went anywhere without.

"Where shall we go, Sir Christopher?" I donned a faux British voice as I sat in the middle seat with an oar on either side of me. "Your wish is my command."

He sat in the stern seat and chortled. Whereas I was blonde and blue eyed, he had almost black hair and green-flecked brown eyes. Despite the surface differences, we had a lot in common, being the most accommodating and easygoing ones in our family. Chris was always smiling and I was always reading. We usually let others take the lead, but this time we would make our own adventure.

"I don't know," he said. "Where do you want to go?"

I looked around. The floathouse sat above a small stream below the forest, its float logs that made up its raft dry, since the tide was halfway out. Opposite it was a smaller floathouse that we used to go to school in, before our dad built a school for us on land.

The small, sheltered cove suddenly felt restrictive since it was the only part of the old cannery we saw on a regular basis, and there wasn't much of the old cannery to see, just some pilings sticking half out of the water.

"Let's go to the ruins," I said.

He gazed at me raptly. The main cannery site had been built next to the large salmon creek and sat on the other side of a high-ridged peninsula from the little bay our floathouse was in. We rarely got to visit it because the salmon creek was where the bears roamed. But we would be safe in the skiff, I told him.

Chris bounced on his seat and nodded excitedly.

I dug the oars into the silky green water and we headed for the big rock that partially protected our little cove from the storm-prone bay. Mom had made it a law that we were never to get out of sight of the floathouse, but Mom wasn't there.

I dipped the oars into unexplored waters, rowing past the weathered grave marker of some unknown cannery resident. Tall black bluffs loomed up at the same time a swell rocked us. There was nowhere to beach the skiff now, if we needed to... we were committed to continue.

Chris gripped the aluminum seat and stared at me, silently asking if we were really going to do this. I nodded.

Each pull of the oars took us farther away from the homey familiarity of the floathouse and its confined bay. We were exposed to the full effect of the wilderness now, the enormous sky above, impermeable, towering bluffs washed by waves to our left, and the endless waterways of Southeast Alaska on our right.

My back was to the view ahead of us as I rowed. I was getting tired, but I didn't want to admit it to my little brother.

Chris sat up straight on his seat and pointed. "Look!"

I turned my head. Up on the rocky bluffs ahead of us was a huge steel cylinder with a peaked roof. Its original, unpainted gray could be seen through the rust of untended decades. It had sat sentinel there, below the tall mountain, with few humans visiting it or seeing it since the cannery burned shortly after World War II.

Awed, we stared at it, and then I turned to the oars with renewed energy. I kept throwing glances over my shoulder. I didn't want to miss the first glimpse of the ruins.

And then there it was, the old cannery site.

A forest of fire-scorched pilings, one with a stunted tree growing on it, stood between the forest and the bay. The blackened timbers of a building's foundations remained below the evergreens' skirts and giant concrete blocks stood out whitely above the rust-colored beach. Amidst the pilings were strange, rusty skeletons of former machinery. The creek rumbled past all of it.

The ruins.

"It looks like it was bombed," Chris said. "Like an atom bomb was dropped on it!"

"It does." I tried to picture what it would have looked like when it was whole and people lived and worked at this remote location. The buildings, like all the canneries in Alaska, would have been cannery red (the color of chili peppers) with white trim, glowing in the water-reflected light. The sound of machinery would have competed with the constant rumble of the creek and men and boats would have been working above and around the pilings of the wharf as clouds of shrieking gulls filled the air.

"If we could time travel," I said, "we could step into their world when the cannery first operated and watch the fish being packed into cases to be sent out into a world that didn't know atom bombs could exist."

I didn't try to row us closer and Chris didn't suggest getting out on shore. We could see big, dark moving things in the creek that we knew were bears. I didn't want to draw their attention because, although I didn't mention it to Chris, I knew they were powerful swimmers and could probably overtake us if they'd wanted to.

We sat in the small skiff with the water lapping against the aluminum sides, rocking in the swell, and gazed at the ruins of a former world, gone long before we were born.

Then I turned the skiff around and we headed for home, promising each other we wouldn't tell anyone about this adventure. This one was just ours.

• • •

MEYERS CHUCK, ALASKA
35 MILES NORTH OF KETCHIKAN
SPRING 1980

We were supposed to be a group of intrepid families braving the apocalypse. Our unified mission: to homestead the ruins of a bygone civilization and resurrect and transform them into an off-the-grid, self-reliant wilderness community.

The adults spent long kerosene-lamp-lit hours poring over the maps, studying the remains of the old cannery that had burned nearly half a century ago. None of them had seen it in person, but they marked out where each home would go, the supplies they'd need, the school they'd build. They figured out how they would barge fuel in, what kind of generators they'd need for electricity, if they could arrange a mail drop way out there in the wilderness far away from all human industry.

When I overheard the talk, I felt like I was overhearing plans for moving aboard a generational starship that was going to explore and colonize deep space.

My family of seven in our tiny thirteen-foot Boston Whaler skiff, overpowered by a fifty-horsepower Mercury outboard motor, went alone on the reconnaissance expedition. Together, we would be the first ones to scout the old cannery.

We whipped past the green forest that seemed to stretch from here to the moon as it climbed a ridge on one side. Across the glassy strait was a vast island covered in snow-capped mountain ranges, headland after headland disappearing into a pearly blue distance.

That was Prince of Wales Island where Dad worked as a logger at the largest logging operation in the world. There were enormous bald patches in the dense green hillsides, giving the island a mangy appearance at odds with the pristine, breathtaking beauty of sea, sky, and the unmolested mainland we skimmed along beside.

Our uncovered skiff, about the length of a Volkswagen Beetle, was a speck.

The world was big; I knew that from school lessons. But the wilderness was bigger. There was no end to it. We were the only humans in it as we sped across the gigantic white-cloud reflections. Ahead of us, a mountain lay on its back, a giant Easter Island head with its stern nose pointed toward the sky, toward space, toward the orbiting planets around the sun, and beyond.

And my family was heading toward it and the slumbering ruins that it had shadowed for decades.

I turned my face into the wind, my hair whipping into a knotted mess around my head as I leaned forward. The bearded man with his hand on the tiller handle of the outboard had decided he was going to go to the ruins, and I knew nothing, not even all this wilderness, was going to stop him.

This was, after all, a man who had stopped the Vietnam War. For an entire day.

He told me years later that when he'd just turned twenty-one, married one month, he had arrived in Vietnam during Phase 1 of the Tet Offensive. In the span of twenty-four hours he saw a bustling metropolis, the Asian people living in it as they had for generations, become a bomb-blasted landscape of skeletal buildings and streets filled with smoking rubble.

After seeing the effects of war close-up, one of the first things he did was to build himself and his fellow grunts a sturdy shelter—a bombproof igloo, so to speak—out of cast-off rocket ammo boxes that he directed his companions to fill with sand for the walls. For the roof he used PSP (perforated steel plating) with more sand-filled rocket ammo boxes on top.

No one had thought of building such a thing, even with screaming missiles and mortars constantly overhead. Everyone else sweltered in flimsy tents or buildings with uninsulated steel roofs that acted like ovens. His igloo was the only comfortable building in the muggy jungle heat. He and his friends had it for three months before the officers evicted them and took it over for themselves.

Dad was a helicopter mechanic (the sole mechanic available for the Huey; a group of mechanics serviced the other helicopters) and it was his job to say which helicopters were fit for duty on any given day. Every day some helicopters didn't come back—and friends and companions disappeared or were brought back bleeding, maimed, or dead. One day one of his best friends was killed.

The next morning he put an X on every single Huey, grounding them all. Without the support of the Hueys none of the other helicopters could fly, and without air support the ground war couldn't progress. That day he wasn't going to allow anyone else to die in an ugly war no one really believed in or knew what they were fighting and dying for.

His commanding officer said to him, "You know you can't do that, Gary. You have to take those Xs off."

Dad just looked at him. The Xs stayed. There was no war that day.

Across from him in the back of the skiff, hugging her youngest child, Mom couldn't believe she was there, that she was living her childhood dream of Alaska as few people had ever gotten to experience it.

Despite her obsession with fashion, music, the arts, and her dream to become a Parisian club singer, she had always felt a fey-like affinity for wild creation and the animals in it. As a teenager she'd gone for day-long walks in the rural Montana countryside with her Belgian Shepherd named Gretchen, spinning dreams out of the Big Sky sunshine.

In her own words:

"We lived on a ranch high in the hills. I would get up early, have breakfast, feed Gretchen and the horses, then I would sit my record player on an old wooden chair on the porch, put my Bob Dylan album on at 'Like a Rolling Stone,' and Gretch and I would go, hearing the music all down the old dirt road."

Her most thrilling moment in her dawn-to-dusk rambles with Gretchen was when the deer came over the mountain.

"It was a large group of deer—until that moment I hadn't realized that they would all travel together like that. Bucks, does, and babies. They all came straight to where Gretchen and I stood, quivering. I stretched out my arms to them and they walked quietly on both sides of me. Not as if I wasn't there, but as if they understood that I belonged to, and with, them.

"I stood there with my arms outstretched for quite a while as the herd passed on either side, my hands on their backs as they went by, one by one, my hands sliding along backs and haunches. Bucks, does, fawns.

"They felt like… 'alive' feels. The only alive I wanted to be. I never wanted anything so much as to turn and go with them…"

And now here she was an adult, with her husband, a man she barely knew after Vietnam—they'd married one month before he went, and the man who came back was not the funny, laughing man she'd married—and five children, heading into the heart of the most remote country she'd ever seen, setting out on an adventure to rival any adventure or experience she'd ever had or read about. She was so excited she was shivering.

· · ·

How was I to know at nine years old that this journey, toward the Old Man mountain staring up at eternity, was to become one of the favorite things of my entire life? I never imagined on our scouting trip how many times I would make it, with my family or alone.

In the skiff, the loudness of the outboard and the wind whipping at our faces made it hard to hold a conversation, so each of us retreated into our own private worlds. On every skiff ride to the cannery, I'd sink down turtlelike into the canvas-over-foam shell of my lifejacket for its comforting, tight embrace, and chew on its black plastic piping, salty from seawater. From this haven I'd look around at the dreaming faces, at the interior eyes, and I'd wonder what each person in my family was thinking as we rode silently through time, from one world point to the next.

We would always start in a place of daily bustle, of talk, of goals and intentions. Then we'd climb into the skiff, and within minutes we were in our own solitary time-out bubbles surrounded by the steady engine noise and the sky and water, suspended from human interaction until we reached the other world point where goals and talk and intentions continued. We might as well have stepped onto a transporter pad and had our constituent parts disassembled and

Jamie and I in the front of our Boston Whaler on the very first trip to the ruins.

then reassembled on the other side of the skiff ride.

Besides my parents, on this particular skiff ride there were "the babies" as we still called them, my two little brothers, sardonic Robin (five) and smiling, generous Christopher (four)—or Mitmer-the-Usurper, as Robin thought of him. Chris had displaced him as the baby of the family and the natural center of attention and affection. ("Mitmer" was Robin's pronunciation of Christopher and soon the whole family used it.) Robin, clever and stubborn, never let anyone forget the wound of this usurpation and the babies spent all their time butting heads, wrestling, and punching.

Then there was Megan (eight), my sister, best friend, and closest companion in age. People thought we were twins since we rarely did anything apart and we were both fair haired with blue eyes. Megan was artistic and sensitive, so softhearted that one time when she stepped on a slug on the narrow gravel trail as we were on our way to school in Meyers Chuck, she had to turn back. Though we were almost to school, she retraced her steps and put the slimy, squished bug out of its misery, all the while sobbing bitter tears.

Her polar opposite was Jamie (eleven), the oldest, who had been born when Dad was away in Vietnam, who had in infanthood considered himself the man of the family and had never known how to stand down from that patriarchal position after the real man of the family returned. Jamie had coopted all of Mom's time, attention, and affection from birth and wasn't shy about letting the Intruder—who Mom called "Gary"—know who ran the show.

When Dad would take his wife and small son to dinner at a friend's, Jamie would decide when it was time to call it a night. He'd put on his outdoor clothes and plant himself in front of Dad and announce, "I'm weddy, Gowwy." If Gary should, inconceivably, ignore him, Jamie would make himself more visible and raise his voice: "I said I'm weddy, Gowwy."

This assumption of authority in his small son didn't go over well with a man who was struggling with PTSD, the demands of a ready-made family, the cold callousness of some of those close to him who made it clear they had no use for Vietnam vets, and the requirements of holding down a job and providing for his family.

Whether it was caused by Dad's antipathy or not, Jamie developed an interest in torturing those around him and then studying their reactions. Once, as a preschooler, he rigged a hallway with fishing line and watched as Mom became entangled and struggled like a fly caught in a web. Another time an older kid came over to play with Jamie when he was two. Moments after Mom left them together, she heard the neighbor kid yelling that he wanted to go home. When she went to check to see what was happening, the boy was rattling the kid gate, demanding to be freed. He couldn't explain what had happened and Jamie just stood in a corner, smiling.

It was a smile we all learned to dread.

And me? Some of my earliest memories, when I was three or four years old, are of getting up every night to pad to my parents' bedroom door. I would step inside and listen to them breathing. I remember the need to do that, to make sure they were both okay. One of them because he was broken, and the other because she was unknowing.

I couldn't bear for anyone to feel diminished and humiliated, to experience loss, for anyone to suffer. Mom tells me that when I was two or three she read me a story about a baby horse that overcame becoming an orphan to live a happy life. At the end I was sobbing. She was bemused. "What's wrong, honey? It's a happy story—see the little horse grew up to be strong and happy!"

"But the mama horse is still dead," I sobbed.

Now, at nine years old, I was the family observer, the mediator, and the chronicler of all of our adventures.

• • •

The Union Bay cannery operated at the mouth of Cannery Creek on the eastern shore of Union Bay, which is located on the east side of Lemesurier Point at the southern entrance to Ernest Sound. It existed about halfway between the cities of Wrangell to the north and Ketchikan to the south, and was unable to be reached by land, only by water and air.

Local fishermen sold their catch to the cannery, which then sold in bulk to Japan. In the 1920s there was a saltery for mild-cured king salmon and later a herring reduction plant and floating clam cannery that operated seven miles away by water in Meyers Chuck, on the west side of Lemesurier Point. In pre-WWII years, Meyers Chuck's over one hundred residents supported a post office, store, machine shop, barber shop, bakery, and bar.

Both the cannery site in Union Bay and the fishing village of Meyers Chuck are on Cleveland Peninsula, which is a part of the mainland. The Coast Mountains, with all their glaciers and snowy ramparts, separate the peninsula from Canada.

Their location on the mainland is unusual. Most communities in Southeast Alaska are on islands. The Cleveland Peninsula terminates at Lemesurier Point, which juts into Clarence Strait, a feared branch of the Inside Passage, and stands across from Prince of Wales Island where one of the few road systems in Alaska's Panhandle connect a variety of small towns.

The cannery had been built in this isolated place in 1916 by Union Bay Fisheries Co., going through two other owners before it was sold to the Nakat Packing Co., which was owned by the son of the Norwegian founder of the city of Petersburg and a partner. They owned it until it burned in 1947.

Burned canneries were not an uncommon sight in Southeast Alaska. Between 1878 and 1949, 134 canneries were built. Sixty-five burned and were never rebuilt. Ours was one of them. The few photos Mom has of our first day at Cannery Creek are gilded with sunshine. We're in our lifejackets, discovering the miracle of that rarest of all rare embellishments in rocky Southeast Alaska—a true sand beach.

Above it are the usual seaweed and barnacle-covered rocks. In the photos Dad is behind us kids as we explore; he's pushing the skiff off and anchoring it in the current of the creek so that it won't go dry as the tide recedes.

Jamie's dog Moby is out of the frame: he's already taken off, nails clicking and scratching over the rocks, to do his scouting ahead of us. Jamie is watching over the two little ones while my sister and I stand together out in front. The bay stretches out behind us kids and Dad to a shimmering, hazy horizon, as if we've stepped through a curtain into another dimension, into a different experience of time.

The ruins of the cannery were on the other side of the creek from us. Dad had decided against landing the skiff there since fallen machinery littered the entire beach and could extend for some distance underwater. He didn't want to foul the outboard's propeller, leaving us stranded.

Once Dad secured the skiff, he led our family up the sandy beach and into the rocks.

The limitless forest of cedar, spruce, and hemlock lined the creek. Evergreen scents sharpened the air over the sun-warmed beach grass. The amber-colored creek, pierced with sunshine, tumbled over the stones and boulders, rushing past the rocky bank we stood on. Up a ways, on this side of the creek, a small cabin dappled by the shadows of alders was the sole building left standing. Its faded red paint was the color of Southeast Alaska's historical canneries.

Opposite us, on the other side of the creek, we could see the ruins of the cannery proper, with its broken and blackened pilings and giant, rusting fuel drum on a point of rocks. Great chunks of weathered concrete stood in the creek between us and the ruins. They stood against the flow, refusing to crumble to the double-barreled forces of time and water. They had probably once supported

Megan and I in the front, Jamie and the boys behind us with Dad anchoring
the skiff in the creek's current as we first set foot on the old cannery site.

and anchored a bridge.

When we got to the edge of the rushing creek, Mom and Dad
carried the younger boys from stone to stone in the shadow of these
concrete monoliths of a long-gone world, telling us older kids to
be careful as we followed. Moby, a Sheltie with a touch of Cocker
Spaniel, ran ahead, pausing and looking back with a panting grin
from every dry perch.

I wonder now at our lack of fear as we tackled that abandoned
place, where the bears, both black and brown, had reigned unopposed
for decades; where there was no hope of help, no one to hear us or
come to our aid if we were harmed.

Instead, we pushed forward, all of us, eager for this exploration.
And the ruins? They'd been there a long time... waiting.

This had once been a community, as many as a hundred men
and women living here cut off from the world, telling their stories,
thinking their thoughts, dreaming about their futures. They played
cards, drank, danced, sang, and worked and worked and worked as

the cannery rumbled, with fishing boats and freight boats coming and going. And in the background the unending thud of the pile driver pounding in pilings for piers and fish trap.

This was a place that had known people, that had made room for them. But after the fire, after the scars and disfigurements, the people had left. For many silent years this place was visited infrequently by fishermen and by locals who came to scavenge—who sawed off what was still good of the burned pilings that had once upheld the wharf and cannery and towed them away to use as foundations under their village homes.

The Forest Service had also been there shortly before us. They'd been surveying the area for a possible logging project. They'd built a sauna beside the foundation beams of a building that no longer existed, and laid down boards to perch their pre-fab temporary shelters on. But in the end, they left too, taking the pre-fab buildings with them but leaving the sauna and the planks behind.

US Steel, the company that had bought the property after the cannery burned, had checked for profitable ore and, finding the extraction and transportation expenses cost prohibitive, abandoned the venture. They left behind a rock pile and stacks of core sample holders in a core shack, and up on the mountain concrete pads, cable, and other debris.

The ruins had watched and waited for life to return, for people to return for real. I felt that as we wandered through the scorched and blackened remains. I felt that we were being welcomed and encouraged to stay, that the ruins wanted us there.

We accepted the invitation and made ourselves at home. We kids could not be dissuaded from stripping down and swimming in the creek, though it was so icy it burned, fed by mountain snows. Our shrieks and laughter floated out over the twisted, rusting metal on the beach, over the solid concrete blocks barren of their former buildings, over the cannery's retort door, its giant rusty circle half-buried in beach gravel.

When I left the water behind, shivering, teeth chattering, it was to find Mom standing in the ruins beside the creek. All around her were stark foundation pilings and rusty steel frame beds, twisted into agonized shapes from the intense heat.

The forest had taken over everything, underbrush and strangling second-growth growing rampant over what had been the bunkhouse, where only rotten boards and foundation pilings remained. Yet she stood there visualizing aloud in word-pictures what our future house, almost a mansion, would look like.

"Which bedroom would you like, honey?" she asked me, as if it were already built.

I stood there looking at the overgrown apocalypse and wondered at her ability to see the same thing and not notice the practical impossibilities of what she was saying. It felt like sheer, breathtaking madness to make real her grand designs out there on the edge of nowhere with her children and husband for skills and labor.

Dad, listening silently from behind his glinting glasses and the beard he'd grown in defiance of the clean-cut conformity that had sent him off to war, noticed the obstacles. But he considered them a challenge and saw the practicalities, not the impossibilities.

• • •

The cannery's wide-open view of Union Bay meant that it was pummeled by savage northwesterly storms—something we discovered within hours of our arrival.

At first it was cat's paws ruffling the bay. Then little wavelets lapped at the ruins as the tide rose. The wavelets transformed into a rushing, curling crash of heavy surf as the wind thrashed the evergreens and careened through miles of forest with a rising, freight train roar.

Dad fetched the skiff from where he'd anchored it and tied it to the remains of a Forest Service outhaul: a rope and pulley system that allows skiffs to be kept out in deep water so they don't "go dry" (beach on the ground as the tide recedes), and can be pulled in as needed.

There was no way our little thirteen-foot open skiff could battle against the expanse of white-capping rollers marching toward us as the afternoon gave way to dusk. We were stranded, marooned in the shadowy, burned ruins without food, bedding, or shelter.

• • •

I don't know how you're supposed to feel about being marooned beyond the last fringe of civilization, beyond help or assistance. Fear seems appropriate, or at least unease, a troubled awareness of all the ways that two adults and five children could die alone and disappear in the wilderness.

My parents set us to work on clearing the land where Mom visualized having her home built, next to the creek, since she'd always dreamed of having a home near rushing water. As Dad chopped seedlings and undergrowth, we hauled them down to the beach in a big pile, working up quite a sweat, not to mention hunger.

We tired finally, and as the wind blowing in off the bay chilled the sweat on us, we huddled together for warmth. Shivering amidst all those reminders of the destructive power of fire, that was all any of us wanted at that moment: a good, rousing blaze.

We had no matches or lighters since neither of my parents smoked, but Dad did have his .30 carbine with him. The gun was a concession to the dangers of the wilderness, a concession made despite both of my parents' issues with guns.

Dad was reminded of the war, and Mom had never gotten over her first introduction to firing a gun when she was a teenager. She hadn't gripped it tightly enough and the recoil had caused the gun to fly up and strike her in the forehead. The pain and shock had been magnified by the deafening report. She'd developed a terrified aversion to all guns to such an extent that she would shake when she was near one and grow sick when she had to handle one.

We watched as Dad ejected a shell and used his pocketknife to dig the bullet out. In a place protected by the wind, behind the pile of brush we'd collected, he dumped the powder onto a rock with dry sticks and moss ready to catch fire. He put the cartridge back in the chamber and fired the primer at the powder, hoping to spark it into flame. However, it blew the powder off the rock.

Eventually—almost, it seemed to us kids, inevitably, as if the elements had no choice but to yield to his angry determination—he got flames to devour his kindling. Now we had a fire to warm ourselves, though nothing to cook on it.

We slept that night in a shelter Dad put together from planks and plastic sheets scavenged from the Forest Service's leftovers. It was cold, with the wind roaring and the trees cracking and thrashing their branches against each other. The wind switched to the south and it rained in the night. Megan and I were envious of Jamie, who had Moby lying on his feet and keeping him warm. The boys were put in the middle and slept warm and toasty. Mom cuddled the boys, wide awake, too amazed at where she was and the adventure she was living to sleep.

Dad also got little sleep, getting up to check on the skiff as it rode the waves too near the rock cliffs for comfort, the big swells coming in and dashing the small craft forward, only for it to be yanked up short by its line tied to the outhaul. He tended the fire, hunkering down near it for warmth, waiting for first light, for the ruins to come back into focus. Despite the stress of worrying about the skiff, at least he wasn't being shot at, and the scream of incoming mortars was far away.

We returned to the fishing village the next day, but the ruins called to us.

"WE'RE GETTIN' OUTTA HERE!"
—Skip Robinson in the 1975 movie *The Wilderness Family*

CHAPTER TWO

WHEN MOM explained to Linda, Uncle Rand's girlfriend, that she and Dad still planned to homestead the old cannery in the wilderness despite their friends dropping out, Linda tried to dissuade her.

"Romi, you have to have more faith in people," Linda said. Maybe she was thinking that it was another instance of the rapidly-becoming-a-cliché story of a Vietnam vet alienated from humanity, dragging his family off into the wilds of Alaska.

But it wasn't like that, not entirely, Mom thought.

They trekked the bare dirt trail that circled the village under mist-laden skies. The community trail's narrowness only allowed people to walk single file under the towering canopy of evergreens, tendrils of overcast trailing into the treetops. The air was intoxicatingly fresh.

"You can't just go off into the wilderness like this. People aren't the enemy," Linda assured her.

Weathered wood-frame houses hugged the hillsides above the winding path or perched beside it on barnacle-studded pilings over the beach. Every now and then boards corduroyed a boggy spot and Linda's and Mom's boots clomped onto them, the mud beneath slurping loudly. Sea gulls screeched from the small harbor that glinted hard and mirrorlike through the trees and crows answered them from deep in the moss-damped forest.

Mom kept to herself her "unworldly" reactions to the mystery and romance of the ruins. She'd long since decided that other adults, even the ones she connected with the most, never understood what she experienced. Places had personalities, they lived and breathed and either welcomed or scorned you. The ruins wanted her family.

Despite the fact that Linda had grown up in San Francisco while Mom had grown up on traplines, farms, and ranches in backroad regions, it was the city-girl Linda who was able to "do" the rural Alaskan lifestyle in a way Mom never could. Linda tackled trapping and flensing a skinned otter, steering Rand's fishing boat, and everything else the men around her did with panache, while at the same time finding the time to crochet, sew, and design quirky, feminine crafts.

Mom wouldn't know—and didn't care to know—how to do what the men did, and though she wore a floppy, boiled-wool, faded-thimbleberry hat that looked like she'd knitted it herself, she'd bought it in a thrift store, allured by its wacky-cocky personality. The sewing arts were a deep, and deeply uninteresting, mystery to her and always had been.

She was not one of the millions of young people who, in the 1960s and '70s, felt driven to spurn the materialistic world in the Back to the Land Movement. Despite her love of novelty and fashion and whatever was current on the modern scene, she, like Dad, were traditionalists and had no interest in the drug culture, free sex, or any of the other ideas of other people their age who dropped out and "went back to the land."

According to Eleanor Agnew in her book *Back from the Land*, these back-to-the-landers thought that by going back to a simpler life and living close to and off the land, they could be better stewards of the world than the exploitative capitalist society that had given them the kind of privilege that allowed them to toss it all away on a fervent wave of idealism.

There were many of these free-floating idealistic types who latched onto Mom and Dad for their stability. My parents were young, but they were a married couple at a time when many young people derided the concept of marriage as being old fashioned and too restrictive.

My dad and mom, happy that they're moving to the ruins, leaving civilization behind.

Mom was a stay-at-home wife while Dad—despite his rebellious long hair and bushy beard (he was once mistaken by a Hell's Angel member as one of their own)—always held down a steady job. They wound up, time and again, taking care of and providing bed and board for any number of youthful wanderers existing in a liberated, drug-induced daze with no thought of jobs, responsibility, or providing for themselves.

These drifters were the children of "The Greatest Generation" that had saved the world from the Great Depression and Nazism... which was a lot to live up to. Dropping out was easier than competing, not to mention nobler—if you could spin it that way. And if you could find a steady young couple, who were in sympathy with the idealism of the times but maintained a traditional way of life, to keep yourself safe and afloat, all the better.

There were plenty of those types in rural Alaskan communities, including Meyers Chuck—"hippies" who were drawn as much to the drug culture and liberation from age-old moral standards, as they were by the validation of living a simpler life. And, at that time, Alaska stood out as a state that welcomed eccentrics, non-traditionalists, and made the private use of marijuana legal.

Neither Mom nor Dad, even in their most antiestablishment moments, had been drawn to that culture. They didn't even smoke cigarettes, though their parents and most of their peers considered it normal to do so. And when old-fashioned crafts became a fad that young and fashionable townspeople followed—sewing or crocheting one's own dresses had a certain cache at the time—Mom, a sucker for almost any hip fad that came along, was immune to the appeal.

She supported individualism and nonconformity, but her idealism remained restricted to the mind and heart; she spurned all labor-intensive manifestations of the zeitgeist. It didn't matter to her that this was not a particularly practical point of view for someone who was determined to live in the remotest heart of the wilderness.

"You should have seen how happy and free the kids were," Mom improvised to Linda.

"The kids will do fine here in the village with other kids around them and a school to attend." Linda was so certain in her opinion that Mom had a low-level sense of panic at the thought of being forced to give up the lonesome blackened pillars and rusting remains of the old cannery.

"You don't know what it's like having five kids in a place this small," Mom said. "It's like having a target painted on you. People are always complaining about every little thing they do, and I don't want them to grow up being squelched all the time. I want them to be free, to do whatever they want to do, be whatever they want to be."

As if on cue, a woman from the village steamed up the path toward them. Before she reached them, glimpsing Mom's floppy hat behind Linda, she barked, "Do you know what your kids are doing down at the dock?"

Mom didn't get a chance to reply.

"They found a whiskey bottle on one of the boats, filled it with water, and are pretending to drink booze!" The woman huffed.

Linda turned and looked at Mom and acknowledged, "I see what you mean."

There were no more arguments after that. Her floathouse home, Southeast Alaska's version of the covered wagon of Oregon Trail fame, would be towed to the ruins.

. . .

When loggers arrived in Alaska and first eyed the timber-rich wilderness of the last great temperate rainforest on the planet, they were stymied by the multitude of waterways that prevented logs and people from being transported by land. They adapted by moving everything onto the water on rafts.

Logging machinery, power plants, stores, schools, and entire towns were built on rafts made of enormous logs lashed together. The floating towns and machinery were towed from one place to the next by powerful, sturdy tugboats that inched along the Inside Passage. (Later, when the logging boom ended, all these floating communities and single floathouses were moored in place and rarely ventured out onto the unprotected passages.)

When we moved to Cannery Creek, it wasn't the first time our single-story, wood-frame house on a raft of giant logs had been towed abroad. It had been towed from Prince of Wales Island to the Ketchikan area and then to Meyers Chuck where we got it. In our keeping it had been towed twice across Clarence Strait, one of Alaska's most unpredictable and dangerous inside waterways.

The first time had been so that Dad would have his family near his logging job, his home anchored in a small bight along the winding passage that leads to Thorne Bay, the largest logging camp in the world at the time. The second time it had been towed back to the fishing village of Meyers Chuck, where Mom's parents and brothers lived. Now it would be towed to the old cannery site while Dad would continue to work at Thorne Bay as a scaler and bucker. The plan was for him to commute home on the weekends across Clarence Strait in the tiny skiff.

Dad had no interest in whatever seasoned arguments there might have been about the crossing being "impossible" at certain times of the year, or hearing that his family couldn't be left without provisions or a man's protection for weeks at a time.

I think there was some relief in not having his family around, demanding things of him he couldn't give. Being a husband, being a father—especially being a father—were skills he didn't possess. His own father, a World War II veteran, had been so harsh toward him that his mother had arranged for her mother to raise him while his siblings stayed at home.

The one time his father had been proud of Dad was when he signed up for the Army. His father wrote him a letter every week, though he wasn't normally a letter writer. Yet, when Dad came back from Vietnam with a beard, his family disowned him. At a time when the mainstream was reviling the war and its veterans, the next letter his father wrote him was "anonymous" (although still in his handwriting), suggesting that it might be better if there was no Vietnam vet in the family.

What did Dad know about being a good father, or any kind of father at all?

He could have asked the old-timers for their advice about his plans for leaving his family in the bush while he worked across the strait, but he didn't. He probably wouldn't have gotten much.

When they first arrived at Meyers Chuck, he and Mom attended a community "town hall" meeting where they realized from the awkward silence that fell at their arrival that they and their five kids had been under discussion. They were invited to participate, but when they spoke up they were seen as overopinionated newcomers.

Besides, even if the locals had taken Dad under their wings, the old-timers' ever-so-reasonable and knowledgeable arguments wouldn't have impressed him. He'd long been accustomed to thinking that, as he liked to joke-but-not-joke, "Where there's a Gary there's a way." No matter how impossible something seemed to be, he could find a way to make it work.

Surviving a war with a Purple Heart Medal, which he refused to accept, had solidified his certainty in his ability to carry out what he'd decided on. He didn't balk at the dangers or the brutal load of hard labor that would be required; holding down a physically demanding job all week and homesteading the wilderness on the weekends suited him just fine.

• • •

Although we kids didn't know it at the time, we almost didn't get to live at the old burned cannery because the other families got cold feet and dropped out.

Fortunately, the company that now owned the cannery, US Steel, was willing to let my parents take over the entire lease with payment due on a yearly basis. It would be easy enough to keep up with since Dad's logging job was a well-paying one for the times.

The woman who had originated the plan, the village school teacher, felt so guilty at leaving my parents high and dry that she arranged for friends of hers, Muriel and Maurice Hoff, who had their own cabin cruiser called the *Lindy Lou*, to go with us.

The Hoffs were typical back-to-the-landers who'd come from the realm of academia to live a simplified, rustic life on a boat in the Alaskan wilderness. Muriel would stand in as a teacher since Mom knew she wasn't up to coping with our education needs.

The Hoffs' boat would come in handy when it came time to move the floathouse. Two of Mom's brothers, Uncle Rand and Uncle Rory, also volunteered their commercial fishing boats to help us make the move.

The moment it really struck me that we were leaving all of civilization behind for the foreseeable future was when I had to return the books I'd borrowed from the village "library," a bottom shelf in the tiny, one-room general store.

I squatted down, pushing the old clothbound books into place, and my eye was snagged by two more books that I longed to read: a Roy Rogers Western and a book about a horse and a dog going on a forest adventure. I couldn't borrow them, Mom explained, because there was no telling when I'd be able to return them—if ever.

That made it starkly real. I emerged from the store into the late afternoon light and stared around in awe at my last glimpse of people and houses, hearing the private generators rumble and the bells on the fishing boats' trolling poles ring out. The red strobe light on top of the telephone tower that serviced a single community phone mounted to a tree, a light that used to lull me to sleep at night, was beaming out a hi-tech message of goodbye.

• • •

We left at the break of day, before it was full light, to catch the tide.

The *Velvet* towing our floathouse and wanigan out of Meyers Chuck to the cannery.
My dad is in his 13-foot Boston Whaler watching to make sure everything works.
The *Wood Duck* and *Lindy Lou* (out of sight) push from behind.

Not that any of us kids were awake when it happened. We were snuggled up in our bunks while the adults moved quietly around the damp decks outside, the dripping forest muffling most sounds.

They coiled up the huge, heavy mooring hawsers that had held our home to the trees and then ran a towline out to the *Velvet*, Uncle Rory's and Aunt Marion's commercial fishing boat. (It was a black-hulled boat with a white cabin and orange-red trim. When the *Velvet* was decked out in longline buoys in circus balloon hues—orange, pink and blue, and yellow—it was a sight to behold on Southeast Alaska's remote fishing grounds.) Uncle Rand in his own fishing boat, the classy little *Wood Duck*, and the Hoffs in their cabin cruiser *Lindy Lou* settled in to push the floathouse from behind.

The photos show that it was a crisp fall day, overcast with smoke from our floathouse chimney wafting behind us as our home was towed out of the long shadows of the tidal lagoon known as the Back Chuck (situated behind the Front Chuck, Meyers Chuck's harbor).

The floathouse was then about twenty-five years old and used to belong to Mom's parents, but Mom and Dad bought it from them when we first moved to Alaska three years before. It was a one-story, regular wood-frame house built in a "shotgun" trailer-house style. Half of the house was a large communal bedroom for us kids, plus the bathroom. The front half had my parents' tiny bedroom, and beyond it was the combined kitchen and living room.

The house was sixteen feet wide and forty feet long, with forest-green ship-lapped siding and white trim around the windows, including the huge bay window that had a bullet hole high up in one corner.

Tied alongside our floathouse was a much smaller, ten-by-fourteen-foot one-room floating cabin called "the wanigan" that my grandfather had built four years before, which Mom had since bought from him. It would serve as our schoolhouse.

The floathouses crept along, testing the lines and what kind of strain the *Velvet*'s engine could take, before they settled on a steady two-knot pace. The adults calculated it would take three to four hours to tow the floathouse to the cannery site.

When we woke up, the floathouse was already underway. The five of us kids and Moby excitedly ran around the house and—when Mom wasn't looking—made a daring run outside to leap across the churning water between the floathouse and the wanigan. Mom had warned us against this feat, telling us horror stories of how a child could get trapped between the two moving buildings and be mangled for life, sawed in half, and/or drowned. As usual, her horror stories encouraged us to test our mettle.

We stood there, listening to the engines of all three boats rumble, hearing the constant splash of the water against and over the logs the buildings sat on, and watched the wanigan tug on its lines like it wanted to escape the solid maturity of the big floathouse.

Jamie, as the ringleader, was on lookout duty to make sure none of the adults were watching. When the coast was clear he'd whisper: "Now!" and one of us would take the exhilarating and frightening jump across the turbulent water to the wanigan.

When the babies insisted on their turn, Megan and I each took a hand of a little brother and jumped them across, hushing them—and our own giggles—when they shrieked with glee. Moby ran along the floathouse deck with his tongue hanging out, his eyes bright and laughing at the death-defying sport.

We were in our lifejackets, of course. We lived in our lifejackets. The one rule Mom was successful in establishing right from the beginning was that no child was to step out of the house without their lifejacket on. It was comforting being encased in protective gear—like a suit of armor against the Alaskan bush's many dangers. At times we even slept in our lifejackets.

The water was millpond smooth, though all the adults knew that the weather in this particular part of Clarence Strait was subject to change without notice every moment. It would have taken weeks of planning, listening to weather forecasts, checking the tides, calculating how long it would take to travel to the cannery site; and then the frustration of having to reschedule the trip when an unforecasted storm raged through.

It would have been a tense time for the adults before and during the tow, looking out for any sign that the weather was about to kick up. These were dangerous waters we were traveling in—shipwrecks on the shores we passed gave silent testimony to that.

Back inside the floathouse, Mom gave us a quick breakfast. We ate while watching the storied Inside Passage glide past our windows with Christopher Cross's "Sailing" playing in the background. Dad was in continual contact with Rory on the *Velvet*, Rand in the *Wood Duck*, and Muriel on the *Lindy Lou* by Citizen Band (CB) radio.

By a freak of bouncing radio signals, truckers from California would break through the squelch with their: "10-4, what's your twenty?" and "Copy that. You're coming in wall to wall and treetop tall." An entire array of twangy CB slang periodically burst through the speaker. The rowdy rap of truckers hauling freight along America's West Coast highways beamed into our wilderness home all the years we lived at the cannery.

The little inlet we headed for was a hidden harbor—it couldn't be seen from a direct approach on the cannery. It was sheltered from the northerly gales, though southeasterly storm surges were free to wreak havoc in there, as we soon discovered.

The harbor was shallow and went dry on minus tides. In addition, there were submerged dangers everywhere, entire forests of pilings (studded with steel spikes that had held long since rotted or scavenged beams in place) that had at one time been the foundations for pre-WWII boat grids and haul-outs.

This harbor was where the superintendent had lived and where the cannery had repaired and stored their fish barges in the off season all the years it was in operation.

The cannery encompassed twenty-one acres of wilderness and had two sides: the "superintendent's inlet" where our floathouse was parked, and "the Other Side," the creek side where the cannery itself had been. They were separated by a high, stubby peninsula.

In the superintendent's inlet the orderly sentinel pilings, silent witnesses to the passing years, stood in marked contrast to the twisted, scorched chaos we'd found on "the Other Side." There had also been a building that had overlooked the superintendent's inlet that was later put on a float and towed the seven miles to Meyers Chuck. There it was put back on land where it still stands today, painted in cannery red, and known locally as "Hotel California" for the hippie inhabitants who lived there in the Seventies.

The *Velvet*, *Wood Duck*, and *Lindy Lou* couldn't maneuver inside the shallow harbor with all the underwater hazards, so they untied from the floathouse and Dad used his skiff to push the house to a central location, tying it to trees on shore and a tall piling on the wanigan side. After it was secured in position, the *Lindy Lou* picked its way inside and tied up to the floathouse on the other side from the wanigan.

There's nothing quite like being in your familiar home and glancing out the window to see not the view you've lived with for years but terra incognito—an unknown, unexplored landscape.

The light shines through the windows differently, making the inside of the house seem subtly strange. There's a continuing, pleasurable, tingling disorientation about it, a breathtaking, awe-inspiring sense of waiting discovery—an almost Alice in Wonderland sense of having fallen down the rabbit hole with all kinds of amazing experiences to live outside the familiar walls of your transported home.

Once the house sat down on dry land, the water gradually receding and lowering us onto the ground as if our house was on a giant elevator, Mom couldn't hold us kids back. She yelled at us to stay within sight of the house as we ran outside. The tall forest of evergreen trees encircled the small harbor, with drift logs, beach grass, and seaweed in a jumble at their heavy skirts.

I don't know about my brothers and sister, but I felt like a *Star Trek* adventurer who had landed on an unknown planet with the remnants of a long-ago civilization to explore. On this side the ruins, although less extensive, were better preserved. All the buildings and barges and anything still valuable had been moved out, so what remained were foundations, wire-wrapped wooden waterlines, and an old winch for hauling out the cannery barges.

We found signs of ancient Native occupation in the form of a "fire tree." The tree was a huge silo of a cedar tree burned hollow in the center. It was outside the part of the cannery that had burned in 1947, and it wasn't a lightning-struck tree since the only burned section was the interior. It was so huge that I could walk around inside and stand in the middle without being able to touch the sides. I used to wonder at the mystery of it, why it had been deliberately burned hollow inside. Later I read that modern researchers hypothesize that the Tlingit tribe used such trees as a way to preserve their precious communal store of fire from the persistently rainy climate.

Our greatest, most awestruck discovery was a grave. It was marked by a weathered and rotting wooden cross on the point that overlooked the bay. (Later we found another one farther back in the woods.)

Who was buried here? What had been their stories? There was no one to ask so we were free to imagine our own stories. There was plenty of scope for a child's imagination in the ruins that we now called home.

"4th grade correspondence
our 4 children school
housing our 4 desks with the attached
chairs
and open up tops
and rusted 50 gallon gas barrel stove.

Outside, beyond the lapping
of the water
Against the worm-eaten logs
of the wanigan
I hear my father's chainsaw
We will haul wood for recess."

—my Fourth Grade poetry composition

CHAPTER THREE

THE *LINDY LOU* was hauled out of the water and held upright by
a wooden cradle Dad built for it near where he eventually moved our
floathouse, so high on the beach that our home only floated during
the highest tides of the year.

After Dad did some repairs to it, Muriel and Maurice moved
into the sole remaining, still-standing cannery building on the
property, the little red cabin we'd noticed on our first visit as it stood
on the edge of the creek across from the ruins.

The Forest Service had marked a trail between the two sides of
the cannery. Dad civilized it by cutting down some small trees and
laying them down over boggy spots, and overall made the trail easier
for the Hoffs to follow. Muriel took it every morning to teach us in
the wanigan.

The wanigan was tiny. It was one room with a small loft. It had
a front and back door that slid in wooden troughs, like a boat door.
There was a hand-hewn counter at the back with a sink that had no
running water, and a four-paned window above it. In one corner the
wood stove, made from an old fuel drum, squatted.

The interior and exterior were all raw wood, unpainted, with
visible nails and hammer dents in floor, walls, and rafters. But this
was common to Southeast Alaska where the timber-loving men in
the area disliked splashing paint around and strongly resisted all

attempts to put anything but varnish on floors or walls.

The small building had served as a home for my grandparents while they built a house on land, and from the first my brothers and sister and I loved playing in and on it. Mom handwrote on lined yellow paper a story called "The Wanigan Kids" and each of us, plus our cousin Shawn who came up in the summers to visit his dad (Rand), had a starring role in the story.

It was a *Wizard of Oz* story, but instead of our house being whirled away by a tornado, in Mom's version the wanigan broke its mooring lines during a high storm tide when just the six of us kids were aboard, and we floated away from adult authority. Instead of the fantastical sights and experiences of Oz, Mom asked each of us to contribute an idea to the story and we decided on adventures of coping with the real and present dangers of the Alaskan wilderness.

She read many books to us and we loved all of them—but we loved none more than "The Wanigan Kids," which we clamored for her to read all the time.

The small, weathered wood floor of the wanigan was scuffed by our four desks. (Chris was too young to attend school yet.) With only three small, four-paned windows to let the light in, we had to have a kerosene lantern burning to be able to read and write, especially in the morning and in the afternoon during the long dark winter months.

On wash nights the desks were pushed to the back to make way for a large tin washtub, oval in design. With water heated on the stove, clothes and bodies were washed. The clothes, washed first, were hung on lines strung below the roof. In the cozy yellow light of the lantern, the windows turned opaque with steam as we scrubbed and splashed below the dangling legs and arms of the clothes, each of us getting a turn. The clothes would continue to hang over our heads when we did our schoolwork.

Dad built a long floating walkway to shore so we could get off to play at recess or go home for lunch. When school first began with Muriel as our teacher, we were given tests by the regional school district that would oversee our education by mail and floatplane visits. The tests were to see where we were at, academically. In between each segment of the testing we were allowed to run around outside for a few minutes to let off steam. The tide was high so we

Megan's watercolor painting of the wanigan, for which she
won first prize in a statewide art competition.

ran across the floating walkway, listening to the water splash under
our assault.

We'd been warned never to go far into the woods, and under no
circumstances were we to use the trail that connected the two sides
of the cannery. There was bear sign everywhere and my parents said
that we shouldn't go on the trail without an adult who'd carry a gun.

At this point, Muriel announced that she didn't believe in guns.

"They're anti-intellectual," she said. "And they're counter-
productive. The reason that people get mauled by bears is because
they take aggressive weapons into bear territory. Bears are intuitive.
This is their world, their land, and the onus is on us to live by their
rules and be respectful of their rights and feelings."

"You're saying we shouldn't carry guns?" Mom, as much as she
disliked guns, couldn't find it in her heart to embrace the idea. Not
with five kids to protect.

"There's enough evidence out there that bears can sense the
hostility of negative and aggressive thinking by humans. They're

tuned into our individual auras. Maurice and I won't carry a gun into the woods. I advise you not to either."

Even I, nine years old at the time, thought this was an argument that bears would not feel compelled to honor. Dad, as usual, kept his thoughts to himself, while Mom tried to argue with Muriel despite how much she would have liked Muriel's argument to be true.

So my parents, to preempt anything she might teach us on the topic, told us kids that we could only go on the trail when Dad was there with a gun.

This, under Jamie's leadership, meant that as soon as we were let out of school on those short breaks between tests, we had to see how far we could get on the trail running as fast as we could, before we had to turn back in time to do the next test.

The memory of racing along the dry edges of the squishy, muddy trail (so that, as Jamie pointed out, we would leave no tell-tale marks on the trail or on our boots) marked by pink and yellow surveyor's tape, the trees looming above us, the threat of bears around every corner, is vivid in my mind. We giggled breathlessly, exultant at being free of adult supervision, at having outsmarted the adults, at surviving the daring escapade.

Megan and I gripped Robin's hands and raced him along behind Jamie. I was terrified of all the bear stories I'd heard, I had nightmares about them breaking into our house while we slept, but there was a laugh-in-the-face-of-danger joy about those urgent races deep into the verboten wilderness that lingers with me to this day.

• • •

When Mom first met Muriel in Meyers Chuck, she'd admired Muriel, in the way Mom always admired women she saw as more capable and take-charge than she was. Muriel was a registered nurse and saw herself, she said, as an Earth Mother type who wanted to live wholly off the land.

This sounded like the perfect person to accompany us into the wilderness, to shore up Mom's less practical nature and provide immediate medical help should it be required. Maurice was not at all practical and had no wilderness skills, but he was friendly, genial, and intellectual. He tended to smile and nod, backing up whatever his wife decided. Where he shone was in singing folk songs and accompanying himself on guitar, like any back-to-the-lander worthy of his salt.

Muriel had traveled widely and had many hair-raising adventures to share. She found herself, she said, invariably in the position of having to stand up to abuses of power and ethical wrongdoing. "You must always stand up for what you believe in; you must be true to your convictions."

Mom loved this because her instinct was to always stand on principle, no matter what it cost.

Everyone was pleased, thinking the two couples would be a perfect match at the isolated cannery site. But before we left Meyers Chuck, something happened.

A friend of both Mom's and Muriel's was the subject of controversy. When the village women got together to hash out what should be done and the conclusion was that the mutual friend should be driven out of the community, Mom stood up and said they didn't have the right to make that choice; they were all the woman's friends and they should act like it.

Her principled arguments, as always, were made as an emotional appeal and dismissed by the majority.

Muriel was silent on the subject. Mom asked her about it later— Muriel was at least as close to the woman as Mom was. Plus, other women would have listened to Muriel, who was so certain. Why hadn't she stood up for her friend? "After all, you're supposed to stand up for what you believe in," Mom reminded her.

Muriel said it wasn't any of her business and she preferred to keep out of it.

Right then Mom started to have doubts about heading into the wilderness with Muriel and Maurice, not to mention having Muriel teach her kids, but everyone was already committed.

• • •

For physical education (PE) we hauled firewood. Dad split it and we stacked it in rows on the wanigan's front porch.

As it grew colder Dad had his hands full finding, sawing, and then splitting enough firewood for the floathouse, the wanigan, and the Hoffs' cabin. Despite their back-to-the-land, sweat-and-callus aspirations, neither Muriel nor Maurice were interested in harvesting their own firewood.

They said that in exchange for his children receiving an education, Dad should provide them with firewood. So Dad would come home from a full week of hard physical labor as a scaler and bucker at the logging camp, and he'd spend the weekend splitting firewood like a machine. The only sign to us kids that he was human was the sweat pouring down his face and the steam rising from his head in the cold air.

Dad filled Maurice's skiff full of firewood—several cords' worth—and towed it over to Muriel and Maurice's cabin. Dad figured it would last them a couple months at least, since the cabin was tiny and it wouldn't take much to heat it.

The next day, the last day of Dad's weekend before he had to go back to work, Maurice knocked on our floathouse door.

"We need firewood."

Dad stared at him. "I just split several cords for you."

"Unfortunately it had other plans and floated away."

"How could it float away? Didn't you tie the skiff to a tree above the tideline?"

Maurice offered an amused, worldly shrug. Obviously the loss of the firewood was an Act of God. What can you do?

Dad was fit to be tied. But, as Maurice indicated in his indirect, urbane way, they needed firewood, and since the agreement was that Dad would provide it in exchange for Muriel teaching his kids, it was up to Dad to supply it. And resupply it.

• • •

I recently asked Robin what he remembers about Muriel and Maurice. Though he's four years younger than I am, he's often my go-to source for memories because he has the kind of mind that keeps arcane details on tap.

He responded: "I hated her so much that I have no memory of her or him. I erased her from my mind."

I understand perfectly why he feels this way.

Muriel wasn't an easy person to like. She had a curious habit of talking to adults like they were children, and to children like they were adults. She went around braless to indicate her free-spirited feminism that unyoked her from the backward Establishment— while all the time trying to form her own Establishment that everyone else was required to support.

What none of us realized, when Mom and Dad accepted Muriel and Maurice as equal members of the plan to colonize the cannery, was that this agreement would set us on a collision course that would lead to an epic clash of wills. Not between Muriel and either of my parents. No, it was between Muriel and one of her students.

When Robin came along, the fourth child in the family, he was so cute and had so much personality that everyone adored him. He was precocious in a funny way, with an ironical take on life that was ridiculous in one so young. As a toddler he walked around with his bottle hanging out of his mouth and talked around it, like a 1920s gangster talking around his cigar. At the same time he had an infectious personality with enthusiasms that swept everyone along. Up to that point, the only fly in his ointment was when Christopher came along a year after him and knocked him out of the prestigious baby slot.

Chris, one of the happiest, most harmonious babies in history, adopted all of Robin's mannerisms including Robin's inability to pronounce his Ls. Chris's failing in this area spurred Robin to take him in hand and demonstrate a correct pronunciation.

When Chris said something about Muriel and Maurice's boat, the *Lindy Lou*, Robin would immediately deride, "It's Rindy Rou— not Rindy Rou!"

Needless to say, Chris's speech didn't improve.

Muriel zeroed in on this fault immediately. All of her bully pulpit instincts became laser focused on fixing the problem that was Robin's speech. The rest of us kids, self-starters who could teach ourselves for the most part, held little interest for her.

"You're not doing it right. Touch your tongue to the roof of your mouth, press your tongue to the back of your top teeth, and make an L sound." She demonstrated.

I did it myself, surprised to discover a skill I'd taken for granted up until then.

Robin stared at her in the wintry light creeping in through the windows. The little cabin smelled of crayons and finger paint, kerosene from the lamps, cedar firewood, and the seaweed that it rested on when the tide was out and it was no longer floating.

"Do it like this," Muriel ordered, and demonstrated again.

He made a sound through his teeth.

"No, not through your teeth. Open your mouth and do it. No, that's not it either. Try it again. Are you watching me? Do you see how I'm doing it? Tara, show him how to do it."

I looked at Robin's downcast face and uncomfortably demonstrated.

"There, that's how you make an L sound. Do you see how easy it is? We're all doing it. Come on, everyone, show Robin how to make an L sound."

Muriel, Jamie, Megan, and I made L sounds while Robin stared down at his desk. I'd never imagined how taunting and belittling a prolonged L sound could be, when an entire group of people did it toward the youngest person in the group.

"Now you do it, Robin."

Robin remained silent.

"Did you hear me, Robin? You're not deaf, I know you can hear me. Now you're just being obstructive. Do you want to grow up with a speech impediment? Do you want to be the butt of jokes, to look like a backward person? Do you know how that will affect your life? I know, we all know, don't we, kids?"

I looked at Robin, and tried to explain to Muriel. "He knows the R sound he's using instead of an L is wrong, he tries to tell Mitmer how to say it right—"

"His name is Christopher, not Mitmer. And that's another thing. If you don't learn your Rs," she told Robin, "you'll be responsible for your younger brother's speech problems throughout his life. Do you want to be responsible for that? Do you want to make him the butt of jokes, mocked and laughed at by people wherever he goes? It will be all your fault. Do you want to live with that?"

Robin scowled and his lower lip crept downward, revealing

small kindergarten teeth clenched together.

"He tries at home, my mom works with both of them on it," I tried again.

Her pale eyes fixed on me. "Obviously that isn't working, is it, Tara? You're not helping by making excuses for him, and neither is your mother. Robin, neither you nor I am going to leave here today without you learning how to pronounce at least one L correctly. That isn't too much to ask, is it kids?"

Robin never again tried to make an L sound in school. In fact, from that point on he refused to cooperate with her in any way. And she refused to admit that she'd lost his cooperation, continuing to harangue and goad him every single day.

It's probably a minor miracle that Robin learned to speak his Ls without a problem. Her Ahab-like quest to stab at his speech impediment to her last breath made it hard for the rest of us to concentrate on our own work, which she paid little attention to anyway. All her focus was dedicated to getting Robin to give in and submit to her authority.

Robin, five years old doing battle with a college-educated woman in her thirties, never gave in. Instead, he discovered that he could hold his own against even the most self-certain adult. There was no going back after that. His cooperation in anything was almost impossible to win from then on.

In addition to this clash that impacted everything, tensions continued to rise over Muriel's and Maurice's expectations that Dad labor for them and keep them supplied in firewood. Due to their inexperience with a wood stove, they treated the wood he cut wastefully. They overheated their small cabin due to their ignorance of the stove's damper and draft and had to have the front door open to cool the place, burning through the wood Dad provided far faster than he'd calculated. When they ran out they became annoyed that he didn't fulfill his side of the bargain instantly, leaving them with a cold cabin to live in.

Muriel was someone who needed the admiration of others and felt the bite all the more keenly when it was withdrawn, which was what happened with my parents—with Mom in particular, who had been so impressed by Muriel when they first met.

By the time Maurice was offered a job in a town to the north of us a few months after the move to the cannery, relations were awkward and strained enough for everyone to be okay with them moving back aboard the *Lindy Lou* and saying their goodbyes. That was the end of their back-to-the-land aspirations. They never again lived so remotely.

We were on our own.

"Gee, I thought watches floated."
—Chris, experimenting with our only timepiece,
Dad's not-waterproof watch, in a pan of water

CHAPTER FOUR

ONE NIGHT, when the wood box that Dad had built next to the front door was empty... I climbed into it.

I could hear my family inside the house talking, laughing, and arguing. Robin's and Chris's voices that couldn't pronounce Ls piped higher than everyone else's. Their voices were muffled so I couldn't hear exactly what they were saying. They were the only human voices for miles.

It was a moonless night, with degrees of black that only the wilderness knows. Up along the wall of the house was the big bay window with a puckered bullet hole in it, not unlike the bullet scar in Dad's back that he got in Vietnam.

Golden kerosene lamplight spilled out, lighting the railing and gravel beach. The forest stream flowing beneath the logs of our house gurgled unseen, winding down through musky seaweed to the bay. The cannery superintendent's house had once stood not far from where our floathouse was. Oil and kerosene lamplight would have spilled out of its twelve-paned windows on the same little bay, surrounded by the same pointed silhouettes of trees that were a deeper, more impenetrable black than the sky.

I stared up at the stars and thought about time. The light from those stars, Jamie had said after reading one of the science books he was always asking Mom to buy him, was millions of years old.

I focused on a single star. That twinkling pinprick of light had been birthed in a distant part of the universe, before constantly, tirelessly traveling across great voids to reach a girl one Earth night in the Alaskan wilderness, curled up in a firewood box listening to her family. She would see it and acknowledge its existence and have her own existence, a part of the ever-changing, ever-moving universe, acknowledged in turn.

Had a cannery worker looked up and seen an earlier version of this light? If so, the light connected me to him in time. We were fellow witnesses of the light's eternal journey to… where? When? Was it going to return from where it had come, like the spawning salmon in the cannery's creek?

It would continue its journey, speeding in the silent vacuum of space, taking a part of me, this moment, with it. That unknown cannery worker who had looked up and seen the same light was a fellow passenger.

I always felt everywhere I went, in the woods and on the beaches, that somehow some part of the cannery workers who had lived here so long ago were still here, but in their own era, going about a life they'd already lived, but somehow present, too, in our time.

There was a sense of the place being haunted, but not in the usual sense of that word. I didn't believe in ghosts, but I did think that as long as a person was remembered at least a remnant of them lived on. What was a memory-person who could almost be seen, almost touched, almost interacted with? Was there a technology not yet invented that could free their memory-images from time's grip?

The cedar shake walls of the wood box surrounded me as I hugged myself to keep warm and stared up into the twinkling sky.

Did time have mirages like space did? Was the *Flying Dutchman*, I wondered, an example of a temporal mirage?

We owned a large annotated chart book covering British Columbia and Southeast Alaska that all of us, adults and children alike, pored over and discussed. One margin note recounted a sighting of the legendary "ghost ship" in our general area as it was recorded in the logbook of the Alaska State Ferry M/V *Malaspina*.

Like all log entries, it gave the exact day, hour, position, weather, and barometric pressure: Sunday, 6 A.M.; February 15, 1973; sixteen miles south of Ketchikan, abeam Twin Island in Revillagigedo Channel; unlimited visibility with northeasterly winds at ten knots; temperature 28°F and barometric pressure at 29:71.

Chief mate Walter Jackinsky was standing watch on the bridge with the helmsman and lookout when "a huge vessel loomed up approximately eight miles dead ahead, broadside and dead in the water." The appearance of it was so striking that they were careful to write down the vessel's exact position in longitude and latitude, near the south end of Bold Island in Coho Cove, marked by Washington Monument Rock.

The log entry reports: "This vessel strongly resembled the Flying Dutchman. The color was all gray, similar to vapor or clouds. It was seen distinctly for about 10 minutes. It looked so exact, natural and real that when seen through binoculars, sailors could be seen moving about on board."

As they watched, the ship dissolved and disappeared.

Huddled in the wood box, I wondered: Were the cannery workers a kind of mirage, recorded on the land around us, and on the ruins—the same way that spatial mirages of long-dead people and past events were mysteriously recorded and preserved on film?

I longed to know who they'd been, what they'd thought, how they'd reacted to this lonesome edge of the world. After we were gone, would we leave temporal mirages of ourselves behind, recorded on the beaches we played on, to mingle with the cannery workers?

• • •

Once we settled in, on the protected side of the cannery, we hardly ever went over to the Other Side where the burned ruins were, especially when it was just Mom and us kids. The charred wreckage lined the large salmon creek where the bears roamed, undisturbed by the rusty skeletons of machines. It meant nothing to them that once a mechanized world hummed, pounded, and rumbled in this remote outpost.

In my mind, the Other Side came to feel a bit like the Forbidden Zone in the original *Planet of the Apes* where the surf washed endlessly against the remains of a destroyed civilization. Yet, though it retained its strangeness and mystery, it still felt like home. I suppose in the same way an ancient castle with a ruined wing can be a home.

Any visit to the Other Side was memorable, but none more so than when Uncle Lance came to stay with us and act as our tutor for a short while after Muriel and Maurice left.

Although technically he was another adult who could be with Mom and us kids while Dad was away during the week, Lance had only recently graduated high school and Jamie, me, and Megan had shared the same classroom with him in the one-room, all-grades bush school in Meyers Chuck.

He was born late in life to Mom's parents—Mom was a teenager during his preschool years, and while her parents worked she raised Lance. When Jamie was born, Lance was more like an older brother to him than an uncle.

I have few memories of him teaching us, probably because we didn't see him as a teacher since he'd only recently been a classmate. I doubt he took the position seriously himself, but being of an artistic bent he did enjoy teaching us from our art history books. One time he took us on a school field trip into the woods to find leaves and ferns to use in sponge painting and stenciling art.

He was well read with a large, picturesque vocabulary and wised us up less through direct teaching and more through incidental moments. Like the time Megan was appalled when Lance mentioned that he was going to take a "spit bath." She let it be known that she thought anyone who would bathe in spit was just plain gross. Lance, swallowing a grin, explained that a spit bath was one that used little water.

Coming to live in Union Bay with us at the old cannery site was a boon to him—jobs were scarce, and it allowed him to get out on his own. Sporting the long-haired hippie look, he turned the wanigan into a smoky man cave where he could blast his screaming Seventies music so loud the cannery workers probably heard it after it tore a hole in the space-time continuum.

Still, he had a knack for knowing what music suited other people's tastes.

Every now and then Lance would cross the beach in the evening, his boots crunching on gravel, seeing by the moon, starshine, and

Lance attended the same one room school as we did in Meyers Chuck
and was more like an older brother than an uncle.

the lamplight falling out of the wanigan's windows on one side of the
beach and the floathouse's lit windows on the other side. He'd burst
in on us while we were playing board games with Mom (Chinese
Checkers, *Sorry!*, *Yahtzee*, *Monopoly*, *Risk*), or when she was reading
a book to us before bed (*Down the Long Hills*, *Little House on the
Prairie*, *Five Little Peppers*, *The Hobbit*, "The Wanigan Kids").

Without so much as a greeting, Lance would insist, "You have
to hear this!" He'd go straight to the car stereo that Dad had rigged
inside the floathouse to a marine battery and shove a cassette in.

We'd sit at attention for the entire album, completely absorbed
by the music in the yellow lamplight: Kim Carnes with her broken,
rusty voice sang "Bette Davis Eyes," or Shot in the Dark's inspired
guitar/flute duet on "Playing with Lightning" chimed out. We
immediately fell in love with and played these albums, and others he
introduced us to, on endless repeat until they became the soundtrack
to our wilderness life.

During the daytime he and Mom had lengthy discussions about

the books they were reading. Though in Lance's case, it wasn't exactly a discussion. He'd give a blow-by-blow account of his book. He'd follow Mom around the house, describing every scene with photographic clarity, following her down to the bathroom, despite her laughing protests, where he'd continue his rant outside the door. There was no escape.

Or he'd come over to share a long-winded, off-color joke that Mom would do her best, to no avail, to head off at the pass. Or he'd entertain us kids by producing the sound of flatulence with nothing more than his hand in his armpit, working his arm industriously. The boys were deeply impressed. Another time he came over to bedazzle Mom with an illusion where he turned his back to her, wrapped his arms around himself, and managed to conjure a woman madly in love with him.

He and Mom also loved playing "Name That Tune." While we watched, they took turns putting a cassette in and allowed a song to play only a snatch of music. They were both good at recognizing who the artist was from the barest riff, but Lance usually won in the end. He was merciless with his disgust and disillusionment when Mom missed one, though she just laughed.

After he left the wilderness to live in the city of Ketchikan, he never forgot us and sent out mixtapes with the latest hits: "The Breakup Song" and "Jeopardy" by Greg Kihn, "Physical" by Olivia Newton-John, "Seven Year Ache" by Rosanne Cash, "Morning Train" by Sheena Easton, "Don't Go Breaking My Heart" by Elton John and Kiki Dee, and so on.

He also recorded directly off the radio, particularly channels that offered a "blast from the past" line-up of hits from Mom and Dad's youth. Through these albums of Fifties and Sixties songs, our parents' era also became a part of ours. We heard these songs at least as often as the modern Eighties ones.

The most memorable recording that Lance sent out to us was Jeff Wayne's rock opera of HG Wells's *The War of the Worlds*, brilliantly narrated by Richard Burton. We never tired of listening to it. We sang the songs from it while we played in the woods and on the beach. Megan and I, with doubtful harmony, crooned "No, Nathaniel, no, there must be more to life" at the drop of a hat as we rode pretend horses around the beaches and built our forts in the woods.

And, with ghoulish relish, all of us intoned the eerie Martian war cry: "Ulaaaa!" It rang off the fortress-like wall of trees and the shore-lapping bay at all hours. We loved to do it at least in part because Mom hated it; she tried to ban it, with zero success. Creeping her out added to the entertainment value.

The story of Earth being taken over by aliens, torching civilization with their death ray, resonated with us almost as much as it had terrorized the victims of Orson Welles's infamous 1938 radio play. While his audience believed it to be a real, live program and panicked, racing away into the night in a mad scramble for survival or stuffing rags in the cracks of doors and windows to escape the fumes of the Martians' deadly poison gas, the five of us kids listening to a recorded rock version of that show nearly half a century later could have easily been convinced that it was true.

My parents could have told us that the world had been destroyed by an alien race or nuclear warfare, with only a few pockets of humanity surviving on Earth, and we would have believed it—because we saw nothing around us to disprove it, and plenty to suggest it was true.

The Other Side seemed to confirm it.

• • •

While Lance was staying with us, he and Mom cooked up an expedition to the ruins.

Unlike our practical, work-oriented father, Mom and Lance were fascinated in a purely aesthetic sense by the atmosphere of the ruins. Their excitement about the illicit trip into ceded bear territory infected us kids. Though they were both adults, Dad's influence tended to dampen risky, arty whims even when he wasn't there. The sense that we were on a covert trek only added to the thrill of it.

We set out into the forest. The narrow dirt trail was marked here and there by giant moss-covered, rotting stumps. At some point in the past the cannery superintendents had fallen massive spruce and cedar trees surprisingly deep in the woods, but for what purpose it wasn't clear. Had they milled their own lumber to build the boardwalk? Or had they somehow hauled the enormous trees down to the water to be used in making fish traps?

Because these large trees had been cut down in the middle of the peninsula that separated the two sides of the cannery, and many trees had been cleared to put in the wide boardwalk connecting both sides, oddly enough the deeper we went into the woods, the more open and airy and bright it became. There was a strangeness to it, as if we were stepping into a zone where the natural laws of the temperate rainforest ceased to exist.

Porcupines clambered clumsily up slim, young trees that had sprouted in the absence of the big trees' shadows. Moby barked at the prickly, comical beasts, but after having one dropped on him when Lance shook it out of a tree, Moby learned that he wasn't interested in a closer acquaintance.

Mom made no effort to stifle our young, high-pitched chatter, believing that human noise warned away bears. She'd attached bells to our life jackets for that purpose and told us to talk loudly, whistle, and generally make a lot of noise whenever we were in the woods. This was one of the mandates of hers that we zestfully obeyed.

The forest was brilliant with every shade of green, the moss a spongy verdant ocean that waved over fallen trees, rocks, and hills. Far below the canopy, giant-leafed, almost tropical, stands of banana-yellow skunk cabbage colonized boggy areas, and shyly curled fiddlehead ferns lined the trail and windfalls in thick profusion.

When we broke out of the woods, we went from comforting color and life to a scene of black-and-white desolation.

Under a leaden sky the ruins were stark. The creek, hidden by the trees, rumbled monotonously. The tide was way out, probably a minus tide, and the blackened pilings stretched in broken rows down yard after yard of rocky beach. Amidst them, the frames of the cannery's machinery lay where they had fallen decades ago when the floors, decks, and pier were engulfed in flames.

We picked our way through the debris field, like divers exploring a deep sea wreck. The minus tide added to the strangeness. I imagined old-fashioned wooden freighters tied to the pier these pilings had supported, floating far above my head as they took onboard tons of canned salmon.

The abundance of metal in odd shapes appealed to both Mom's

and Lance's creative natures and they enthusiastically fitted them together into modern art steel sculptures right there on the spot. We kids were encouraged to follow suit, as an ad hoc school fieldtrip.

Back in Meyers Chuck when Lance was fourteen, he and his friend Norman Miller (one of my Aunt Marion's five brothers) used to act as city architects on the beach building entire metropolises, beginning with a rusted-out starter they found as a town power plant. Inspired by these memories, when Lance investigated the ruins that day with us and saw a rusty bedframe complete with bedsprings and a headboard, all concretized together, he knew that he had to build a car.

He used it as his platform and Mom and the five of us kids pounced on tortured rusty shapes, calling out "car parts" and dragging them to him. We watched in delight as the junk turned into a jalopy, as Mom called it. Lance positioned four huge gears on both sides as wheels, and a wheel valve attached to a long steel pipe as a steering wheel. He built up seats, the hood of the car, and a trunk.

When he was finally satisfied, his collaborators were sweaty and grungy, covered in rust, but elated with the results of their labors and Lance's vision. Mom lamented not having film in her camera to capture the junk jalopy as it rested on the rocks, far from any road, with the expanse of the bay and the distant mountains of Prince of Wales Island on the horizon beyond it.

Nevertheless, we posed on it, riding in the back seats as Lance drove and Mom took pictures with squared fingers held up to her eye.

"Where should we go?" Lance asked, jauntily honking an invisible horn.

Each of us kids got to shout out a destination and Lance made engine noises. We leaned when he leaned, taking sharp corners around precipitous drop-offs, laughing as the jalopy careened into one imaginary story after another.

The jalopy remained on the beach long after Lance left, eventually scattered by heavy storm surges. It remains in my memory, ready for us to climb aboard and drive off into adventure amidst the cannery ruins.

A friend: *What's the song that spoke*
most to you as a child?
Me: *"I'm So Afraid" by Fleetwood Mac.*

CHAPTER FIVE

THERE WAS a lot to fear where we lived, and while all of us kids
were afraid of bears and storms, each of us had specific things we
worried about. Megan and the boys were afraid of the dark. Jamie
was afraid of wolves. And I was afraid of burning to death in my bed.

My fear emerged as a result of Jamie's interest in science.

As a teenager Jamie became obsessed with fantasy, but during
his preteen years when we first moved to the cannery the only books
he was interested in were scientific ones. "Don't give me anything
that isn't true. I want fact books," he insisted to Mom.

Jamie, regrettably, misused his wide-ranging collection of
scientific facts.

Like the night Jamie, Megan, and I were playing in the back
bedroom by the glow of the kerosene Coleman lantern hanging from
the ceiling with a round soot spot above it. Megan was subject to night
terrors and had to have the light on all night, though when everyone
was in bed my parents turned it down to a mellow glimmer. The
long, eight-paned window that faced the forest was black with night,
reflecting back an image of the room with us in it.

To stop Robin and Chris from bothering us older kids, they were
restricted to one walled-off corner of the large room. Because Mom
was softhearted and she didn't want them to feel left out, she had
Dad not panel the wall to their room so they could look out on us

older kids as we played.

The unintended result was that the boys looked like they were zoo animals in a wooden cage or enclosure. They loved to scamper up the framework of the open walls and perch at the space at the top, peering down at us, heckling and jeering at us, and throwing their toys at us, like feral monkeys.

This particular night Jamie, Megan, and I were playing Jamie's own special version of poker in which the rules—forever after immortalized as "Jamie Rules"—were complicated and subject to change without notice. And, let it be noted, always resulted in him winning. Years later I saw the original *Star Trek* episode "A Piece of the Action" and recognized Captain Kirk's "Fizz-bin" as Jamie's version of poker.

As Jamie was explaining to me why I couldn't make the exact same discard he'd made moments earlier (a spade could never be discarded when a club was turned up, unless a heart had been discarded three turns previously; or if it was a Friday night), he paused and stared at me without blinking.

I shifted uneasily, dreading the appearance of one of his disturbing smiles.

The smile didn't appear. Instead, his stare became more and more clinical. I did not find this a reassuring development.

"Interesting," he said. "Did you know that the way some people store fat on their body can be evidence of a lethal combination of chemicals in the stomach? Hold out your arm."

Warily, I looked at my arm.

He picked it up, squeezing it experimentally. "Uh-huh. That's what I thought. You have the thick-skinned subcutaneous fat layer profile of the type of person who is scientifically most likely to suffer from spontaneous human combustion."

I looked at Megan. She stared back at me wide eyed. She looked glad that she didn't have a thick-skinned subcutaneous fat layer profile.

"What, you ask, is spontaneous human combustion?" he continued in a professorial tone as he shuffled the cards. "It begins with a steady increase in temperature due to self-heating reactions caused by chemical processes in the stomach, followed by thermal runaway. This self-heating accelerates to higher and higher temperatures until finally... auto-ignition." He dropped the cards and shoved his hands widely apart, miming a conflagration. He added sound effects of a fire burning.

I knew it was better not to understand what he was talking about. I always regretted asking him to explain. "You haven't dealt out yet. Mom's going to tell us to go to bed pretty soon."

He picked the deck back up and dealt the cards out with slow deliberation as he kept his eyes fixed on me. "That means you ignite and burn hotter than a furnace. People who spontaneously combust burn so hot that there's nothing left of them but their hands and feet. The furniture they're on barely smolders, but the person burns up completely."

I pictured Megan waking up one morning, in the bottom bunk we shared, with my hands and feet lying beside her. At least she'd barely be singed.

"What can I do about it?" I picked up my cards, trying to keep it casual. Fear was like blood in the water to Jamie.

He consulted his science books. After a while, as I waited with outward composure, he slapped the book shut. "Nothing. There's nothing that can be done. You're one of the rare subsets of humans born with the body type that leads to spontaneous combustion. Science has no cure." He stared at me for another long, clinically interested moment, then shrugged. "So, how many cards do you want?"

I lay in bed that night, staring at the glowing lantern and the shadows in the corners of the room, listening to the even breathing of my brothers and sister. The window, so close to the woods, always unnerved me at night. It seemed an unnecessary, open invitation to every bear in Alaska to come in and enjoy a midnight snack.

Many a night I'd lie there and hear a deliberate, crunching sound, like footsteps in hardened snow, and I'd try to convince myself that it was my heartbeat, not a bear prowling around, sniffing out its next meal.

That night I heard the rhythmic sound go faster and faster. It was my heartbeat all right, and it was laboring so fast and hard that it seemed to shake me in the bunk next to Megan. Was this the first sign of spontaneous combustion? Sweat popped out on my brow and

I went rigidly still. There was no question now: I was getting hotter. And hotter.

The more I thought about it and tried not to get hotter, the more heated my body became.

I stared in fascinated horror at the flame burning at the end of the wick in the lantern. My subcutaneous fat layer would make me burn like that wick. I'd char to crusty blackness right next to Megan as she slept obliviously.

Why me? What had I done to deserve a subcutaneous fat layer? Tears leaked out of my eyes as the heat built upward, right into a ball in my throat.

The silence of the house, of the wilderness outside, turned an indifferent eye toward my sufferings as the furnace inside heated to the point of inescapable ignition. I think I passed out from terror.

The next morning Jamie leaned down from the top bunk to do an inspection.

"Oh. You're still here. I thought you might have spontaneously combusted and I wanted to make a record of it. For science." He considered. "Oh, well, there's always tonight."

He smiled. That smile.

• • •

I was about four or five when my parents took us three older kids—the babies not being born yet—to the theater to watch *The Wilderness Family* (as it was originally titled when it was released in 1975), during the height of the Back to the Land Movement.

It's the story of a family that leaves smoggy Los Angeles to homestead remote mountain territory beside an alpine lake, reachable by floatplane. There's the dad, Skip, a denim-clad construction worker who can't hammer a nail in to save his life; Pat, a long-haired, too-glamorous-for-my-gingham-skirt former beauty pageant runner-up as the mother; Jenny, the earnest, asthmatic blonde girl who needs to escape the smog to survive and should have won an Oscar for her performance; and Toby, the giggling little boy who gets into generic mischief and has to be surreptitiously elbowed to remember his lines.

The movie is low budget, with endless images of innocent wilderness play set to saccharine songs and back-to-back montages of DIY cabin building and homesteading to save on paying a scriptwriter. Half the dialogue sounds adlibbed on the spot.

The little girl looked like a cross between my sister and me. I promptly identified with her to the full of my preschool heart. There she was on the enormous screen, playing with the wildlife, running joyfully through wildflower-strewn fields in her Seventies bellbottoms, wearing the exact same ribbed tank top I owned, her long blonde hair waving behind her.

Then, all at once, there she was, being chased by a huge, roaring grizzly. In one of the most traumatic instances of my entire life, I watched as the little blonde girl splashed through the creek and desperately hid in a shallow cave. The bear was on her in an instant, clawing at the roots and reaching for her as she screamed for her mother...

Mom says that my sister and I had cowered in her arms and refused to look at the screen until the bear was chased away by the faithful family hound, Crust, the only real hero of the series.

This was my introduction to bears. A few years later my family moved from the Lower 48 to Alaska, to a location eerily reminiscent of the one in *The Wilderness Family*. We reached it by floatplane. Everyone used a radio to communicate, like they do in the movie. My parents were talking about going farther out to homestead the wilderness.

And there were bears. Everywhere.

Not that I saw one immediately, but they were one of the most frequent topics of conversation amongst the adults. I overheard blood-chilling, hair-raising tales that brought back that terrifying image of the little blonde girl racing for her life as the monstrous beast loped after her.

I suffered nightmares about bears every night of my wilderness life, when I wasn't hyperventilating over the possibility of spontaneously combusting. Sometimes I dreamed of both. It did cross my mind to think that it would serve right whatever bear crashed through the window and into our bedroom to snatch me out of my bunk if I spontaneously combusted in its belly like a bomb.

I'm sure Mom had her own nightmares. After all, during the weekdays while Dad was away logging, she was responsible for five kids who weren't known for their adherence to all the rules she dreamed up to keep us safe.

The cannery site was a veritable bear magnet with its large salmon-spawning creek. And, since the site was part of the mainland, we got both black and brown bears. (In the Alexander Archipelago of Alaska, bears practice island segregation—all the brown bears on one island, all the black bears on another. The mainland was a desegregated zone, and we were right in the middle of it.)

Mom had heard all the bear horror stories too, but her fear of them warred with her more visceral terror of guns that amounted to an uncontrollable phobia. To get around this problem, she had Dad string open jugs of ammonia around the outside of the house and where we kids played.

And she taught us the conventional bear-country safety rules: make lots of noise, don't run from a bear (a bear can run faster than you), don't try to jump in the bay to escape it (a bear can swim faster than you), play dead if it attacks you, back slowly away and get home immediately if you smell a horrible stench, wear your bear bells, blow your bear whistle, climb thick trees with lots of limbs to impede a bear's tree-hugging climbing abilities or its ability to push a smaller tree over...

She made bears sound like supervillains who we had no hope of escaping, with diabolical superpowers no mere human child could hope to defeat. This did not, by the way, improve the quality of my sleep.

Not content with the conventional, she got inventive. And, wisely or not, turned the stuff of our nightmares into playtime.

The bear drill, as she called it, appealed to our athleticism and our competitive instincts. That was how she framed it: "Let's see how fast you can do the drill, from the moment I call 'Bear!' to the moment you're all in the attic."

Her plan was to get us all tucked into the cramped, dark attic of the one story floathouse if a bear ever roamed too close to the house or tried to break and enter. Though a brown bear, if it was determined enough and sniffed us out, could have torn the ceiling apart to get at us. I'm sure she thought that at least it would keep us kids from being underfoot and running loose in the event of a bear assault.

We never knew when Mom would instigate the drill. We'd be going about our business of building forts, attacking each other with bristly yellow skunk cabbage cones, swimming, rowing in the blue plastic rowboat that looked like one of the boys' Fisher-Price toys, climbing trees, and generally living about as free and close to nature as kids could get without turning entirely feral.

When we heard, at any time of the day, "Bear!" we had to drop whatever we were doing, grab the hand of the nearest "baby," and force ourselves to walk sedately to the floathouse before galloping up the ramp with its raised wooden stops and along the railed, narrow front deck to the front door.

On one typical bear drill we burst through the white-painted front door and Jamie jumped on the table and shoved the loosely fitted attic door (a square of plywood) to one side.

Megan grabbed Chris and tossed him to me and I handed him up to Jamie, who snatched him and threw him into the dark hole above his head. Robin came next, and he, too, was flung into the darkness. I pushed Megan onto the table and Jamie heaved her into the hole. Then he grabbed my hand and yanked me onto the table and shoved me in amongst my sweaty, giggling brothers and sister. Jamie athletically pulled himself into the attic and immediately slammed the door into place.

The five of us huddled together, panting in the hot and dusty darkness. We were supposed to wait as silently as possible, without moving, until Mom gave the all clear.

There was no light up there, and other than our breathing and the rustle of our attempts to get comfortable on the bare ceiling joists, it was quiet. It smelled dusty and mildewed with boxes full of magazines, paperback romances, eight-track cassettes, clothes from the Seventies, and other things that we couldn't see but knew were there.

I imagined a camera with an outside view of the shining aluminum roof of the floathouse and the camera ascending, taking in the rectangular floathouse's lengthwise perch on a small mud flat at the edge of the forest with a stream flowing out from under the house's float logs down a gravel beach, past the old pilings down to the broad bay.

The view expanded to show the endless forest climbing ridges and mountains as far as the eye could see toward Canada. On the other side of the peninsula where the floathouse was, the remains of the cannery sprawled black and rusty in the tumbling, golden creek and on the rocky beach. Rising higher the camera took in the breadth of the bay that merged with Clarence Strait, an integral part of Alaska's Inside Passage.

In all that space, there were no other humans. Just us.

But there were a lot of bears, some of them fishing in the salmon creek amidst the twisted cannery debris, on the other side of the peninsula from the floathouse. There were more bears than humans in this land.

Then I pictured the camera cutting back to the hot and dark attic.

"I think that was our fastest yet," Jamie whispered.

I nodded, pushing at the hair stuck to my overheated cheeks and forehead. "I don't think we can get any faster."

"I wonder if Mommy was surprised?" Megan said.

"I wonder if she'll give us a treat?" Robin speculated.

Chris responded, "I'm hungry," and our bellies grumbled. We were always hungry.

The bears were hungry too, of course, but I never felt any sympathy for them. Not when my brothers and sister and I were potentially on their menu.

• • •

There were other things besides bears and spontaneous combustion to fear in our wilderness home.

We quickly found that the first storm we'd encountered at the cannery on our reconnaissance visit was not an uncommon event. Even inside our more protected harbor the wind could find us. And in the winter when the tides were high, blown up higher by a terrifying, roaring wind, a monster storm surge wreaked havoc on everything that floated.

The floathouse in Union Bay. Opposite it is the wanigan with pilings
on either side of the bay. The white spots are our skiffs.

Firewood logs broke loose, skiffs broke loose, the walkway to the
wanigan broke loose, and one night during a hurricane-force storm,
our floathouse broke loose.

It was a night when Dad was home. He was the one who knew
instantly when the swifter cables holding our floathouse to shore
snapped in the surge. He yelled for us all to get outside. Mom only
stopped long enough to make sure we put on our lifejackets and then
we scrambled out.

With only flashlights, we faced the black gale. Mom and the five
of us kids, from oldest to youngest, were ordered to the back of the
float where we had to grab hold of one of the broken cables to stop
the floathouse from being sucked out into the larger bay. We planted
our feet as best we could and our hands burned on the rusty, twisted
steel strands that formed the cable. Our arms were almost yanked
out of their sockets as the many tons of floathouse surged.

Dad jumped into our thirteen-foot Boston Whaler, puny looking
against the sixty-foot length of the heavy float. He had all the force
of the fifty-horsepower Mercury outboard at his command as he

turned the throttle up and pushed against the house, trying to force it back far enough into position so that we could get a wrap of the cable around the brow log to hold it in place.

Wind whipped at our bodies, buffeting the little ones so hard it was a wonder they didn't get blown away. Maybe only their grip on the cable kept them in place. A mix of rain and spray splattered us. The tree branches of the surrounding forest rose and fell in the gusts almost as violently as the floathouse rose and fell in the heavy, sucking surge.

For every foot Dad managed to push the floathouse up when the surge was with him, the water took back two more as soon as the surge went the other way. We kids with Mom were never able to move fast enough to get the stiff cable bent around the brow log to form a loop before the slack was yanked out of the line, almost yanking us into the turbulent bay with it.

If any of us fell in, we'd be sucked under the logs of the floathouse and crushed under it when the surge ground it onto the beach. Our lifejackets wouldn't protect us from that.

We tried to harness the house. Again and again and again, until we were drenched and shaking and the little ones were crying.

We could hear Dad swearing over the thunderous combination of wind and waves. He was screaming at the sky, screaming at the wind, at the waves, and, without putting it into words, at Vietnam. At the futility of trying to live in this world that never gave you any quarter, that worked to destroy you every time you turned around or tried to accomplish anything.

Finally he screamed at Mom: "Get me the gun!"

She didn't know if he meant to shoot himself or all of us, or shoot it to relieve his feelings. Whatever the case, she was done. Without a word, without looking at him, Mom flung the cable down and stomped back to the house.

We followed her.

We didn't know what else to do. We didn't know if our house was going to be dashed to pieces, or be sucked out into the churning storm swells and washed off the float to sink with us in it. The house shook and the windows rattled when the surge dropped us hard on the ground, and the roof sounded like it was about to be torn off in the wind. But it seemed safer inside the house than out there with the storm and Dad.

We didn't get sucked out into the bay that night.

Dad pitted his war rage against the raging elements... and won. I don't know the particulars of how he managed to keep the floathouse from being torn out into the bay, except maybe by just pushing against the float with the skiff until the tide turned, but he did it.

I don't think it surprised any of us kids. His rage was deeper, fiercer, more unforgiving than the worst storm. Nothing could stand against it.

No one sat us down and told us about Vietnam. But we all knew about it. We knew it as a bleak, ugly presence that was there whenever Dad was there.

Dad never hit us—he rarely spanked us. In fact, I can only remember one time he disciplined us with corporal punishment, when we were playing with fire. And I think Mom insisted on it so that we'd learn to never do it again.

He never hit us with his hands, but we dreaded his moods more than we dreaded bears, storms, and spontaneous human combustion. We dreaded his rages and his furious contempt. His intolerance for ineptitude, for things not working, for kids not rising to the occasion, made us avoid him whenever possible.

Maybe when he was away from us he liked us, because when he came home from work he'd have a huge, olive-drab Army backpack stuffed to the brim with Hostess treats, so excessive in their kid appeal that they seemed cartoonish: bright yellow Twinkies with an oozing white-frosting heart—plain, or with strawberry zebra stripes—pink snowballs so sweet they could give you a stomachache just looking at them, chocolate cupcakes with the white scribble of frosting on top of the chocolate frosting, Ding Dongs, half-moon pastry pies in a variety of flavors tasting of starch and shortening and sweetness. There was a mountain of cartoon treats.

But once the goodies were handed out, all of our loud kid antics and our demands on his wife's attention got on Dad's nerves. We took the first excuse to run outside, leaving Mom—our companion, while he was away, in kid adventures and entertainment—to deal with his moods and his unhappiness to be home with us, having to do all the things that had to be done on his weekend after a hard week of heavy labor at the logging camp.

It was backwards for Dad, I think. The weekdays were his escape, when he was happiest. Weekends with us were the slog, his duty, the real work. When the black moods reigned.

He had a sort of stand-in family across the strait in Thorne Bay, twenty miles away. At the logging camp he was teamed with Gerald Pitcher, or "Pitch" as he was known by everyone, who operated the "shovel" that picked up the logs that Dad scaled and bucked off with a chainsaw.

Pitch was a Vietnam vet too. He'd been a helicopter door gunner. Dad was a helicopter mechanic and door gunner and crew chief. They fought in different years, but it was the same war, and they understood each other and what the other man had gone through. They were, in a lot of ways, mirrors of each other, but in ways that complemented rather than antagonized. They became best friends.

Pitch had a wife and three girls, and Dad often had dinner with them as a much-loved "Uncle Gary." I think he was able to be more comfortable and accessible with the girls, more playful and fun, as he only occasionally was with us. They didn't demand fatherhood of him and he could relax and enjoy their company in ways he never could with his own children.

I think it was a relief for him to cross the strait back to Pitch and his other family, a family with no demands, no expectations, just affection and acceptance.

We rarely saw Pitch and his family, but I liked them. I could see why Dad was so comfortable with them. They were salt-of-the-earth people, direct, humorous, pragmatic with definite opinions—larger than life, in Pitch's case—and the girls were instantly lovable.

They helped Dad regain a lot of his humanity and a sense of normality lost in Vietnam. They made him happy.

Thinking back, I'm surprised that he came home every weekend. But he did. Almost without fail he crossed one of the most treacherous bodies of water in all of Alaska every weekend in an open, thirteen-foot skiff. One time the crossing was so rough that one of the large Alaska Marine Highway ferries, seeing him battling the big seas in his tiny skiff, went off their route to break a trail for him through the heaving swells.

Doggedly, he drove through whatever weather was thrown at him to reach us and shower us with goodies, his wilderness skills and labor, and his war rage.

When I wandered the cannery ruins as a teenager, looking at the desolation, the twisted, scorched remains of a once smoothly, industriously functioning unit, I wondered if it was a visual representation of my dad's inner world.

"If you ain't dyin' you ain't livin'." —Rand

CHAPTER SIX

MOM DREAMED of moving to Alaska her whole life. Her mom, Pat, had read every James Oliver Curwood book she could get her hands on. The Far North, the word "Alaska," resonated with romance and adventure for both of them.

Mom's dad, Frank, was a footloose adventurer, but he had a lot of places to get to before he finally made it to Alaska. Mom and her two brothers were perpetually the new kids at school—when they were near a school—as Frank took his kids, Romi, Randy, and Rory, and his wife, Pat, down every back road he could find.

Mom grew up following him on his remote hunting and trapping trails while her mom stayed at home, sometimes in nothing more than a tent, sewing all their clothes and making meals out of nothing. (Mom's dad insisted on making meals out of the animals he trapped, like beaver and muskrat, that nobody but him could tolerate eating. It was hard enough smelling it.)

Barely out of her toddler years, Mom was delighted to find little piles of "raisins" on the trail left especially for her by the deer as she followed along in her dad's big footprints. She was disillusioned when her father told her that the deer hadn't left her edible gifts; the soft round pellets were something else entirely.

They crossed from Montana (where Mom was kissed by Dad under the bed when they were both five and she thought he'd made her pregnant) to the Great Lakes, and then back to Montana again where Mom married Dad when they were both twenty-one.

Frank worked in the US Merchant Marine on the Great Lakes whenever the family was hard up for money. He parked his wife and kids near Duluth, Minnesota, in 1957, the same year the freighter *Edmund Fitzgerald* was constructed, so large that it was within a foot of the maximum length allowed for passage through the almost-finished Saint Lawrence Seaway.

Later he would sail on "the big Fitz" years before she sank with all hands in a storm on Lake Superior in late 1975. I grew up singing along with Gordon Lightfoot's ode to the disaster, "Wreck of the Edmund Fitzgerald."

Pat tucked her children in bed and sang them an old folk song about the *Titanic*: "It was sad when the great ship went down / Husbands and wives and little children lost their lives / It was sad when the great ship went down."

She had a large stock of these kinds of folk disaster songs from her own childhood. Her children thought nothing of how the lyrics might relate to their father, who was so often away on the big ships plying the stormy lakes. "I just remember a cozy feeling as I was tucked in and she sang," Mom reminisces.

Pat (Priscilla) had been a semi-professional singer with two of her sisters, Ginny (Virginia) and Babe (Nila). They'd been the Irwin Sisters and had sung for weddings and local events, including in big hotels to keep the Eastern tourists happily entertained during the summer season. They even took second place in an Amateur Hour talent show.

Despite Pat's bona fides as a singer, Mom, in the way of all cool-obsessed teenagers, cringed when her mother sang the songs from her Sixties rock 'n' roll records, putting that way-back 1930s warble on them. "Now I'd probably love to hear them sung that way," Mom says wistfully.

When Frank was briefly back home, on one unforgettable outing he took his kids to visit one of the boats he worked on. They climbed the endless ladder to get to the deck of the freighter and were shown all over the ship, including down in the engine room where the enormous engines made a lasting impression. Mom doesn't remember which ship it was, but I like to imagine that it was the *Edmund Fitzgerald*.

And all the time, Mom badgered her dad, from one side of the continent to the other, to take them north to Alaska.

Her chagrin was great when he finally decided to make the move to the Last Frontier with Pat, Rory, and the newest addition to the family, Lance, in tow—by then she was married and had two kids, Jamie and me.

• • •

"Rather than waste time at the dock untying, we just cut the ropes and headed out. We [made] it around the point, but were rolling really bad… we did most of our searching from Lemly Rock to about a third of the way into Union Bay. We [had] to come back to calmer waters [because] it was really severe, but it seems to me we didn't come back to port for 3 days… maybe we did refuel and get food, but I thought we were out there 3 days along with Bob Hunley, Rod Maddox and a few other fishermen and Search & Rescue."
—Lance, in an e-mail about the night of February 13, 1981

• • •

Rand was married as well, to a tall, blonde young woman named Jan, not yet in her twenties, and they had a baby son, Shawn, whom Rand adored. Some of the time they lived with my parents, when they all lived in Anacortes, Washington. Jamie, Shawn, and I were born there, in that order.

Mom and Rand had grown up inseparable as children, best friends in the way siblings could be when they lived so remotely that the humans they interacted with the most consistently were family members. She and Rand did everything together, shared all the same 1950s kid adventures, shared the same imagination even.

"One time," Mom reminisces, "when we were little, Rand and I got up early to surprise our mom by making her breakfast. We decided to jazz things up with food coloring, but…" She laughs ruefully. "Even we couldn't eat the gray-green pancakes."

After separations of teen years and marriage, they were still close. Their enthusiasm for music and art kept them tight, and they could talk for hours about anything and everything under the sun, sometimes agreeing, sometimes arguing, but always laughing. Their entire family had a well-developed love of the absurd.

Rand didn't reach his full height of six feet until he was in his twenties. He grew up small and was the oldest son of a six-foot-four, larger-than-life father who personified hypermasculine adventure, a man who had run away from home at the age of twelve, rode the rails as a teenager, survived the waning days of the Wild Old West (once almost hanged, mistakenly, as a horse thief), and had a career as a boxer who had never lost a bout, before being shipped off to fight in World War II. As such, Rand always seemed to feel like he had to prove himself and went out of his way to dive into reckless, law-defying, life-endangering pastimes.

One time Rand and a friend drove Mom to a grocery store to do her shopping. She came out a little while later with her bags in her arms to hear Rand yelling at her.

"Get in the car, Romi! Get in the car now!!"

When she stopped and stared at him uncertainly, he jumped out and tossed her into the back seat. Her groceries went flying, landing on the backseat and floor of the car. She was only partly in, her legs sticking out with the door hitting them when he jumped back in and gunned it.

He and his friend laughed maniacally while she yelled at them. When she sat up and looked out the back, she saw that they'd stolen an entire tub of cabbages that had been on display in front of the store and shoved them into the trunk. The trunk door was open and the pilfered cabbages were bouncing out and rolling all down the street behind them.

"You never knew what to expect," she says after every Rand story.

He wound up spending much of his free time hanging out in jail. The local cops adored him, as most people did, and left the jail door open for him to come and go as he needed. It was no secret that Rand was intensely loyal to his friends—some of whom did not deserve, and did not return, such loyalty—and he took the rap for whatever crimes they all got up to.

A few years after Frank moved his family to Alaska, he came back down to show Rand the way up from Anacortes. Jan and Shawn flew to Ketchikan while Rand brought up his first fishing boat, the *Janet One*. He and his dad made it safely, but it was a rough trip, a hint of the kind of weather Rand would be dealing with when he'd make a career for himself as an Alaskan commercial troller.

• • •

"I looked at Gary and we both just knew it was time to let go.
That there was no point in continuing."
—Mom, about the night of February 13, 1981

• • •

At the same time Frank and Rand made the trip by sea, my parents attempted to reach Alaska by land, via the Al-Can Highway (as the Alaska Highway was then called). Dad built a live-aboard van for the occasion that Mom painted in the typical garish Seventies colors of lime green, orange, gold, and brown, and christened it "the Gypsy Wagon."

They made it as far as Boston Bar, British Columbia, when the van broke down. They had no money, but Dad was hired by a local garage owner who asked no questions about a visa until Dad had worked there for a few months. By then the garage owner knew what kind of an employee he had and was eager to keep him. He pushed Dad to get a visa and live in Canada permanently.

Mom and Dad had fallen in love with Canadians and the country, so they agreed to give up Alaska. Dad crossed the border back into the US with Mom, Jamie, and me, and visited the office that handled visas. The officious bureaucrat behind the desk had a lot on his mind, and at the sight of my Bohemian-looking parents he decided to unload it on them.

"We're tired of all the lazy, no-account draft dodgers flooding our country," he told them. "We don't need any more."

Dad said, "I'm no draft dodger. I can show you my discharge papers."

The bureaucrat wasn't interested. "You draft dodgers skip out on your own country. You show no loyalty to it. And you expect us to believe you'd be loyal to our country? We don't need your kind." He went on in this vein and ignored everything Dad had to say about his Vietnam service. Dismissed it. As if all that he'd lived and lost meant nothing. Deliberately refused to believe in it.

Until Dad lunged across the desk and grabbed him by the throat.

Mom, who had never seen, and would never again see, Dad lay hands on anyone in anger, never forgot it. The bureaucrat didn't either. Once Dad was persuaded to let him go, the red-faced man ordered them out of Canada immediately, to leave their belongings and get back to the US where they belonged.

Mom pleaded with him—everything they owned was in the Gypsy Wagon. She wasn't someone who cried in the face of adversity, but unbeknownst to her she was coming down with tonsillitis, and under the stress of the moment she burst into tears. The man became uncomfortable enough by her tears to relent and say that they could get their belongings, but then they had to leave Canada.

It was several years after this before they finally made it to Alaska.

In the interim, before my parents made the move, Mom periodically visited her family. I remember my first impression of Ketchikan, when Mom visited Rand and Jan and Shawn who were already living there.

The city was like nothing I'd ever seen before.

Ketchikan, Alaska, was bathed in extreme, late northern light during an endless evening that turned everything gold. The air tasted of things I couldn't name, but it made everything more vivid than it already was.

The streets were narrow—some of them were wooden, some went right over the water built on telephone pole stilts, and some climbed sheer, forested hillsides with barely a pause between hills. Everything was raw and wood-frame and still retained the frontier flavor. There were totem poles right in the middle of the downtown shopping area.

I felt like I was visiting a different world.

• • •

> *"I offered to go with him to move the boat but he said no*
> *and he would be right back... After a bit I knew in my*
> *'knower' that things were not good. I mean, I really knew!"*
> —Linda, in an e-mail about the night of February 13, 1981

• • •

I loved Rand. I loved everything about him, especially the way he was with Shawn. I was in awe of a father who couldn't get enough close time with his boy, who loved to hold him, ruffle his blond hair, joke with him, and get right down on the floor to play with him.

Rand had enough love to go around and delighted in spending time with his nephew and nieces. He loved children and children loved him back. In fact, I don't know anyone who didn't love Rand. He had the gift of moving between a child's world and an adult's world effortlessly, perhaps because he never entirely grew up.

In an adult setting he could be a quiet observer, or he could be a dynamic opinion giver. He had a soft, low voice, with a hint of the Deep South in it that was a source of bafflement to his family, since he'd never spent any time in the South.

Like everyone in his family, discussions that could turn into all-in arguments were a staple of life for him. He could be persuaded to a different point of view, but never bulldozed. His mom was known to try, grinding relentlessly on one opinion to the point where he felt the need to bang his head on the table and plead to her, "Just shoot me. Either stop talking, or just shoot me!"

Rand was artistically gifted, but he was modest about it. I was impressed with everything I saw of his, including a painting of a sailboat and an odd ink drawing on a conch of a Gollum-looking scholar surrounded by scrolls and books, writing on a scroll with a feather pen. It was fantasy and realism strikingly wedded, and I always longed to see more images drawn in this style.

He wasn't without vices, typical to the time and place. He swore, smoked, and drank—I remember him with a cigarette sticking out of his dark beard and a beer in the mitt that was his left hand. In an unguarded moment, when Dad and Rand had worked in the shingle mill in Anacortes, Washington, Rand had lost all the fingers and the tip of his thumb to the saw and was rushed to the hospital. Dad looked for the missing fingers to have them sewn back on, but they couldn't be found.

I'd never, in my childhood, known him to have fingers on both hands, so I accepted their absence as normal to him. It was a part of who he was, like his beard or his uniquely helpless laugh. And it certainly didn't stop him from doing anything he felt like doing. He lived the remote fishing and trapping Alaskan life as fully as anyone around him.

Tolerance came in extremes for him. In a friend he could tolerate almost any behavior, no matter how much hot water it landed him in. He could accept other people's opinions, even of himself, and he could—somewhat dryly and with satirical enjoyment—understand people's prejudices and self-deceptions.

But there was one thing he absolutely could not tolerate, and that was boredom. Boredom was easily worse than death to him, and he needed constant amusement. Because he rewarded his entertainers with enthusiasm and his helpless, infectious laughter, people loved to entertain him.

The times I remember my dad being his most playful, laughing the most, and really enjoying himself were when Rand was there egging him on.

Like the time Rand urged Dad to get on the radio and prank everyone in Meyers Chuck. The entire area during this time communicated by CB radio. Dad's handle was a nickname he'd picked up in the Army: "The Walrus."

Disguising his voice, Dad keyed the mic and said he was captain of a one-hundred-foot vessel named the *Sea Cucumber* and he was in rough weather with engine trouble. We all provided sound effects, rattling aluminum flashing for thunder, banging on a bell to mimic the sound of a ledge marker in rough weather, not to mention throwing in a few lonely sea gull cries for color. Dad asked if there was room at the village dock for his boat.

The locals got on the radio to confer with each other and discuss which boats to move to make room for the huge *Sea Cucumber*.

Grandma Pat recognized Rand's laughter in the background when Dad was talking. She got on the radio. Donning a Texan twang and calling herself "Clam Digger," she pushed Dad to more and more ridiculous heights of fantasy. At last, the locals caught on—fortunately, before they went out into the night to move the boats around at the dock. All but the most humorless got a laugh out of it.

• • •

"I was shouting his name, but it wasn't 'Rand.'
I was yelling: 'Randy, Randy, where are you?'
In my mind he'd reverted to being a little boy."
—Mom, about the night of February 13, 1981

• • •

My parents also liked to prank Rand, like the time he and his girlfriend Linda came over for dinner and they had me greet them. My parents combed my waist-length, straight blonde hair over my face and had me stand in my boots facing the wrong way.

When I didn't respond to their greetings, Rand shook my shoulder, then walked around me and realized what we'd done. He loved it. When music was put on, "Slow Dancing" by Johnny Rivers, he took me by the hand and slow danced with me—with my hair out of my face and my boots on right. I thought he was the most amazing man who'd ever lived.

When we moved to the cannery, Rand had been divorced from Jan for a few years and was living with Linda, who'd grown up in San Francisco.

I remember when I, along with the rest of Rand's family, first met Linda. We were all at Grandpa Frank's and Grandma Pat's house in Meyers Chuck, the adults seated at the round table with its shiny yellow plywood top over a large barrel, in the captain-style wooden chairs circled around it. The tall Aladdin lamp in the center shed golden light on the shelves of books on one side and bounced off the black paned window on another side.

Cigarette smoke from my grandparents' ashtrays floated toward the peeled log beams overhead, as did the coffee and hot chocolate steam rising from brown-and-gold mugs placed near elbows. The adults were wondering what Rand's girlfriend was like, how to handle their sense of loyalty to Jan while respecting Rand's right to move on, not to mention how a woman from a sophisticated city like San Francisco would take to living on a cramped fishing boat.

A few minutes later Rand pushed open the back door and strolled over the hallway's gold and cream linoleum floor. Following him was a slender woman wearing a black turtleneck under her jacket, her long brown hair held back in a thick, shining braid. I thought she was striking, with a sense of style and a charisma that complemented Rand's casual dynamism.

Within minutes of being introduced to Linda Miller (no relation to Rory's wife, formerly Marion Miller), Rand's family found out she enjoyed the same love of the absurd that they did, and once they all started laughing together at something ridiculous and self-deprecating she shared, she was a permanent member of the family.

When Mom no longer had a tutor for the five of us kids, Linda said she would take on the job, against Rand's advice to "never work for family or friends." But she insisted, so they moved into the cabin on the creek side. He kept his new boat the *Wood Duck*, a thirty-two-foot wooden trolling boat built in 1964, in a tiny bight to the north of us.

• • •

"When we found the skiff, you could see the painter had been cut with a knife… we figured the way it was blowing and considering his only having one hand, the skiff was probably instantly snatched away."
—Lance, in an e-mail about the night of February 13, 1981

• • •

I was the first of us kids to wake up that night when I heard my parents talking on the CB radio. The wind was roaring through the trees, pummeling the house and making the panes in the window near my bed rattle. It screamed under the eaves at a pitch that sounded like nothing earthly.

The glow of the lantern hanging from the ceiling didn't reassure me as it usually did whenever I woke up during a storm. I crept out of bed and found my parents in the front room.

It wasn't until I heard his voice coming through the speaker that I realized Rand was out there in the storm. He hadn't been able to settle in for the night, thinking about his boat moored in a tiny bight a quarter mile to the north. Mom and Dad had spent the evening at the cabin with Rand and Linda, sharing beers and opinions about which version of the song "He Ain't Heavy, He's My Brother," was the best.

Mom insisted that the Hollies had the best version, but Dad was a staunch Neil Diamond fan and wouldn't back down. Rand sided with him, as he tended to do, even if he might have agreed with Mom. He had a deep vein of sympathy for how Dad had been treated after his return from Vietnam. "You're right, buddy," he said, almost gently. "Diamond's got the best version."

As the evening wore on and the wind continued to pick up, Rand became worried about the growing storm and decided to take the *Wood Duck* to a different anchorage.

He didn't get far before he ran into trouble. The seas were massive with hissing white combers on top, and the little *Wood Duck* was taking wave after wave over the bow. The seawater exploded so continuously against the small wheelhouse's windows that he could barely see which way to steer to keep the bow pointed into the waves. If he was turned broadside to the waves, he was certain the boat would either swamp or capsize.

His voice was calm, if a bit dry, but still tinged with that warm Southern accent as he related his problems. Typically, in severe weather, a trolling boat would let down its trolling poles and toss out anchors attached to them called stabilizers, or stabies, because they tended to stabilize a boat's roll.

But, as he told my parents, he didn't dare leave the wheel long enough to do that.

Dad talked to Rand at first, but I think post trauma from Vietnam overcame him and he couldn't speak. He handed the mic to Mom. Besides, she'd been insisting that he ask Rand to put on his survival suit, if he had one.

It was the first thing she told him when she got hold of the microphone. "You need to get into a survival suit."

Rand holding up a monster lingcod in the cockpit of the *Wood Duck*.

By then, Megan, feeling my absence in the bunk we shared, had joined me. We sat huddled on my parents' mussed bed, listening to the wind and the crash of the waves and our uncle's voice on the radio. The other kids joined us one after the other.

It was hard to tell what Rand said next, either that he didn't have time to put on a survival suit, he didn't have one, or he wasn't able to fully suit up in it. He kept having to let go of the microphone to deal with problems in the wheelhouse. He said things were coming loose down below and his gear was being washed off the decks outside. At one point he left to make sure the dinghy, the small lifeboat, was still lashed overhead. Through the radio we could hear the boat's engine and the cacophony of the struggle the boat was going through.

In Meyers Chuck everyone heard the conversation and knew Rand was in trouble. Someone called the Coast Guard while Rory and Lance raced to Rory's boat, the *Velvet*, and cut the lines—rather than take the time to untie them—and powered up the engine to pull away from the dock as fast as they could.

Grandpa Frank wanted to go too, but he was persuaded that leaving Grandma Pat was not an option. At that point my grandfather had suffered several heart attacks and no one thought it was a good idea for him to head out into that kind of weather.

The *Velvet*, unfortunately, had a bad tendency to roll more than most boats during a following sea, even with the stabies out, and as soon as Rory turned the corner to head down into Union Bay, the huge swells laid his boat over again and again. Lance, out on the bow, hung on for dear life, trying to peer through the wind and stinging rain as Rory maneuvered the spotlight, searching for the *Wood Duck*.

I could hear the tense grimness and frustration in Rory's usually drawling, easygoing voice when he got on the radio and said he had to turn back to less violent seas.

The Coast Guard had also sent out a Search and Rescue vessel, but they were turned back not that far from Ketchikan by the ferocity of the storm. This despite the pride Coast Guardsmen take in their unofficial motto: "You have to go out, you don't have to come back."

Back in Meyers Chuck, another fisherman, Bob Hunley, headed for his own boat, the *Sunrise*, one of the best riding and largest long-liners in the Meyers Chuck fishing fleet. Everyone felt that Rand's best hope at that point was for the *Sunrise* to reach him.

Minutes later Bob Hunley's laconic voice said over the radio, "We're going to be delayed. Our tanks are dry. Someone siphoned the fuel out of the boat's tanks. We have to refuel."

On the radio Rand said the *Wood Duck* was being swamped, that there was water coming in everywhere.

"She's going down," he said.

Mom tried to convince him that he could hang in there.

"She's gonna roll and she's not gonna come back up," he said matter-of-factly. "I'm out."

The frightening finality in his voice made Mom reassure him strongly that people were working to get to him, that they'd find him. "You're going to make it, Rand. You're going to be okay."

He said, "I'm going to get the skiff off the boom."

· · ·

*"It was really dark and the wind was howling. I remember
all five of us kids standing on the front deck, or maybe inside
in front of the big window, and seeing our parents go out into
that horrible weather in that tiny little skiff and wonder if they
were coming back. If they didn't, what would happen to us?"*
—Megan, about the night of February 13, 1981

• • •

I don't remember my parents arguing about it when they decided to
go out in our thirteen-foot Boston Whaler to try to reach him. They
were impelled by the absolute necessity to save Rand. Mom told me
later that as they ran down the beach, she was screaming to Dad
over the wind: "The kids, Gary, the kids!" She said he just looked at
her and they kept running down to the skiff.

Mom's fears of making her kids orphaned were confirmed once
they were out in those towering seas, in the dark, in the tiny open
skiff. For once, the fifty-horsepower outboard, normally way too
much power for a skiff that size, came into its own as Dad powered
up the mountainous swells. On the other side they dove down into
the trough, and then labored back up in the hissing, screaming
blackness only to swoop down again—a nightmare rollercoaster full
of terrible, real-world consequences.

In between shouting for Rand, though she knew he wouldn't
hear, Mom thought about her kids, that they could be orphaned. "The
wind and the seas that night… it wasn't like anything I'd experienced
before. It felt different. It felt malevolent," she recalls.

Dad never describes that night, or their attempt in the skiff to
get to Rand.

"I knew when we lost him," Mom says. "We both knew. That's
when we turned back."

When they returned home, Mom stumbled out of the skiff, her
clothes soaking wet and stiff with saltwater, and crossed through
the woods with her flashlight to reach the cabin and tell Linda
what had happened. Neither of them admitted that the unthinkable
had happened, though Linda revealed later that she, too, had had a
moment when she felt Rand was gone.

They returned to the floathouse, bolstering each other up with denial-fueled hope. Inside the floathouse we listened with them as Bob Hunley in the refueled *Sunrise* turned the corner and headed into the maelstrom that was Union Bay. His boat took a pounding as he watched his radar. Tentative excitement swept all of us when he narrated the search over the radio, eventually saying, "I've got a blip."

"What's a blip?" Mom demanded.

Dad said it was radar-speak for a positive contact. It was probably the dinghy, with Rand in it.

"You're calling him a blip? You can't call a man a blip!" Mom said through wavering laughter.

"That will be his nickname. We'll call him Blip from now on," Linda wisecracked.

Mom and Linda laughed until they cried. Between breaths they offered more absurd sentences using Blip as Rand's new name. They held onto each other as they laughed hysterically while the rest of us watched them in the kerosene lamplight.

I pictured Rand getting the small dinghy down. I could see him struggling to launch the dinghy off the swamped boat with all the gear and everything surging around his legs, with the wind roaring and icy waves spitting at him. I imagined that the boat felt unstable, the way a dream can, when you have to hug the ground to keep from being swept away to something terrible.

I imagined him getting in the dinghy and tying himself to it so he wouldn't be separated from it as the huge, salty seas crashed down over him as he peered into the darkness, hoping to see a light coming toward him. I imagined his shivering relief when he saw the *Sunrise*'s green and red running lights, its spotlight turning the night into day as it swept over the waves toward him. Rescue was so close, he was almost there.

Dad, to give himself something constructive to do and to help get Mom and himself dry after they were soaked by sea spray in the skiff, stuffed cardboard boxes in the stove to throw out some heat. The chimney, apparently caked with creosote, caught on fire. Dad cursed and headed outside to take care of it while Mom and Linda found this latest threat hilarious.

It felt like the world was coming apart at the seams.

Bob Hunley's voice said on the radio: "We've got the dinghy alongside... it's empty."

• • •

*"I remember us being in a kind of denial that evening and the days to
follow. We scoured the beaches yelling his name while
the Coast Guard searched out in the deep."*
—Linda, in an e-mail about that night and the days following
February 13, 1981

• • •

Everyone looked.

Everyone in the area who had a boat came and searched.

It was surreal how calm the weather was the next day, and the days after that. The Coast Guard came out in their orange-and-white helicopter and landed on the beach near the floathouse during low tide.

None of the adults were there. They were all out looking for Rand, calling his name.

My brothers and sister were too shy to deal with the strange men in their astronaut-looking orange suits and helmets stepping out of the metal and plexiglass bubble, the rotors chopping at the air. I stood on the end of one of the big logs the house sat on as a slow-trudging, reluctant man approached the floathouse. I looked down at him when he stopped in front of me.

He craned his head back and gave me a searching, oddly vulnerable look, as if he was scared to talk to me. I realize now he must have been very young. "Are your parents home?" he asked.

"No, they're out looking."

He hesitated, then gave his name and described where they'd already searched and found nothing. Then he told me where they were going to look next. It was obvious he was uncomfortable talking in this businesslike way, the way he'd been trained, to a nine-year-old girl about a family tragedy.

"Can you tell them that?" he finished. I think he wanted to add something personal, to say he was sorry that our family was going through this, but he didn't know how to say it.

"I'll tell them," I said.

He looked at me again searchingly, as if expecting something more from me. Maybe to make it better for him, but I didn't know how. Finally, he put his helmet on and trudged back toward the helicopter and the waiting pilot, the gravel and clam shells crunching under his boots.

I watched the two suited men rise up into the air, staring down at me and the floathouse. I could picture myself and the house getting smaller as they rose, until they were whisked away back to continue the search on the broad, reflective bay.

The five of us kids, left alone, didn't know what to do with ourselves or our feelings—or what our feelings were. We ran around screaming and yelling at the top of our lungs, jumping on the furniture, and doing the bear drill until we were exhausted.

When our parents got home we clamored around them insistently, demanding attention, food, attention. Dad stalked off wordlessly, ignoring us, hating the world and everything and everyone in it. Mom, physically, emotionally, and all other ways exhausted, yelled at us. "I just lost my brother! I've been out there hour after hour yelling his name until I'm hoarse, and you're asking if I'll cook you macaroni and cheese?"

I don't remember if it was the Coast Guard or one of the boats in the fishing fleet that finally found the *Wood Duck*. It was all but sunk, only the bow out of the water, held up by a pocket of air. It was suggested that people have been known to survive boat disasters by breathing in pockets of air like that, so for one last instant of hope, the Coast Guard dove on the wreck, but found no one aboard.

The *Wood Duck* was near enough to shore to be beached and salvaged and it would have become the property of Rory—but he was repulsed by the idea of benefiting from his brother's death. For the same reason he refused to sell it. Instead, he and Dad put halibut anchors on its bow and stern and towed it into deeper water.

Rand's family, not counting the kids, boarded the *Velvet* for a memorial ceremony of sorts as Rory got the mostly sunk *Wood Duck* under careful tow. Judy Collins's album *Colors of the Day* was playing on the stereo's speakers.

The *Wood Duck* sank entirely, pulling the stern of the *Velvet* down so that they had to cut the towline, as Judy Collins sang "Farewell to Tarwathie." I wasn't there, but I pictured it from what I overheard said among the adults, and now whenever I hear Judy Collins sing I think of the *Wood Duck*'s slow drift downward from beams of light near the surface, down through fathoms of darkness until it settled somewhere on the bottom.

• • •

"I never thought of that. That never struck me before."
—everyone interviewed for this chapter, when I said that my grandmother could have lost all her children that night

• • •

For many, many years I pictured Rand surviving. I had fully fleshed-out fantasies of him making it to an island that the searchers had overlooked and being picked up by a passing tourist boat, or maybe smugglers, shadowy criminals who didn't want to reveal themselves, and him suffering from amnesia so he couldn't tell them where to take him. I imagined bumping into him in one of the towns around here. I used to look for him even when I was an adult wherever there were crowds of people… all the way into my late twenties.

Some people were bothered by the fact that the *Wood Duck* went down on Friday the 13th, but my parents weren't superstitious. To counteract the common superstition that might affect us kids, they made a point of paying attention to every Friday that landed on the thirteenth day of the month after that, and nothing bad ever again happened to our family on that day.

The truth is, it's incredibly easy for fishermen to lose their lives in Alaska. That year alone, in 1981, eighty-eight fishermen lost their lives, and four Coast Guardsmen died when their helicopter went down in a storm while attempting a rescue. Thirty-six years later, to the day that we lost Rand, the US Coast Guard suspended its search for the six-man crew of the ninety-eight-foot crabber *Destination*, which was believed to have sunk approximately two miles northwest of St. George Island.

I looked up the sinkings that year online at alaskashipwreck.com:

> February 13, 1981 – The trawler *Wood Duck* sank near Union Bay with the loss of one crewman [sic].

And, scrolling farther down, boat after boat lost, crewman drowned, I found:

> October 30, 1981 – The 54-foot *Gem* sank near Cape Spencer. David Miller, Larry Miller and another brother were picked up by the Coast Guard in a C-130. The fourth crewman, Tim Blake, was lost.

These three Millers were my Aunt Marion's brothers, Rory's and Rand's brothers-in-law, and Tim Blake was a close friend. Dick Miller named his oldest son after him.

Three years later:

> Sept 30, 1984 – The 48-foot wooden fishing vessel *Curlew* sank in a rescue attempt of fishing vessel *Kelly Ann* in the Shumagin Islands. The *Kelly Ann* cut the towline as the *Curlew* foundered and managed to start her engine, avoid the nearby rocks and save Ray Miller from the sinking *Curlew*. Lost from the *Curlew* were David Miller... Jeff O'Donohue and Phil O'Donohue.

David was Aunt Marion's oldest brother, nicknamed Dobbs. Ray was her kid brother who my siblings and I grew up with. He was the same age as Jamie. Ray married Liz O'Donohue; and his and Marion's brother, Norman, married Sheila O'Donohue. Liz and Sheila were sisters to brothers Jeff and Phil, lost on the *Curlew*.

If there is one constant in a commercial fishing lifestyle, it is that there will be boats that go down and family members and friends lost. I doubt there's a fishing family in Alaska who hasn't been affected by the sinking of someone close to them.

My Aunt Marion and Uncle Rory each lost their oldest brother.

If that wasn't bad enough, all of my grandmother's children were on the water that night, and they might all have been lost. Her husband, Frank, could have been lost too if he hadn't been persuaded to stay behind.

Now I wonder what my grandfather thought, if he wondered why his son would be lost when he himself had survived so many years on some of the world's stormiest lakes, oceans, and inside waters.

He'd survived a war where many sailors and soldiers lost their lives, he'd been there at Iwo Jima when Japan surrendered, crossing a vast ocean to be there, and crossing it again to get back home. Yet it was his son who went down, not him.

• • •

"I was numb. For a long time I didn't feel anything at all.
While we were looking for him in the skiff, when I was going out
alone in the canoe and searching the beaches, calling his name for
weeks, I felt nothing. It was the first time in my life I experienced
no emotions, at all. Until I hurt my foot—and all at once
I could feel again. I felt it then. I felt his loss."
—Mom, about the days and years following February 13, 1981

• • •

I didn't know it at the time, I don't think anyone did, but my mom sank into depression after we lost Rand. She became a different person, turned inward, writing, always writing in journal after journal.

This is an entry from one of her journals:

He was so little when he first gave me his loyalty. Those
days when he manfully ate the mud pies I made for him,
when he ran away with me if I told him that that was what
the situation called for. He shared everything with me, and
he talked serious stuff and so did I… how we felt… how it
felt when we lost Smokey, our favorite person who happened
to be part Cocker Spaniel… How it felt when our parents
fought… How it was being "the new kid" all the time in
school after school after school…

How—life—felt.

Later, when he thought he was almost a man, and I thought
him my little teenage brother, he brought to me the spoils of
his first theft and dumped the dime store glitter of $1.50 jewels
in my lap. I told him off and he told me not to worry. He told
me not to worry so many times. He was some swashbuckling,
laughing highwayman set down in the wrong age.

Rand (at age five) and Mom (at age seven), best friends in Montana.

He was just a little older when he came to me and asked if I was "a slut." His first experience of disillusionment with women had come. A girl he'd really liked had been found to have "feet of clay," or was it "round heels"? I guess he just wanted to know if all women would let him down. He had what were once called "ideals" (at least about women he had them). I told him "no" I wasn't "a slut" and he believed me just because I told him. Because—I—told him. I liked him for that. And for so much more... I could fill books with what I liked him for...

He kept on growing, and growing beyond me, and away from me, but I always liked him as much as anyone I ever met, and more than most.

We would still meet and talk sometimes and we'd tell each other that we loved each other. We'd argue sometimes and he'd tell me not to worry.

His family meant a lot to him,—everything, I think.

I was his past. His memories. I stored them for him so that he could say: "remember when?"... And have it all vividly come back in a second. Something we remembered together (which always came back in those conversations)

*was about a time on the road (moving again, "new kid"
again) when we stopped at a gas station.*

*There was a group of kids our age there, on bikes, they'd
known each other since birth, you could just tell. They got
soda pops out of a cooler and laughed and joked with the
old man there fixing a tire. Small town life. We always
remembered them together, and the old man fixing that tire.
And we both felt it so odd that they meant something to us
when they never even noticed us.*

*Memories that only he and I shared. I could say to
someone else ... "once I saw a group of kids on bikes drinking
pop and an old man fixing a tire." What would it mean?
Nothing. Only he knew what it was—that feeling.*

*And he was loyal. So loyal. He would have died for us or
killed for us. No question. I believe that.*

*He did die, when he was still young. More than twice his
age when he died is what I am now. He always said ... "don't
worry"...*

I don't have to now. He's safe—forever.

• • •

For myself, I can't help but think of how strange the world is, how
terrible it can be.

I think of Rand as a brown-haired, blue-eyed little boy, feeling
safe, warm, and cozy in a lamplit bedroom as his mom tucked him
and his siblings in while she sang, "How sad it was when that great
ship went down, how sad it was...."

CHAPTER SEVEN

THERE'S A scene in *The Wilderness Family* where the Robinsons are working at building their log cabin home next to an alpine lake when they hear a plane.

The Robinsons drop everything to run toward the shoreline as the plane drops something in the lake. Skip paddles out in the canoe and picks it up while the kids and Pat hop with excitement on shore. They call out to him, asking who it's from.

As he paddles back, Skip tells them it's from the school board.

"Oh, no," Toby groans.

"How'd they ever find us out here?" Jenny mourns.

Skip smirks so hard it almost flips the canoe. "I squealed."

"Oh, Dad!"

My siblings and I never understood it. When our huge boxes of school supplies arrived through a Southeast Islands School District (SISD) homeschooling program, all of it belonging to no one but us kids—separate packages for each kid, categorized by grade—we were beyond thrilled.

We'd rip the boxes open and gloat over the tablets, pencils, loose paper, drawing paper, construction paper, file folders, rulers, clay, crayons, finger paint, pipe cleaners, glue, tape, stapler and staples— even the paper clips filled us with possessive awe. It was all ours!

But, best of all, for kids whose mother had instilled in them a love for the printed and bound word, there were entire boxes filled with nothing but books.

We sat down on the floor at the open boxes and started reading. The course was put together by Calvert's Correspondence School with books that had been written for my parents' generation. They were old fashioned with an emphasis on the classics and on history, but we didn't care.

We read everything. No, we devoured it. Four-hundred-page history books, illustrated world architecture books, workbooks. I read the math books, hunting through the pages to find the word problems.

I always disliked them as math problems, but I loved reading about the kids in the broader world doing exotic things like boarding trains at different times to go to different locations. I liked imagining a world where you could travel by land over great distances and meet people wherever you went. And I loved it when Mary, Pete, or Bill would drive to the grocery store to help their mom buy varying amounts of oranges, bananas, and apples. We, by contrast, got our fruit once a month from the Fruit Boat that stopped in Meyers Chuck (it also sold shoes, and various other items).

I could picture these strange things because I'd once lived in that world before I was six, but my little brothers could not. When problems or stories involved farms, for instance, they were clueless. When asked where milk came from, they insisted that it wasn't from some weird, fat-deer animal they'd never seen before, and it certainly did not come in liquid form! That was laughable. It came in a box, all nice and dry, and you added water to it to make it liquid, according to taste. A much more humane arrangement than squeezing it out of some poor animal.

I scoured the science textbooks for each grade searching for the cure, or at least a management program, for Human Spontaneous Combustion. And was always dejected when I failed to find it. I couldn't help feeling that whoever had written these science books were asking all the wrong questions, never getting to the really important things in life.

There were fiction classics like *Robinson Crusoe*, whose titular character I found it easy to relate to, having no problem picturing a shipwrecked person being forced to live all alone off the land. And then there was *Lorna Doone* with its dialect-heavy, seventeenth-century derring-do on the dark moors of England. I loved to sneak it out from under my covers where I'd hidden it and read by the dim glow of the lantern when everyone was sleeping.

On these nights, it felt as if the cannery workers, existing in a shadowy, temporal mirage, were reading over my shoulder. By some curious alchemy, the arbitrary markings on white paper transmuted in my brain into a country on the other side of the continent and an entire ocean, filled with people as alive as I was, engaged in remarkable adventures that I was allowed to ride along with.

Another book that took us to faraway places and times in a particularly visual way was a textbook on art history that was accompanied by a packet of cards with famous paintings on them by artists such as Da Vinci, Goya, and Van Gogh, among many, many others.

We pored over these paintings, swept away into history, meeting people from long ago who'd lived in silks, velvets, and lace, imagining their inner and outer worlds by any little clue in colors and brushstrokes. Megan, in particular, who had a deep love for anything art related, lost herself in these photographs of the works of great masters.

She'd sit at the new school's table, her chair resting on the brown braided rug on top of the black tarpaper floor, and go through them slowly. The barrel stove crackled behind her and to the right the plexiglass windows provided a view of the raw wilderness, the unbroken forest, and the bay beyond where sea lions snorted and whales spouted. Inside her mind, she was touring Gauguin's Tahiti and Goya's sixteenth-century Spain.

We read all the books within weeks of getting them, and then read each other's, and then reread our favorites. When it came time to send in reports, workbook pages, and tests, nothing could have been simpler. We knew all the answers (excluding the dreaded subject Arithmetic).

For a while, before Rand was lost, we continued to do school in the wanigan with Linda teaching us. We loved her way of teaching. She had such infectious enthusiasm for everything, and could be counted on to laugh at our every wisecrack, no matter how lame.

She made allowances for our fluid wilderness idea of time to a certain extent, not being too strict about how long each class ran. She was flexible and allowed us, if a particular lesson was exciting, to go past the allotted time with it, figuring to make up on the next lesson the next day. For the most part, she had eager, compliant students.

There was one exception: Robin. After his experiences with Muriel, his attitude toward school was, to say the least, skeptical. He made a point of letting everyone know he'd learn on his own terms or not at all. While everyone else managed more often than not to get to the wanigan on time for school, he was always late.

Linda came up with the inspiration of promising a cupcake to anyone who made it to school on time.

Despite his deep reverence for all things frosted, Robin was not to be bribed out of his hard-won ascendancy over adult rule.

While us older kids got there on time and munched on our cupcakes, the kindergartner strolled in pointedly well after school was scheduled to begin. Linda took one look at Robin as he sat at his desk glooming at the frosting mustaches on his sibling's faces and caved.

"How," she recalls, "could we all eat cupcakes in front of him?" She excuses her weakness by saying, "He was so darn cute!"

He was never on time for school, so far as I know, and ensured that the rest of us were tardy in later years.

• • •

One weekend we watched Dad use a mallet and froe to cut a huge pile of red cedar shakes. The next weekend he came home from his logging job with the skiff full of lumber, rolls of tarpaper, rectangles of plexiglass, boxes of different-sized nails, and other building supplies, with Lance seated on top of it all.

We kids and Mom helped haul the lumber and other supplies up to the building site above the beach to the right of the floathouse: a row of foundation pilings that once supported a platform where the old cannery barges used to winter over. We did minor fetching and carrying, but for the most part we stood by and watched as, with businesslike efficiency, Dad and Lance put up our new schoolhouse in two days.

A short flight of stairs near the floathouse went up to the deck, and the floor went down quickly on top of it. The wall frames made of two-by-fours were nailed briskly together and pushed up, and then the low ceiling joists and rafters went up, held together by a sixteen-foot long ridge beam. Once the sturdy skeleton was in place, the floor and walls were wrapped with tarpaper, the thud of the staple gun ringing out throughout the afternoon.

When Dad took on any task, he became a machine. I felt a sneaking pity for Lance, though jobs were scarce and he was getting paid. I knew from experience how hard it was keeping up with Dad, who gave no quarter to youngsters of any age. He seemed unaware that his bruising pace would be difficult for other experienced men his age to keep up with, let alone a teenager or five under-teens. His dark impatience with any "slackness" was something to be avoided at all costs.

The next day the roof and walls were sided with the shakes, and the plexiglass was fitted into the holes left for the windows. Dad had brought home with him several large sheets of thick white cardboard with silvery backing that he nailed up for a ceiling.

We struggled with a large, oval braided rug, lugging it awkwardly up the new steps, and laid it down on the tarpaper floor in the center of the open, sixteen-by-sixteen-foot room. On top of the rug we settled a veneer-over-particleboard oval table. Against the windowless back wall that faced the forest we hung the chalkboard and bulletin board that SISD had sent out to us. They'd also sent out a teacher's desk and a filing cabinet. Both of those were fitted in at the back wall, near the door.

The wall opposite the door, with a single window in it, had a long, waist-high bookcase painted white. Jamie's desk, a "skookum-built" desk that Dad had crafted when he was sixteen, was set against the front wall, near one end of the bookcase.

The most massive piece of furniture that took much angst and effort to move out of the floathouse and up into the woods, up the stairs and maneuvered through the door into the school, was the old wooden counter that had come with the floathouse and that Mom no longer wanted to have in there, since it took up so much space. We finally fitted it against the front wall, with the sink—which

We're standing in front of the homeschool Dad and Lance built.
Left to right: Chris, Linda, Robin, Megan, me, and Jamie.

was never hooked up to running water after it left the floathouse—
under the two plexiglass windows that had a view of our
fifty-five-gallon drums of fuel for the generator and beyond that the
beach and bay.

Mom painted "Boomin' Union Bay School" in rainbow-hued
letters on a white-painted board and hung it outside beneath the
front windows. It was an ironic salute to the original idea of several
families moving to the Union Bay cannery site and making it "boom."

Instead of a bustling community filled with children, there
were the five of us kids, and Linda as our teacher.

• • •

Since she didn't want to live all alone by herself in the ruins, on the
other side of the property from us in the old cabin, it was decided
that Linda would move her belongings into the wanigan and live
across from us in the small inlet.

The new school felt much more official than the wanigan, since it
had been built for the specific purpose of being a school. However,
it was still heated by a barrel wood stove—the plexiglass windows
fogged up fiercely when the fire was first started on cold winter
mornings—so we continued to haul and stack firewood for PE.

Since we older kids had already done most of the year's work
before the first day of school began, Linda felt free to include

wilderness skills in her curriculum. This reached Robin's heart immediately. She'd worked a trapline with Rand and taught Robin how to set the smallest trap, bait it, and catch a mink, and then how to skin it and dry the skin.

Meanwhile, she taught Megan and me—Jamie picked it up as well—how to crochet potholders, hats, and purses. Mom was in firm retreat from all the sewing arts (Dad had taught us how to sew with a thread and needle, a skill he'd learned in the Army), so if it hadn't been for Linda we wouldn't have learned the skill of turning yarn into useful, decorative objects.

She had a wonderful, wholehearted laugh that made her bend over in helpless hilarity and there was nothing we loved more than to trigger it. One morning, relying on her sense of the absurd that was not untouched by a twisted appreciation for the macabre, Jamie set the school up to look like a horrific massacre had occurred.

Using a liberal hand with a bottle of ketchup and putting to ghoulish use his skills in weapon making and noose tying, he arranged for his siblings to sprawl in various death poses, oozing ketchup onto table and desks and counter.

We were giggling under our breath and trying to maintain our grotesque poses when we heard Linda's footsteps up the stairs and across the deck. Holding our collective breath, we heard the door open.

There was a brief pause as she took in the scene in front of her. Then she doubled over and there was that laugh.

One of the things that amused her the most was our reaction to the sound of a floatplane. It was, without fail, SISD's plane with Tom Aubertine on board, the man who visited all the remote-lying areas under the school district's oversight. It was his job to keep track of everyone's progress and troubleshoot any problems.

We'd become more than a little feral by then, rarely bothering to brush our hair, tidy our communal mess of a bedroom (which Linda took to calling the Baaack Room in spectral tones), or do any other chores around the house. Mom, after Rand's loss, didn't enforce any of these things, relying on the threat of Dad's weekend visits to have the place somewhat decent looking when he came home.

But when we heard that distinct airplane engine sound different from a boat, we'd yell "Plane!" and rush around getting the place in shape for a Town Visitor. We looked on it as a variation of the bear drill—there was at least as much terror and exhilaration involved. Maybe more, because unlike the bear drill when we never really had a furry monster bearing down on us, Tom Aubertine *was* going to make an appearance.

Within the first moment of hearing the distant plane to when its pontoons splashed down in our little bay, we'd tear around the house shoving everything out of sight. Dirty dishes went in the oven, clothes and books under the couch, toys flung into the growing pile on the Baaack Room's floor with the door heaved against and pounded on until it could be closed.

Mom would tame our wild locks, scrub our hands and faces, and shove us into the cleanest clothes available so that we'd meet Tom Aubertine with innocent, shining faces and studious eyes when he'd finally climb out of the plane and up the beach to the floathouse.

He was the only regular visitor we had, and I remember him as being self-contained and encouraging in a low-key, observant way. He certainly never put any pressure on us kids, maybe because we were eager students and it was obvious we could easily handle the workload.

Tom Aubertine insisted at the end of every visit that if we had any problems we were to let him know and he'd see what he could do to resolve the issue. But the one thing he couldn't help us with was the content of the textbooks.

These books were written for a post-WWII world, so perhaps it was understandable that they propagandized war as noble, if it was being fought for freedom, which all "good wars" were. One book quoted the poem "War Song" by Thomas Moore (1779–1852):

No, Freedom! Whose smile we shall never resign,
Go, tell our invaders, the Danes,
'Tis sweeter to bleed for an age at thy shrine,
Than to sleep but a moment in chains.

But I wasn't buying it. Not with the specter of Vietnam hanging around my dad. I had constant post-traumatic proof of what war did to men and got passed along to their families. Dad was in chains to it for more than a moment, as were all of us with him.

One book of legends promoted the tales of knights and chivalry of old. Linda gave me a book report to do on one of the chapters, on sports that knights played. She gave me the assignment verbally rather than wrote it down, and didn't indicate that it was from this book.

What I heard was: "Write a two-page report on nightly sports."

It seemed like a strange request to me, but I rallied to the challenge and came up with the most outrageous, ridiculous nighttime sports I could think of, and added an illustration in full Crayola color.

Linda laughed and gave me an A for creativity before explaining the mistake.

Later, when I thought about it, I was glad I'd misunderstood. I didn't want to glorify knightly sports that were play battles, men playing at war, making it sound honorable and free of consequences. I was glad that I'd accidentally spoofed it.

• • •

Because neither Mom nor Linda was confident of their math skills, it was left to Dad on the weekends to help us through the arithmetical labyrinth.

The problem with this was: 1) Dad had zero patience for fumbling, intimidated kids, and 2) Dad didn't know how to teach—he knew how to do a thing, but not how to explain it. He would do one of our math problems while we watched and then figured that would be sufficient for us to pick it up.

"I learned by watching others do things. So should you," he'd say.

This didn't work for me. I had to know the why of a thing before it made sense to me. I loved the idea of math. I loved that there was a language of numbers that could describe everyday things around me, that could describe the universe, space and time, but I needed to know the logic behind the rules.

He didn't have the words to explain it.

Instead, I studied the books, digging and figuring, until I could answer my own questions and work out how to get the same solution he had. Later, as I grew up, I learned to keep asking him questions that would eventually make him give me the piece I needed to make it all make sense. I learned by making connections, not by watching and then doing.

Which was interesting in itself. There are different ways of learning. Each person is reached by something else, I thought, suggesting that we construct our perspectives of the world with different tools and materials. No wonder no two people see the same event the same way. No wonder there are so many misunderstandings and wars in the world.

And then I was presented with the paradoxes in my math book's appendix, apparently put there to mess with students' minds just as they figured they'd learned what the world was about.

The writers of the math books ripped the rug right out from under us by going on about an ancient philosopher who mathematically hypothesized that motion and change was an illusion.

Speedy Achilles and the slow tortoise have to cover the exact same distance, so no matter how fast or slow they go neither ever gets ahead of the other.

Or something like that. I couldn't quite get their point because it seemed to me that they were leaving out necessary, real-life facts in their illustration. Change and motion were not solely physical. There were intangibles present that couldn't be grabbed and pinned like an insect to a board to be studied with a magnifying glass. Motion and change involved some sort of transformation, a breaking through the barrier of space, some way to merge space and time to provide movement and change.

These were concepts I felt but couldn't argue because I didn't have enough knowledge. I had the feeling I was meant to be intimidated into submission by the authors referencing a Greek named Zeno who'd lived in 490–430 BC "The Ancients," after all, were to be revered and never contradicted; at least that was the impression I got from the Calvert's Correspondence Course designers.

Just learning about "BC" should have been a mind-trip. Modern time, the time we lived in, flowed forward, according to our calendar dating from Jesus's first birthday; while time marched backwards from that date for the long dead ancient world.

In other words, time could flow in both directions, despite our science books only teaching a single direction of time, from past to future.

The truth was, I had no problem with time flowing in either direction. In fact, my mental image of time was of a river flowing from the future while our bodies were temporal units meeting that turbulent current of possibilities. However we reacted to what that river of time brought to us—in that split second there were countless options—the present was created by whatever action we took. What flowed behind were the consequences of our actions: they became the irreversible past.

Since no teacher insisted it was otherwise, taking it for granted that we all viewed time the same way, I grew up with this idea of time. It set me on a collision course with the outside world that would one day traumatize me for a long time to come.

"'You are incorrigible,' he exclaimed. Lucretia, walking up the staircase in front of him, had the last word. 'Is that not a much more interesting thing to be than conformable?'"
—*The Bored Bridegroom* by Barbara Cartland

CHAPTER EIGHT

WE COULDN'T expect to keep Linda with us forever, and so it went. A local fisherman friend named Art Forbes snatched her up, and once more it was just Mom and the five of us kids.

Mom sank deeper into depression and became more of an absentminded companion than a mother. She immersed herself in books after a brief enthusiasm for redecorating the floathouse's living room (painting the floor aqua and laying down a blue-and-gold oriental rug that covered almost the entire floor, situating large pink and turquoise vases near the two couches that faced each other, hanging a Dutch wall clock—with heavy brass weights—that had to be wound daily).

After all the years of dreaming about Alaska and then finally having the dream come true, she lost herself in a world other than the one she lived in.

We adapted to the change and took shameless advantage of her state. We'd wait until she was deeply into one of her books before casually asking if we could help ourselves to some rationed item of food.

"Hmm?" she'd say.

We'd repeat our request.

"Mm-hm. Sure." Her eyes never budged from the page. Later, when she came up for air and realized we'd eaten what we weren't supposed to, we were able to tell her truthfully she'd given the okay.

One of Mom's favorite subjects was English history. She had shelves full of books on the kings and queens of England and talked about them like they were modern celebrities. She had a major crush on Charles II. Anne Boleyn, whom Mom seemed to identify with, was another obsession. Besides the weightier tomes, her need for escapism demanded lighter fare, so she had subscriptions to British paperback romances: Harlequins and Regency novels.

Megan and I dove headfirst into the world of Barbara Cartland and became enamored of the Regency period. We developed as a character a snobby, aristocratic matriarch named Madame Moonlea. We'd swish majestically around our Alaskan floathouse home that was perched above the tide surrounded by evergreens, and peer down at our younger brothers through pretend lorgnettes, saying all manner of stuffy, superior things to them in our best upper-crust British accents. We let them know that odds were not great that they'd be invited to Almack's for the supper dance.

We tooled around outside on driftwood logs, pretending we were in phaetons and curricles, snapping riding whips (thin red cedar limbs divested of needles) over the horse's backs, and chatting about the latest balls and plays at Covent Garden. We sat side saddle (in our ragged jeans that magically transformed into gorgeous riding habits of the finest satins and silks) on logs with weathered, broken branches, hooking our leg around ones that took the place of a saddle horn, and trotted around Hyde Park exchanging witty remarks and the latest on dits.

"Lady Dalgliesh has behaved insupportably," I shared, my voice a languid, congested drawl. I moved my body on the log as if I was aboard a walking horse. "She was quite in her cups during the Michaelmas Ball, I gather."

"Oh, not Lady D again." Megan yawned delicately, patting her lips with her pinky raised. "If I hear another word about her, I daresay I shall be bored to distinction!"

I cleared my throat in my most genteel manner. "Pray forgive me, m'lady, but I believe you mean bored to distraction, or possibly extinction?"

Megan caught my eye and we burst into laughter.

Naturally such delicious young debutantes had admirers. We

each had one in particular, two Lords of the Realm named Smith Darcourt (for Megan) and Reuben Challonly (for me). They were more of the athletic, Corinthian type rather than refined dandies. They were always betting on things like pig races.

Megan and I managed to keep up with them when they went out steeple chasing—though we didn't really know what that was about. We gathered that it meant a lot of galloping around the beaches, so we held invisible reins in our hands and jumped logs or the creek that ran beneath the floathouse. We artistically lurched when we leapt, acting out a body's movement on the back of a horse in motion.

We also had a few duels. We stood back to back holding our driftwood guns sternly in front of us, while Robin and Chris stood by as our seconds. As one of the boys counted off, we marched with measured strides away from each other, the gravel beach and clam shells crunching underfoot, the musk of seaweed in our nostrils. Off to the side the tar-blackened pilings of the old cannery haul-out marched down the beach in soldierly formation arranged by size, from tallest to shortest.

On the count of ten we turned and shot. Somehow we survived to do it all again, though we weren't so bourgeois as "the babies" who ran around shooting each other with their fingers and yelling "new guy" every two minutes. ("New guy" was their magical reset phrase that allowed them to unceasingly come back from the dead while playing cops and robbers.)

SISD had sent out clay with our school supplies, and while we all loved to make food from it (hamburgers and hotdogs were particular favorites) Megan and I focused on using it to mold an entire London Season's worth of ton people.

We had men in tails and top hats tapping crops against their high Hessian boots. Ladies who perched side saddle on prancing steeds (splayfooted so they'd stay upright) wore flowing riding habits and hats with veils. Little boys in sailor suits chased after barking dogs, and people of all descriptions in their Regency attire (and, anachronistically, Victorian dresses complete with exaggerated bustles) strolled about or rode in two-wheeled, open vehicles pulled by one or more horses.

We filled the plexiglass windows that overlooked the raw beach and bay with these preening clay people from Barbara Cartland's world.

I wondered what aristocratic Barbara Cartland would think, as she drifted about her ornate British mansion, if she could see two ragamuffin wilderness girls lifting lines from her books to put in the mouths of our clay people and Barbie dolls.

All that Barbara Cartland reading would come in handy in future school years, we found. Her books were packed full of historical facts and settings, and when it came time to study Western European history in high school we were way ahead of our schoolmates and aced every test.

• • •

I loved horse books, having the typical girl obsession with horses. I'd devour a book about a cowgirl at the rodeo, and when it was finished I'd race onto the beach and do tight turns around the double lines of pilings that marched down the beach.

When my little brothers asked what I was supposed to be playing at, I thought they were incredibly dim. "Barrel racing—obviously," I'd retort, and whip that quarter horse around the next piling more tightly than the last one.

While Megan sketched pretty much everything and liked to work with water paints, I stuck to mainly horses, sketching them with pencils, or writing the kinds of equine stories I wanted to read and then illustrating them with brightly colored pens. I stapled or sewed the pages together and read the results to my indiscriminating little brothers.

Megan liked books about girls our own age, ones with a moral or a principle to be learned and upheld, like *Blubber* by Judy Blume.

"You have to read this," she told me after she finished it. "It's got an important message. I think every kid should read it." There was a zealot's gleam in her eye that didn't bode well for my enjoyment of the book, I was sure.

I did try. I wasn't able to finish it. "I didn't like any of the characters."

She shook her head at me. "They're not supposed to be likable, they're relatable!"

"I didn't find them relatable. I found them a bunch of rotten, stinking, selfish bullies."

"But that's the point! You're supposed to realize that any of us can be bullies if we're not careful." Megan was always trying to pass on these lessons she gleaned from books to our little brothers—without notable success. If anything, they went out of their way to do the exact opposite of her helpful pointers.

I was more in the "let them learn by example" camp, so they favored me since it allowed them to follow their own course. This worked well for happy-go-lucky, always-smiling-and-singing Chris (he liked to make up lyrics on the spot about whatever was happening around him and sang all day long). Robin, however, could only take this for so long. He understood, if no one else did, that a growing, perpetually-up-to-no-good boy required boundaries and needed some discipline to maintain them.

He'd push and push and drive everyone crazy with his deliberately escalating bad behavior. But Mom was the furthest thing from a disciplinarian. She tried all the noncorporal punishment, child psychology tricks she could drum up, but Robin always saw through them. She tried threatening that when Dad came home on the weekend he'd take care of it. But although we all had a lively interest in avoiding Dad's blacker moods, he wasn't a disciplinarian either.

I finally had enough.

"Pilgrim," I told Robin, adapting a quote from a favorite John Wayne movie, "you've caused a lot of problems and what you deserve is a darned good spanking. But I won't give it to you. I won't, I won't—the heck I won't!" And then I spanked him.

Robin loved it. He loved the humor, he loved the quote, but most of all, he loved the discipline. Afterward he told me, "I love you, Tara. You're the best sister ever." And he'd be a perfect little boy for a week or so, before he started pushing to receive some more of that good old John Wayne discipline again.

In addition to the book subscriptions Mom got for herself, she also got Jamie started on The Hardy Boys, me on Nancy Drew, and Megan with The Bobbsey Twins—but we all read each other's books, just as we had with each other's textbooks.

Mom also got a subscription for Dad. He'd been brought up on TV Westerns—it was the one thing he shared with his own dad—so she had Westerns written by Louis L'Amour arriving in every batch of mail. When I tired of Barbara Cartland's mannered Regency world, I dove headlong into the two-fisted, gunslinging, cayuse-riding world of L'Amour's Old West. It was a toss-up which one I liked more, but in the end L'Amour won the contest.

For one thing, I related more to the people in his books. They used kerosene lamps like us; the frontier they lived on had few people scattered throughout a huge, empty land. Women were left alone with their children to homestead while the men went off to make money. Guns were an accepted tool of life and people had to cope with the weather in a visceral, life-and-death way. Food and other luxuries were hard come by. And books, anything written, were treasured more highly than money.

Before bed, Mom read to us *Down the Long Hills*, the one book L'Amour wrote primarily from a kid's point of view. The grizzly encounters in it did not help my sleep issues, but there was no lack of identification we felt for the young protagonist, who, in a lot of ways, resembled Jamie.

Despite Jamie's various ways of torturing us, we never questioned his survival instincts or his resourcefulness, like the kid in the book. And even the boy's protectiveness and care of his little sister rang true. Though Jamie wouldn't have been anywhere near as kind and patient about it, there wasn't a one of us kids who doubted that he'd be there for us and risk his own life to save us.

He was only about four when he saved my life during a family outing on a lake in Montana. The moment our parents weren't looking I crawled into the water and would have drowned if Jamie hadn't gone after me. When Mom checked on us she nearly had a heart attack when she didn't see either of us on shore. Then she looked in the lake and saw Jamie standing in water lapping at his face, holding me above the surface. His head kept going under in between waves, but he never let me drop.

I suppose this gave him a certain proprietary attitude about me, like in the saying that if someone saves your life, you belong to them. Perhaps that's why he felt free to torture me with the news that I was in the top ninety percentile of humans mostly likely to suffer spontaneous combustion.

• • •

We older kids loved school and didn't require much oversight after Linda left. Robin and Chris resisted, but Jamie, Megan, and I loved to go up to the school and follow the course program on our own.

This allowed Mom to be an on-again, off-again kind of teacher. She did it in spurts and we, naturally, took advantage of this. To prank her we deliberately filled our workbooks full of random words, crazy phrases, and whatever stray thought entered our brains. We knew the right answers, but what fun would writing them down be? Every few weeks she went through our textbooks and was beside herself at our apparent laziness and/or lack of intelligence.

We had to erase everything and put in the right answers before Tom Aubertine made one of his surprise visits; but it was worth it to us, and we did it all over again to win one of her ever-reliable baffled tirades.

Mom was a woman of extremes about any of her enthusiasms, even during the worst of her depression, so when she took on something she tended to go all out. Like the time she showed up for school one day to teach us about her favorite subject: Literature.

She chose Robert Louis Stevenson to talk about, since she was reading us *Treasure Island* every night. She became animated as she shared snippets from a biography she had about him, scratching out points on the chalkboard, and analyzing in great detail every single book he'd ever written, fitting in how they had emotionally affected her.

It was a college-level, thorough lecture, and at the end of it she asked, "So, can anyone tell me what Robert Louis Stevenson wrote?"

Robin said dryly, with a touch of bitterness, "Too much."

• • •

There were times when we spent days and days, week after week, trapped indoors when Southeast Alaska's inclement weather (we received about 170 inches of precipitation annually) poured an endless deluge down, pounding on the tin roof and hitting the floathouse's deck so hard it seemed to rain upward as well as downward.

To keep us all focused and quiet, Mom sat in the rocking chair and read *Anne of Green Gables* all the way through from beginning to end in one day, having to raise her voice over the rain, until her voice was hoarse. It was a good choice; even the boys were entranced by the too-imaginative and easily triggered girl who got herself into trouble every time she turned around.

Robin and Chris were young enough that they forgot what the sun was. When it finally made an appearance, after weeks of overcast and rain, it didn't go well.

Robin was sitting on the floor near the big bay window playing and listening to one of the books on tape Mom put in to save her voice (we had *The Time Machine*, *The Hound of the Baskervilles*, *Wind in the Willows*, *The Railway Children*, *The Lost World*, *Strange Case of Dr. Jekyll and Mr. Hyde*) when a beam of golden sunlight shot down and lit up the floor next to him.

"What is it? What is it?" he yelled, scooting away in panic.

To Robin it was an extraterrestrial light beamed in from outer space—which, come to think of it, was exactly what it was.

Once its harmlessness was demonstrated he adapted quickly, and we all ran outside to embrace the return of the prodigal sun.

Mom, as the only adult amidst piping young voices demanding her attention, was driven stir crazy during the sunless shut-in days.

"Do not call me Mommy!" she finally snapped. "My name is Romi. Call me Romi!"

It felt a little strange at first, but again we quickly adapted—until she decided it was too creepy to hear her name being called all day long by kid voices and she told us to stop.

That was when she'd turn the VHF marine radio to the telephone channel so that she could listen to adult voices talking about adult concerns. Back then you could hear both sides of a conversation. Later, the person making the call was beeped out while you could still hear the one responding.

We soon tuned in for weekly calls by our favorite fishermen calling home. We got to know the names of all their family members,

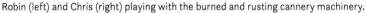
Robin (left) and Chris (right) playing with the burned and rusting cannery machinery.

their pets, the happenings of their family life—the ups, the downs, and the crises. They never knew we existed, but they and their lives were our entertainment.

Mom felt a particular need to hear the lower timbre of men's voices. "It was an actual craving," she remembers. "You can get starved for that lower male register. No wonder the pioneer women in sod houses went crazy listening to nothing but high-pitched prairie winds and kid voices all day, every day."

During those indoor days, after reading from Laura Ingalls Wilder's books, she would attempt to be the conventional homemaker in the wilderness. One time she determinedly decided that she was going to sew some cloth dolls for Megan and me, the way her mother had when Mom was little, and her mother's mother before her.

Mom doubled the piece of white cotton, drew the outline of two dolls on it, cut them out, and sewed the two pieces along their cut edges, stuffing the dolls with cotton as she went. She used pastel-colored yarn (pinks and turquoise) for the hair and drew on the faces. We were impressed that she'd managed this much, but she insisted on finishing the dolls by sewing clothes onto them. She sewed and sewed, stabbing herself repeatedly, muttering, but finally declared she had pulled it off. With a flourish of triumph she lifted the doll to show us—only to discover that she'd sewed the doll to her shirt. She collapsed into hysterical laughter.

That was her last attempt at sewing anything, I think. The dolls remained uncompleted ghosts of dolls. They were a bit eerie and we weren't sure what to make of them, but we kept them around as backups.

She was more successful with our paper dolls. Mom was an excellent artist and loved fashion. She designed stylish ensembles for our paper dolls (from *Gone With the Wind*, Dolly Dingle, Barbie) and colored them, complete with strategically placed tabs. We cut them out and had stacks of clothes with which to dress our paper dolls. She also drew and colored paper furniture and wall art for us to decorate their cardboard grocery box homes.

Mom was often more like a babysitter than a parent, playing board games, jacks, pickup sticks, and putting together jigsaw puzzles with us. She also taught us a multitude of card games, which came in handy since they helped us with our math studies, our one continuing weak spot as students. Cribbage in particular was a great game for teaching us to add and multiply by five.

Often the favorite time of our days was at night. Mom always read to us from one book or another and we loved to sit around, or lie on the floor, and listen to her read in the mellow glow of the kerosene lamplight, with the wood popping and shifting every now and then in the stove. The windows were pitch black all around us, with the wilderness beyond them, but it was warm and cozy inside as her voice took us on adventures far away and sometimes a long time ago.

Or, if she didn't feel like reading, she played music and we'd all dance, trying to be as creative as possible in our moves. Megan had, by far, the strangest set of moves I have ever seen. Experimental ballet is creatively bankrupt in comparison. That scene with Audrey Hepburn in *Funny Face* where she dances in the Parisian club—her kooky moves look tame in comparison.

Megan's idea of how to get her groove on was to jump in place and spank herself with both hands. She was right on the beat, I'll give her that.

Fleetwood Mac was always a favorite on these nights, particularly their double album *Tusk*. The titular song's beat was one Jamie liked to pound out on every surface, everywhere, at all hours of the day. Another song from that album, "Not That Funny," was somehow interpreted by one of us kids—family lore says it was Megan, me, or Chris, but no one knows for sure—as "Stop that Farting," which became the lyrics we loved to shout when that song came on.

Sometimes we didn't dance. Instead, Mom would blow out the lamp, and we'd listen to an album on the cassette player in the dark, like Phil Collins's *Face Value* album, and talk about anything under the sun (including trying to figure out what the lyrics to "In the Air Tonight" meant).

Everything was grist for the discussion: what we'd read, what we'd discovered, what we thought, what we thought the future would be like. Mom would let us talk far into the night until our voices dragged and we fell asleep.

We never grew out of this—right into adulthood, to this day, there's nothing any of us like more than to sit around in the dark, listen to music, and talk about everything and anything with her. Dad tolerated this pastime when he was home, and he still does.

• • •

In addition to her random appearances at school, Mom roused herself from her book reverie with conscientious effort from time to time to have a Bible study with us.

To our delight, on nice days she took us out to the big smooth rock where Megan and I had one of our forts. Around the corner, heading toward the cannery side, were the mysterious grave markers.

We'd sit on the enormous rock with a view of the spacious bay and the faraway, logged mountains of Prince of Wales Island. In all that expanse we were the only beings who could talk about what we were looking at, what we were experiencing.

As Mom studied with us, geese honked in V-formation above us while humpback whales did their bubble feeding out in the bay surrounded by shrieking sea gulls. The snorts and Darth Vader breathing of sea lions carried to us across the water. In the deep forest behind us, squirrels chattered and songbirds joyously serenaded the sunshine.

"Do you think all of this and our ability to enjoy it could have happened by accident?" she asked.

We looked around and breathed in the familiar, musky tidal scent wedded to the earthy aroma of the sun-heated forest. The interconnection we felt between all living things around us was too complex to be accidental, we thought.

She gave us thought experiments to consider while we interrupted her with important, clarifying questions.

"What if you were lost in the woods," she said, "and you came across a cabin stocked with food—"

"What kind of food?"

"The best kind of food," Mom said. "So you come across a cabin full of the best foods, and firewood—"

"Already split?"

"Yes. And—"

"Already hauled and stacked?"

"Yes. The cabin is set up perfectly for human needs. Now when we step inside and look around and see how snug and well built it is—"

"Not built by Skip so the shakes on the roof don't blow off," one of us quipped and was rewarded with a gust of laughter from our siblings. Poor, well-intentioned, incompetent Skip, from *The Wilderness Family* movies, was often the butt of our jokes.

Mom laughed too. "Right. So do you think this cabin in the wilderness, with all of its provisions, just sort of sprouted out of the ground, possibly over a really long period of time, building itself from the ground up? Ask yourselves: did it happen by accident—or did someone build it?"

We thought that was the dumbest question ever and didn't hesitate to share this opinion with her, our youthful shouts echoing off the rocks and bay.

She waved us down. "You might think that's an obvious answer, but do you know that many people, very educated people, think that our planet home with all of its provisions to support life, happened by accident? They don't believe that anyone designed it or built it."

It was the first we'd heard of it. Our Calvert's textbooks either hadn't stated this outright, or had glossed over it in a way that had passed us by. The concept seemed like nonsense. We wondered if Mom had gotten her facts wrong. But she insisted that there were people who believed everything we saw around us had just... happened. Over many, many, many years.

But that wasn't how time worked. We saw that in the ruins of a past civilization all around us. Instead of anything appearing and forming out of nothing into something new and sophisticated over a long period of time, everything decayed, broke down, and disappeared.

Later, when I thought about what she'd said, it made even less sense. For one thing, what about math? I loved math, however bad I was at it, because it was the language of the universe. How could life, the planets, the universe, time, happen by accident... and have a language to describe how it was formed, to define what laws regulated all of it, perfectly designed so that humans could interact with it and create their own designs based on it? How could laws be accidental? I couldn't make it make sense no matter how I tried.

Although Mom shared her Bible understanding with us, she made it clear that we were to come to our own conclusions, that she wasn't forcing her beliefs on us and we should do our own search to find out what we really believed.

This was how she'd been raised as a young child. Her parents weren't religious, but they encouraged her when she showed an interest in spiritual things, to make a search.

The only time either of her parents attempted to step in was when Mom became fascinated with the theater and ritual of Catholicism. Her father begged her, with tears in his eyes, to go anywhere but to that religion.

He'd been brought up in a traditionally Catholic household, but when he left home at the age of twelve it was partly due to the Church, though he never went into specifics about what had happened. Her stalwart, stoic, and adventurous father crying made a big impression on her, but she looked into Catholicism anyway, and in the end he didn't stop her.

Eventually, though, she felt it wasn't what she was looking for, and she continued searching through a variety of different religions until she was a teenager and began to study with a group that was originally known as the International Bible Students Association. Their goal was to search the scriptures to find out what was actual Bible truth and where manmade traditions had infiltrated Christianity. They were determined to discard the latter and live in accord with the former in order to worship God the way the Bible instructed. (They later adopted the name Jehovah's Witnesses.)

Soon enough Mom was amazed and excited, she told us, to learn that some things that she'd always taken for granted, such as that Jesus died on a cross, that Jesus was God and a part of the Trinity, that a fiery hell for sinners existed... were all human traditions rooted in pagan beliefs, rather than supported by the Bible. She told her friends and cousins, "Did you know Jesus didn't die on a cross? That the word in the Bible for what he died on means an upright stake, not a cross? That the cross was actually a pagan symbol?"

More astonishing for her was how the holidays, even those that were supposedly in celebration of Christ, were not scriptural but had been adopted—with all their child-appealing characteristics (chocolate rabbits and dyed boiled eggs to celebrate Christ's resurrection; a jolly fat man coming down a chimney to leave presents under a decorated tree to celebrate Christ's birth)—by early Christendom in order to win over superstitious pagans as converts.

Mom, always excited to learn, absorbed these in-depth studies. Her intellectually curious parents were intrigued as well, and before long they were studying too. In short order, the whole family was studying.

However, by the time Mom and her brothers had all grown up and everyone ended up in Alaska, Mom was the only one still studying the Bible and learning new things that contradicted manmade doctrines. These she shared with her kids out on a rock overlooking an Alaskan bay, where the humpback whales breached and bald eagles flew.

• • •

Dad had no objections to our studying the Bible. He'd been brought up Lutheran, but in his own way he'd done a search too, questioning

Church traditions that contradicted or didn't follow up on the very Scriptures the adults in charge had him learn. These adults had no specific answers for him, telling him not to ask questions and to just have faith—a response that didn't work for him.

After Vietnam he was so deeply angry and bitter that there was no way the Church he'd grown up with and its conventional faith and lack of answers could reach him. He did study, occasionally, in Montana, with the Witnesses, and he never opposed Mom's studies with us kids in the wilderness. In fact, there were times when he did some of the Bible reading during our studies.

Mom didn't celebrate the holidays because of their unscriptural origins, and Dad dropped them without any resistance or interest.

Since we had no immediate neighbors and didn't see anyone else celebrating the holidays, except in movies (which always felt somewhat mythical—not to mention a bit dumb, like when the Wilderness Family attached burning candles to the fir tree they'd dragged inside their log cabin, a disaster waiting to happen), we didn't miss Christmas, Easter, or any of the holidays.

Mom made sure we wouldn't feel deprived by coming up with an annual Family Presents Day. (In addition, Dad's mother, our Grandma Helen in Montana, sent us a huge care package every winter full of goodies, books, and clothes.)

Mom would let us pore over the Sears & Roebuck catalog and pick what toys and clothes we wanted most, and over a period of months she'd order them. The boxes would pile up to the point that they had to be stored in the wanigan. We would stand on tiptoes and peer in the four-paned windows of our former school and drool over the huge pile of booty.

Mom's plan was always to have the local kids from Meyers Chuck come over. She'd make a lot of treats, including cake, and have presents ready for us and the other kids, without obligation for them to bring any presents. And then the boxes would all be opened.

It never worked out as planned. For one reason or another Mom would inevitably, out of the blue, impulsively decide that it was time to open the presents. Forget about the whole party idea. She'd send us over to the wanigan to haul back all the boxes and then we'd tear into them, shrieking and handing the right ones to each other.

Megan was more into dolls than I was, so she ended up with all sorts of Barbie doll accessories (a bright yellow RV, a red Camaro, a two-story house) and another dollhouse with a tiny doll family. I, on the other hand, scored big time with Breyer model horses, especially the ones that were accompanied by books (*Misty of Chincoteague, Smoky the Cow Horse, Black Beauty*). We searched the catalog for stables and corrals to buy, but couldn't find any. As a surprise for me, Mom asked Dad to build them and he did, much better made than any we could have bought.

The boys got Fisher-Price toys: a little airport set, a train set, a bus, a school, and a barn complete with animals. They also got Hot Wheel cars, cowboy hats, toolboxes, and—the bane of all our existence—cap guns. Robin remembers also getting a toy guitar. Chris remembers a big brown teddy bear and a pocket knife with an eagle on it.

Jamie, nearly a teenager, focused on music. He was the first one to get a boom box and he wound up with an enviable library of cassette albums. He'd take the boom box up to his fort on the big cedar stump behind the floathouse and listen to it for hours, the sound of Queen's *Flash Gordon* soundtrack weaving through the Alaskan forest.

• • •

Mom was always writing. Either in bound journals or on loose paper, like the yellow paper she wrote "The Wanigan Kids" on. She'd leave the house to write so she could concentrate without five kids (and later, half a million dogs—or so it seemed) distracting her with their nonstop cacophony.

On nice days she'd find a rock or log to perch on with a great view, or later when we lived on the cannery side, she'd find a nook somewhere next to the golden, tumbling creek, and we'd see her there writing furiously away, hardly ever looking up, and know we weren't to interrupt her. For a wonder, we didn't.

Probably because we considered her letter writing important. A lady in Ketchikan conducted a Bible study with her through the mail. Mom put so much importance on responding and was so diligent about doing it that we developed a deeper respect for the notion of

Bible study than we probably would have based solely on our own irregular Bible studies with her. Her example impressed us because we weren't accustomed to her being so determined and consistent about anything.

Family and friends scattered far and wide also received letters from her. Whenever I meet them now they always bring up how much they loved getting a letter from the wilderness.

Mom was well known, it turned out, for the pleasure her letters gave people. They were written in cursive and accompanied by a jungle of smiley faces, hyphens, and exclamation marks, not to mention last-minute add-ons and insertions that climbed up the margins and across the top so you had to turn every page in a circle before you were finished with it.

Mom wrote these garrulous letters about our wilderness life to Mr. McKenzie (I never knew his first name). His title was Manager of Remote Lands & Properties, or something like that, and he worked for US Steel, the company that owned the cannery property. He was the one who handled the twenty-year lease Dad and Mom had committed to, and to whom they sent in their payments. Mom disliked the idea of sending in the check cold, so she always added a chatty letter full of all our doings.

Mr. McKenzie must have been surprised when he received that first letter, but he soon began to think of us fondly and developed a personal bond with us. We were his own personal Wilderness Family.

This was most apparent when Mr. McKenzie retired and could no longer keep up with his correspondence and his son wrote to us, assuring us of his father's continued affection and how much enjoyment he—and, we gathered, Mr. McKenzie's entire family— had received from Mom's letters over the years.

Apparently, we were a lot of people's remote Alaskan reality TV show long before that was a thing, thanks to Mom's letters.

"It was like The Hunger Games!*"*
—Delaney Neilson, after hearing stories
about her father Chris's childhood

CHAPTER NINE

LIFE IN the wilderness for us children was all about three things: chores, play, and food. Not necessarily in that order.

Mom loved cookbooks and owned a large selection of coffee table books that featured food. We liked to pore over them, drooling at the glossy pictures. She let us experiment with cooking our own meals—her only rule was that we had to eat whatever we made, no matter how badly it turned out, because we couldn't afford to waste any food.

We made some pretty gruesome messes but we never balked at eating it. Food was food, however it looked, smelled, or tasted to children in the wilderness who knew it wouldn't be easy to get more if we ran out.

Our favorite staples to experiment with were popcorn and oats. There was a five-gallon bucket of popcorn kernels and another of sugar. Meanwhile, flour and oats each had their own green plastic fifty-five-gallon garbage barrel.

The oats we turned into every kind of granola imaginable, adding raisins in the winter and huckleberries in the summer. We put the granola in baggies to keep us powered up as we played outside, from the moment we were freed from home school until dinner time.

Popcorn was more versatile yet. When we ran out of cereal we mixed up some dry milk with water, sprinkled sugar on a bowl full of popcorn, and poured milk over it. You had to eat it quickly because it became soggy fast. We mixed molasses with peanut butter (two more staples we had in industrial amounts) and stirred popcorn into it. Or we broke into the cases of boxed macaroni and cheese to liberate a silvery packet of bright-orange cheese and we sprinkled it on popcorn.

We loved to make cakes and our number one favorite, when we ran out of eggs, was chocolate mayonnaise cake. If you open our family's copy of *The Joy of Cooking*, it falls open to that page, the most floury and chocolate-smeared page in the entire book. I learned from it how to make pie dough and became an expert at it. We had thirty-pound boxes of apples, so I made a lot of apple pies. My secret ingredient was Ronald's Tea, an instant powdered tea packed full of citrus flavoring.

Potatoes and onions, which we had in fifty-pound bags, were a favorite morning food when fried and drenched in ketchup. We also had gallon cans of instant mashed potatoes. I don't know who the genius was who decided to combine them with Tang and stir in hot water, but that was a thing we did for a quick and weird treat.

• • •

When we built forts, they were mainly the setting for the play food we stocked them with. Megan and I built several forts throughout the woods, using the tin and steel core holders from US Steel's core shack. Our favorite fort was set in an indentation in the large smooth rock at the point overlooking Union Bay. We had a couch made of moss and a chair we'd made from a firewood block. The main focus of the fort was the shelf set in the rock wall.

On it we placed an egg carton full of "eggs"—clam shells stuffed with yellow cedar sawdust. There was a can of "chili"—the rich heart of a rotten red cedar tree mixed with water. We had bags full of seaweed; both popweed and the bright green sea salad; sea asparagus; and the pale-green and yellow hemlock tree buds that could be crumbled to add "parmesan cheese" to any dish. Plus, of course, the dark mud behind the floathouse that could be made into hamburger patties and chocolate cakes and cupcakes.

Megan washing cannery dishes to play with in our forts as puppies follow her.

When Linda left she hadn't taken all of her things with her, leaving behind in the wanigan bottles of shampoo and soap, packages of wheat germ, and quite a few dishes and cutlery. Megan and I hauled them off to our fort and used them in our food fantasy life. We could spend entire days cooking on our pretend stove, breaking the clam-eggs over bowls filled with assorted condiments, making it all stick together with shampoo. I still remember the beach and perfume smell of some combinations.

Jamie's first fort was built below the school and he called it "the store." He had his favorite meat, "ham hocks" (sawed-off tree knots) strung up in beachcombed netting, various fruits (different tree cones), grains (beach grass, wild rice), and vegetables (skunk cabbage cones for corn, rocks for potatoes, gravel for peas) stashed about that we could come and peruse.

We saw what he was doing and then gathered our own supplies from the same places he had and created our own stores around his until we had an entire outdoor food market below the school. When his store no longer flourished, Jamie decided that instead of being civilized about food, it was time to switch to the Tooth-and-Claw Stratagem. We would battle each other for the food in our stores and forts!

This allowed him to indulge his fondness for crafting weapons of every description. At the age of twelve he was already an expert in carving spears, wooden swords, knives, and throwing stars, and was particularly good at making bows and arrows.

He made the bows from sturdy tree limbs and filched fishing line and twine from Dad's stores. The arrows he cut from leftover cedar shakes from the school's siding and roof and then carefully shaved until they were perfectly smooth. He slit the ends and fitted in beachcombed eagle and sea gull feathers. For the tips he sharpened stones and tied them in place with twine or Dad's black tape. After dipping them in tree sap and allowing them to harden, the tips couldn't be knocked loose. These were serious weapons and could easily be mistaken for museum artifacts.

He press-ganged Robin and Chris into his army. They weren't the best shots, but they were enthusiastic and didn't mind retrieving arrows or thrown spears. Plus, each of us had big stores of chopped-up bull kelp, skunk cabbage, and pine cones to fling at invaders. Once our defenses were breached it was all about hand-to-hand combat with wooden swords, spears, and knives.

And yes, there were casualties. I remember one hard-fought battle that raged over hills, beaches, and finally into the water. Jamie got in a blow with his wooden sword that I didn't block in time (he was in his small aluminum skiff, I was in the water) and I wound up with a bloody lip.

Retreat seemed advisable. I swam home and Mom was shaken out of her faraway daydream world by the copious amounts of blood I was spewing. It was worth it to me though, because she gave me a cup of her precious Café Français (a powdered latte drink that came in a blue, red, and white tin that was her own personal treat) and a package of Saltine crackers to make me feel better, while Jamie looked on in deep chagrin. My brothers and sister were envious that I'd managed to win real food from the battle.

I settled on the couch, tucked in with a fuzzy afghan, nursing a huge, throbbing lip. I couldn't help wincing when the salt from the crackers got into the cut, but I was quite content otherwise. The tide was high and water bounced off the bay outside and rippled across the ceiling. I could hear my siblings resuming the fight with envy-fueled gusto, their shouts and yells and bangs muffled by the floathouse walls.

Mom put on some music and gave me an old photo album to look at. It was mostly of people I'd never known but had heard my Grandma Pat talk about. The photos were black and white, a bit yellowed in places, pasted to pages of black construction paper. Many of the people in them no longer existed and those still alive were different now, no longer the free-spirited children captured and trapped in their time-frozen world.

Why, I wondered, as I turned the pages filled with bygone people caught in bygone moments feeling bygone emotions, was it possible to snatch and capture moments of time, like Regency ladies netting butterflies and pinning them to a board? Like the way Zeno with his mathematical paradox had attempted to capture and pin motion and change.

Why did time with all its depth and motion become this flat, spatial thing?

What was this urge to spatialize time? To conquer it and physically own it? I turned the pages with a deep sense of mystery and wonder, sipping the sweet, creamy Café Français as Patsy Cline sang about walking along the Nile at night in the background and the water-reflected sunshine rippled all around me.

• • •

Spinach noodles.

Say those two words to any of us and you'll be greeted with an involuntary grimace.

It reminds us of the time it stormed for weeks, preventing Dad from crossing the strait. Every day we stood at the big window, peering out at the thrashing trees as the wind roared through them, and watched the waves pummel the big rock, twenty-foot explosions of spray wetting it down and turning it black.

Every day we willed the weather to moderate, for the maelstrom of white water out on the bay to subside.

And every day, as the food dwindled, it blew harder.

Mom tried rationing when she realized how low our staples were getting and that it might be a while before Dad could reach us, but it didn't do any good. One day we woke up to no food.

Mom was faced with the certainty of not being able to feed her five children—for how long, there was no telling. We made macabre jokes, wondering which of us would be eaten first. We figured Jamie would be the one to make that choice, and it probably wouldn't be much longer either.

We scoured the bare cupboards and every corner of the kitchen obsessively until someone turned up ancient spinach fettuccini noodles in a jar that had been used for décor, never meant to be eaten. That didn't matter; it was food, and our bellies were grumbling.

Mom boiled them. She had nothing but salt and pepper for seasoning, but the important thing was we'd have something hot and filling to put in our hollow stomachs. We watched with keen interest as she stirred the noodles. We saw them clump together into a greenish-gray, lumpy goop. They smelled funny.

Our grandparents had owned the floathouse before us and they were heavy smokers. When we dug into The Green Blob, all we tasted was cigarette-smoked, stale spinach. We normally ate anything put before us; we never turned anything down. But not one of us could manage more than a few bites before our stomachs rebelled.

Jamie picked up Dad's .30-30 rifle.

"What are you doing?" Mom demanded. Maybe she thought the Cannibal Time was upon us.

"I'm going hunting. There are deer all over this place."

Mom didn't like it. She loved deer, felt an almost mystical connection to them, but her impractical heart had to give in to the relentless physical needs of her children's empty stomachs.

She didn't go down without a fight. "You could get lost. Or have an accident. And we wouldn't know where you were or how to find you."

Jamie was impatient to be gone, but he said, "If I get hurt or lost, I'll shoot the gun three times like Dad told us to do in an emergency, every fifteen minutes. You'll be able to find me by following the sound."

Mom had to let him go. The rest of us kids watched as he strapped on Dad's Bowie knife, loaded up with ammunition, and picked up the .30-.30. He struck out for the ridge behind the house where we often heard wolves howling.

A few hours later we heard a single shot.

Jamie got his first deer. He was thirteen years old.

He didn't know how to dress it out so he carried the entire deer down to the beach. When he stumbled out of the woods, sweating and covered in blood, the conquering hero waiting for the accolades to commence—Dad showed up in the skiff. It was piled full of groceries.

"Aw man," Jamie says was his chagrined and exhausted thought. Still, he was glad that Dad was there to show him how to dress the deer and hang it.

Dad, frustrated at not having been able to get to us, built a dock for floatplanes to land at that he anchored to a rock beyond the lowest tide. As it happened, before the year was over he had to charter a floatplane to send us groceries when it stormed again. He sent other supplies as well, and mail. At one point we lost our rowboat and the canoe needed to be patched, so Mom was forced to haul the tin washtub down the beach and row out to the floatplane in it.

An innocence we didn't know we'd had crumbled over the spinach noodles incident. We realized how cut off we were, how scarce food was, and how quickly starvation could threaten us. The result was that Mom began a decades-long obsession with squirreling away extra food "for the famine." Every extra dollar Dad made was put into stocking up on nonperishables.

In addition, she made it a law that no deer could be killed within a few miles of the floathouse. She claimed that she wanted them tame enough to hang around so we would always have a fund of food on the hoof. But we all knew she just jumped at the opportunity to protect the deer while at the same time managing to put a practical spin on it.

Jamie became obsessed too—with providing us with food before we reached famine conditions. Since Mom wouldn't allow further deer hunting, he focused on fishing. We couldn't go far on his fishing expeditions because his aluminum skiff was powered by oars. Plus, Mom had made it a rule that we couldn't get out of sight of the floathouse. We were also never to get out on shore, where bears and wolves roamed.

This seriously limited the scope of Jamie's fishing mission. Only bullheads, perch, and hooligan swam right inside our little harbor. The real fish were out there on the bay. When Dad was home he'd take one of us kids in the skiff and jig up a Red Snapper or a variety of cod an hour before dinner, without fail. So Jamie knew they were out there, in Mom's forbidden zone.

One day, skirting the zone, he managed to snag a halibut.

Mom had told us horror stories about this peculiar flat fish, which could reach gigantic proportions. Some had been caught that weighed as much as a full-grown black bear. They were powerful fish and she told us that fishermen who had hauled even the more moderately sized ones into the skiff with them had ended up with a broken leg or been knocked overboard. It was common for fishermen to shoot a halibut to avoid such dangers. She told us we were never, under any circumstances, to haul a live halibut into the skiff with us. We were supposed to haul it to shore and pull it onto the rocks and kill it before putting it in the skiff.

So that's what we did. The fish dragged us around a bit as Jamie fought to keep it on his line. Megan and I worked the oars and finally managed to bump the skiff into a rocky shore down around a bend from the floathouse.

With the fish between the rocks and the skiff, Megan and I got the net under it. We got out on shore and Jamie killed the halibut, about a thirty-five pounder, with the gaff hook. When it was no longer moving, the three of us struggled to haul its slippery, awkward weight into the boat.

Buzzing with adrenaline and flushed with the good feeling that comes with knowing we'd helped to put food on the table, we hurrahed and yelled and banged on the sides of the boat as we headed for home.

Mom was on the deck shouting too. She obviously recognized the epic moment for what it was.

It was only when we got closer that we realized she wasn't shouting praise and acclaim. She was furious.

Shortly before, she'd been immersed in one of her books, like usual, but something made her glance out the window. She saw us in the rowboat and to her disbelief we were rowing toward shore with the obvious intention of getting out—against her express orders. In moments we were out of her sight, behind a bend in the shoreline.

Megan, Jamie, and I proudly hold up the halibut we caught
to help stock our food supplies.

"That's it. They're never going to be allowed in that boat again!" She stormed out onto deck and was made madder by our carry-on. When we got within hearing range she reamed us out.

"I told you that you were never, *never*, to go to shore, and never get out of my sight! So what do you do? The minute you think I'm not looking, you do both!"

Jamie managed to get a word in edgewise. "You told us we couldn't take a live halibut into the boat with us. You said we had to take it to shore to kill it."

It took a moment, but it finally penetrated. "Halibut?"

We revealed our trophy.

Mollified, and realizing she'd given us conflicting rules, she made up for it by oohing and aahing over the halibut. She fetched her camera to use some of her precious film on our prize. She had us pose with the fish, which we'd hauled up the beach in the tin washtub.

Roman Caesars never felt more triumphant.

• • •

Dad's response to the threat of famine was to plant a vegetable garden. He marked one out in front of the school where he'd turned up some good soil. It was where the cannery had built its barge storage platforms.

The problem was that in the intervening forty years the area had become a virtual jungle of seedlings growing close together, as always happened in any previously cleared space in the rainforest. If that wasn't bad enough, there was plenty of vine-like, entangling salal brush and prickly, painful devil's club.

It looked like an impossible task. And that was before taking into account the way Dad never could bear to spread any project out over more than one weekend. When he planned to do something, he planned to get it done before he returned to work.

Which meant that he was out there from dawn till dusk with the chainsaw and ax, cutting down every tree, seedling, and weed in the plot. Which likewise meant that we were out there from dawn till dusk, fighting off the swarms of bugs as we grabbed branches, small trees, and piles of brush, and hauled it all down the beach to be burned.

Despite how hardened we were to physical work and play, that weekend stands out as some of the hardest work of my entire life. There were almost no rests. We were so tired we drooped over our dinner at night, barely able to chew. Crawling into bed was the best thing ever. But then I'd lie there, aching in every body part, wondering if my back was broken, wondering if I was going to die. I'd fall asleep suddenly, dreamlessly, and sleep the whole night through, only to be woken by Dad, driving us back out to work on the garden.

He didn't bother to pause for lunch, so Mom brought us sandwiches and we at them standing, with hands sticky from tree sap, nails clogged with dirt, clothes smelling of brush smoke. And then went right back at it. Even after the rectangle of land was cleared we weren't done. Dad turned over the soil and we picked out every stone and root he turned up. We spent hours in a bent over position until it felt like we'd freeze that way.

Finally we were allowed to stand (still hunched) and watch, bug bitten, muscles burning and trembling, completely exhausted, while he methodically planted the seeds in long rows. He finished off the weekend labor by building a fence made of posts and fishing net to keep out the deer and—he hoped—the two-legged predators that bore his genes.

Some hope. After having worked that hard for the rewards, we never hesitated to help ourselves, though we had to be cautious when he was home. There was more of a thrill to it—the rutabagas tasted that much more crunchy and delicious—when we managed to snitch them right under his nose. And we didn't even like rutabagas.

The next day when he discovered our depredations, he'd rant and rave and we'd make ourselves scarce. Hiding in the hills, watching from the forest. Biding our time until the next nighttime veggie raid, led by our fearless, carrot-obsessed leader, Jamie.

The following year, after realizing one garden was not going to be enough, since almost everything he planted got snitched before he could harvest it, Dad marked out a bigger garden over near the entrance to the trail that led to the cannery side.

While we were clearing it, we found the remains of the cannery superintendent's house and evidence that another fire had struck years after the one that destroyed the cannery. We knew this because near the new garden plot many of US Steel's core sample holders had been scorched and melted, and the little shed that stood in the pile of broken ore was partially burned. The fire that burned the superintendent's house had to have occurred after US Steel bought the property, and had been limited to one small area.

Near the scorched remains of the superintendent's house we also discovered a hill of coal. Apparently it had been used to heat the superintendent's house.

I loved finding it. No one used coal anymore, but it gave me a tie to Louis L'Amour's day, and also Barbara Cartland's. I made up stories about that hill of coal, picturing Louis L'Amour characters as cannery workers handling it, and it made the labor of clearing the garden much easier to bear. I could lose myself in a mental world while my body was left to fend for itself, a lesson that I never forgot and that made every chore and job after that much easier to endure.

• • •

Dad also wanted to experiment with local wild plants, but Mom saw them all as potentially deadly. "I can't tell you not to eat them, but we're not giving them to the kids. If anything happened, if any of those plants are poisonous, we couldn't get them to a hospital in time."

The only local flora she allowed to be part of our wilderness dining experience was something called Chicken of the Woods, a bright-orange mushroom that grows on rotten trees and has a bright yellow underside.

While it's generally safe, some people are highly sensitive to it—and she turned out to be one of those people. Her body reacted like she'd been poisoned. That was the definitive end of her willingness to experiment with local flora.

"I remember when Dad drew dog names and Junior's name was drawn. Dad took him behind the school in the woods and tied him to a tree while he hid and waited with his rifle. I was sure Junior was going to get eaten and I was crying like a baby." —Robin, remembering when he was six years old

CHAPTER TEN

DURING OUR first year at the cannery we had Jamie's dog Moby for canine companionship. He was a Sheltie (miniature Collie) with a touch of Cocker Spaniel. We all adored him. Moby was the James Bond of dogs: intensely masculine, intelligently suave, coolly courageous, casually on top of every situation… and insanely territorial.

We found that out one day when our nearest neighbor, who lived alone on a mining claim several miles to the north of us, made a visit with his big, dumb black lab named Rascal.

Moby, despite being only half his size, went for Rascal with teeth bared and we had to lock the incensed dog inside the floathouse— where he promptly lost his secret agent cool. He glared out the window, whining and twitching as the invader marked territory all over Moby's domain.

The high-pitched, anguished, enraged noises that came out of him made us laugh, though we tried to disguise it out of respect for his feelings. It was just so funny to see our always cool, calm, and collected Moby losing his mind as he raced from one window to the next, standing on the back of the couch, shivering and bristling, to watch the enemy disrespectfully get fresh with his territory.

When the neighbor and his dog left, we let Moby outside and watched as he almost ruptured himself running around obliterating the other dog's scent.

When Mom and Dad decided to get me a dog, a beautiful golden Cocker Spaniel that Linda and her husband Art picked up in Ketchikan and brought out to us along with some supplies on their fishing boat, we were concerned about how Moby would react.

Our fears proved groundless. Moby and Lady, as I named her, frolicked together, nudging each other; they couldn't get enough of each other.

"Look, they like each other!" we exclaimed happily.

A few months later we quadrupled our canine count when Lady gave birth to six puppies. Moby liked her so much, in fact, that we quickly accumulated about two or three dogs per kid. We had enough to go around for visiting cousins to adopt one or two for the duration of their stay.

We had a lot of fun naming them: Sonya, Little Anne, Bear Killer, Vicky, Junior, Cheerios, Zarkov, Peppermint, Panda, Saber, Sylvester, Butch… Each kid had a different idea of what made a good dog name. Mom chose one white-and-black puppy that she named Wee Macgregor. Dad got into the action by adopting one he named Andy.

Mom loved to stand at the big bay window and watch us kids racing around the beaches with a stream of happy dogs barking and jumping behind us. It was such a picture of youthful freedom, she says, that she still likes to think about it to this day.

We were too busy having fun to notice her watching. The dogs were packed with so much personality that we saw them as friends. They all had distinct personalities: Junior was amiable, Bear Killer was the bad-boy troublemaker, Vicky was sweet and dainty, Little Anne was a gruff tomboy, and so on.

The only ones who weren't thrilled by the new arrivals were the cats. We'd arrived at the cannery with several cats including Betty, Creosote Bill, Duchess, and Linda's cat F.u.b.a.r.

As long as the cats maintained the high ground—strutting along the top rail on the floathouse's front deck beyond the dogs' reach, or climbing around the roof, their claws screeching on the tin as they slid down to jump onto the rail—there were no troubles. But once the cats got down where the dogs were, war ensued.

Lady was obsessively loyal and couldn't bear to be apart from me for any amount of time. My little brothers took advantage of this.

Whenever we played hide-and-seek I'd have to put Lady inside the floathouse before I hid. But the boys would let her out and run behind her as she put her nose to the ground and, yipping frantically, she'd hunt me down within seconds no matter where I hid.

She could swim underwater and climb ladders and thought nothing of fishing in the creek with Moby and chasing bears. On the other hand, she was also terrified of gloves and garbage bags. She went everywhere with me, and was a wonderful mother to her puppies. In fact, while I saw her as my baby, I think she saw me as another one of her pups that she had to keep track of and protect.

Megan might have felt deprived at first, seeing how close Lady and I were, but it wasn't long before she had her own dog, a pretty black female with white markings who she called Sonya. As it turned out, Sonya was a bit of a con artist. She broke her leg and after it healed she'd milk it for all the attention she could get—though she forgot which leg had been injured and would lift the wrong one, whining and looking pitiful.

Megan adored her and went along with her scam. Sonya slept with us after her injury and Mom would come in and see her daughters hugging either side of the bed while Sonya stretched out in the middle.

• • •

Apparently Muriel, our first homeschool teacher, thought about us more than we did her, because a couple years later she returned on a peacemaking mission. Either that or she wanted to show off how happily her life had continued without us, to the tune of having acquired a cute baby in the interim.

I can only imagine her feelings of having fatally miscalculated our willingness to let bygones be bygones when a friend dropped her off in his skiff on the beach at low tide and then motored away, leaving her to face a horde of snarling dogs.

Not to mention the five of us feral kids racing after the dogs screaming at the top of our lungs, "Kill her! Kill her! Kill her!"

The fact was, the dogs' only regular experience of humans was the seven of us. Whenever we had a visitor they went wild, racing down the beach barking their heads off. Mom would tell us kids to chase after them and make sure they didn't bite anyone.

So when Muriel returned with her baby, the dogs went into their "stranger danger" attack mode. We ran after the dogs, yelling at them. Bear Killer was the ringleader so we all yelled at him, calling him by the shortened form of his name: "Killer! Kill-er!"

When we reached Muriel, she stared at us in a strange way and seemed reluctant to hike up the beach with us to the floathouse. But the skiff that had brought her had already left, so she had no choice but to stay.

I offered to hold the baby while she climbed the floathouse's logs, but she sharply spurned my attempt to be helpful and hugged the baby more tightly. Once inside, the whole time that she drank the tea Mom offered her and bragged about how amazing her offspring was, she kept giving us odd looks. She seemed only too happy to leave when the friend returned to pick her up.

It wasn't until after Muriel left that I thought about her strange behavior and the way we'd yelled Bear Killer's name as we ran after him and the other dogs. I said to Mom, "Do you suppose she thought we were yelling, 'Kill her?'"

Mom burst out laughing, but when she thought about it, she had to admit it was a definite possibility.

Somewhere out there Muriel has probably been telling the story of those savage Neilson kids for decades.

• • •

I don't know how it happened, but I was the one who wound up with the job of weaning all the puppies. When they were born sick, I'd stay up all night nursing them.

I didn't have a lot to work with. We discovered when we had rabbits (our parents, not knowing themselves very well, had decided to breed them for food—but neither of them had the temperament to kill cute little rabbits) that acidophilus could save lives. That worked with the puppies, but sometimes it didn't.

I remember one puppy I worked extremely hard to save who needed constant attention. I had to keep her warm and throughout the day and night give her the medicine I'd concocted that perked her up. But one night I fell asleep and forgot to give her the dose. When I woke up in the morning, she was dead. I buried a lot of puppies and every one broke my heart.

It didn't matter how hard I tried or what I did, there was no saving some of them, no matter how much love and care I gave them. This periodic trauma went on during all the years that we lived at the cannery.

Worse than these puppy deaths was when the wolves came down off the mountains and snatched our four-legged companions to kill and eat them.

• • •

One evening, as the sky turned periwinkle and the endless, javelin-tipped forest began to turn black, Mom looked out at the point where the big rock was and saw a lone wolf, big, shaggy, and rawboned, standing there... looking at the floathouse and the kids and dogs playing in front of it.

She sharply called us in from our play.

It was the first time we'd seen a wolf right out in the open.

The dogs didn't have to be told that danger was near. They ran and hid under the floathouse and crouched on the logs with the floor right above their heads. We hoped that the lone wolf would go on his way.

He didn't.

He stayed there, barely moving, staring at the floathouse. It was one of the creepiest things we ever experienced at the cannery. We managed to coax the dogs out from under the house so we could pull them inside before it got dark. The cats hid on the roof and didn't stir from the ridge peak all night.

When darkness fell we lit the kerosene lamps. Everything was silent... too silent... until the first wolf howled. It was right outside, so close that we all jumped and the dogs cowered as close to us as they could get. Some climbed onto the couches with us.

More wolves answered until we could hear them howling in a ring around the house. We stared at each other in the yellow kerosene light that put dark shadows in the corners and blackened

Chris (seated) with Little Mac and Robin holding Junior.
Many of our beloved canine companions were stolen by wolves.

the windows so we couldn't see what was outside.

Whenever our family was in a stressful or scary situation, we usually resorted to humor. "We need Skip to show up and shoot off his gun," I quipped, referencing *The Wilderness Family* movies as we so often did. The others laughed.

"What if it's Scarface out there and they break the windows?" Robin asked, referring to the second movie in the series that focused on the family being terrorized by wolves, led by a terrifying black wolf named Scarface.

"How do we make them go away?" Megan asked.

Mom shook her head. "I don't know." There was no one she could call as darkness fell over the bay and forest, cutting us off from the nearest village. The lights shining out of our windows were the only lights for miles, other than the faint starshine fighting its way through dark cloud cover.

We hugged the dogs, as much for our own comfort as theirs. Moby, who would have been scratching at the door to get out and tangle with another dog on his territory, kept far away from the door and windows, the hair raised on the back of his neck, a growl low in his throat.

The wolves, as if trained in psychological warfare, were quiet just long enough for us to think they'd left, just long enough for our nerves to relax—and then one howled and the others answered, revealing that we were still surrounded. The repeated relaxing and tensing could easily drive a person crazy. The dogs shivered in our arms, their heads ducked hard against us, trying to burrow right inside us.

Were the wolves trying to get us to come out, to send the dogs out to them to eat in return for them leaving? I had the sense that this was what people in an Old West fort felt when they were under siege. I hid my face in the crazy tuft of hair on Lady's head as she quivered against me, and the living flesh and dog smell of her imprinted permanently on my mind as I listened to the predatory howls outside.

Time's malleability first impressed itself on me then, the way it could slow and stretch and refuse to proceed. As I hugged Lady, a phrase that I would use to remind myself of time's inevitable passage and reassure myself in any crisis came to mind and I whispered it to myself: "This too shall pass."

"I wish they would go away!" Mom exclaimed. She had recently read a pioneer woman's diary where the woman wrote about wolves digging at the sod roof to get at her and her baby inside. Mom couldn't get it out of her mind.

Jamie, fearless in every other way, had a horror of wolves. When Dad worked on a farm in Washington State a decade ago, the boss's eight-year-old daughter told preschooler Jamie bloodcurdling tales of wolves stealing and eating little kids.

That night he felt particularly vulnerable because he'd sprained his ankle and was hobbling around with the support of a stick. As the wolves continued to howl, Jamie packed on every weapon in the house, including the ax.

He strapped the .44 in its sheath with its belt-load of cartridges over his chest. Dad's Bowie knife in its sheath was belted around his waist. He hung the .30-30 over one shoulder and gripped the 30.06 in his hands. He probably had more weapons tucked in less visible places as well. He looked like a protagonist from a horror movie ready for every nightmare.

"I need to go out and shoot. That might drive them off." He looked like it was the last thing on earth he wanted to do.

"No. I don't want you going out there," Mom said instantly.

"Somebody has to do it."

"Well, I'm not shooting anything," she retorted. In her fear of handling guns she'd likely hurt herself or one of us kids or one of the dogs, or put a hole in the house, break a window—it wouldn't be good, whatever came of it.

"I'm the one that needs to do it," Jamie insisted.

She forgot about her gun phobia as she realized why he was so insistent. He felt that he needed to face his fears to be able to overcome them. She nodded.

He inched up to the door with the .44 in his hand as us kids watched him with our breaths held. What if there was a wolf right there at the door, waiting for him to open it so it could lunge inside and get us?

He paused a moment to let go of his walking stick and put his free hand on the door knob, breathing deeply. Then he yanked the door open, stepped outside, and pulled the trigger multiple times—the concussive blasts hammering at us and making the dogs flinch and whimper—before jumping back inside and slamming the door shut. His eyes were wide and he was breathing hard, but he'd done it.

The wolves scattered at the shock of the gunshots.

But they came back. They always came back.

When Dad came home and we told him about what had happened, he didn't say much. That night he got to experience the wolf siege for himself when they came down off the ridge to circle the house and howl again. As we dragged the dogs inside, he shone the flashlight into the darkness and we saw a sea of glowing eyes ringing the floathouse.

• • •

Jamie already knew how to shoot, but Dad decided that with the wolf threat hanging over us, it was time to teach me and Megan how to shoot as well. He set up a target on the beach and drilled us with safety and sighting tips. (He'd made sharpshooter status in the Army.)

I held the hard stock of the gun tight to my shoulder, lined up the open sights on the target, and fought to hold the weight of the rifle level. I blocked out Dad's critical eyes, breathed in the smell of gun oil slowly, let it out, and pulled the trigger. I hit the target, though not the hand-drawn bull's-eye.

Megan was up next and, probably too aware of Dad's focused attention on what she was doing, didn't hold the stock tightly enough to her shoulder. When she pulled the trigger, the rifle's kick knocked her straight down to the beach onto her butt. She didn't cry. If anything, it made her mad and a little more focused. She got right back up, shot again, hitting the target, closer to the bull's-eye than I'd gotten.

The boys were too small to learn, and Mom, for the most part, refused to have anything to do with shooting guns. She would, if she felt she had to, hang the .44 in its belt off her shoulder, though she had zero intention of ever shooting it. This became an issue the time a group of hunters unexpectedly showed up. They were strangers to us and, of course, were all carrying guns.

She met them with the gun on her shoulder as Dad had told her she had to in such a situation, and they chatted for a while in a friendly way, putting her off her guard.

Then the man who did most of the talking said casually, "Nice-looking revolver. What is it, a .44 magnum?"

"I have no idea. My husband makes me wear it," Mom confessed.

"Can I have a look at it?"

"Sure." She handed him the gun.

He took it, looked it over, and then stared straight at her. "Ma'am," he said, "don't ever do that again. Your husband meant for you to have that gun to protect you and your kids." He handed it back to her.

Mom sheepishly put it back on her shoulder and laughed later when she told us kids about it.

• • •

The wolves continued to lurk. Whenever we heard them howling at night, we pulled the dogs inside. But they got bolder and were no longer frightened off by gunshots.

They took to appearing in broad daylight. One time when Mom

was walking on the beach, she looked up and saw a wolf standing on the rocks in front of her. She froze, watching him, waiting to see what he would do. As she watched, he disappeared. Dissolved, as if he'd never existed, as if he were a mirage. She must have blinked and, in that nanosecond, he vanished.

Another day while we were outside playing with the dogs, we saw the wolves materialize silently at the top of the small hill at one end of the floathouse, the hill we sledded down in winter.

Rather than howling, the wolves made soft, whining noises and to our disbelief we saw one of the female dogs, Tina (named for Tina Turner), instead of being frightened, trot up the hill toward them.

"Come back!" We ran after her, shouting her name. The other dogs milled around us, confused and panicked. The wolves continued to lure Tina, right in front of us. We finally managed to grab her and raced back to the house, shoving the dogs inside.

When we counted them up, to our horror one was missing. Little Mac, Chris's dog, was gone. The wolves, like master magicians, had stolen him while our focus had been on the dog they'd tried to lure up the hill. We never saw Little Mac again, but he wasn't the last to be taken.

On one of the days when Dad was home, he had to go up in the woods to work on the dam and waterline. He took the 30.06 with him, but he didn't glimpse a single wolf. The dogs followed him, as they always did.

When he returned home, he found out that one of the dogs that had followed him was missing.

It was Megan's beloved, spoiled pet, Sonya.

The wolves had stolen right up behind him and snatched Sonya away without any trouble or alerting Dad to their presence. Sonya hadn't made a sound of protest. It shocked all of us, but it desolated Megan. She was inconsolable and cried for months.

Dad was driven to extreme measures. He put all the names of the dogs in his hat and drew one out. We held our breaths, praying it wouldn't be our dog's name that was drawn.

After drawing out the name, he took Junior, Robin's friendly little reddish-gold dog, and tied him to the back of the school. The ridge that the wolves came down was right behind it.

Dad hid out of sight with the 30.06 and waited. Soon enough, Junior got tired of the unaccustomed rope anchoring him in place. He twisted and fought it, whining and barking, making all kinds of unhappy, distressed noises.

We waited inside the floathouse with the other dogs, listening to poor Junior trying to get our attention, knowing he was wolf bait. Robin was sure that his dog was about to be eaten.

We were all traumatized as we waited for the gunshots that would free us from the terrorism of the wolves, listening to poor Junior yipping and crying while the unseen killers lurked. It probably didn't do Dad's Vietnam PTSD much good either, waiting for an unseen, lethal enemy with a gun in his hands.

But the wolves were too smart and didn't fall for the trap. Dad had to return to Thorne Bay without resolving the threat of the wolves.

• • •

One night Mom woke me and Megan. She had the gun on her shoulder.

"It's the wolves," she whispered.

Jamie, with the badly sprained ankle, and the boys were still asleep. The lantern that worked as a nightlight to ward off Megan's night terrors created a dim glow that wasn't strong enough to turn the windows above the bed black. There was a full moon outside, shining more light into the house than the lantern could.

"You have to run across to the wanigan and put the girl dogs inside. I'll keep watch with the gun."

Dad had built a large cage on the front deck of the wanigan to put the female dogs in when they were in heat, but no one thought it would withstand a wolf attack.

As Megan and I crawled out of the warmth of our bedding, we heard the wolves howling on the ridge. Our hearts beat faster and faster, waking us up completely as Mom hurried us to the front door.

It was bitterly cold outside, but we didn't stop to grab coats or put boots on. We raced out onto the cold boards of the floathouse's deck and then across the frost-covered rocks of the beach.

The whole world was limned with icy moonlight. The forest looming around us was leached of color, in shades of gray, with the blackest shadows beneath the trees. We felt the unseen eyes of forest creatures and ran faster. Mom stood in the open door with the gun. We wondered if she'd be able to use it if the wolves came after us.

The rocks were so piercingly cold that they burned our feet as we ran. The line of seaweed left by the tide crunched when we stepped on it, scraping our soles, sending a musky scent into the still, cold night. The huge empty bay was still, reflecting the moonlit sky.

I felt Megan's terror. Knowing her fear of the night, let alone with wolves added into it, I almost wished she wasn't there beside me. After all, though I did have a sense of urgency and fear, I was more impressed—even awed—by the experience.

All around us the vast lonesome wilderness of forest and sea was lit by the colorless light of the moon. The wolves howled closer and closer as they came down from the mountains. If it weren't for the dogs being in danger and Megan so scared, I might have enjoyed the sheer, pulse-pounding adventure of it, even the icy rocks under my bare feet.

We finally reached the wanigan and clambered up over the slick, wet logs into the shadows under its porch roof. The girl dogs were caught between pleasure at our appearance and fear as the wolves' hunting chorus echoed through the forest. They wriggled and quivered, whining, jumping up on the cage wall.

Megan opened it while I gripped the cold, rusty spike that served as a door handle and used my weight to slide the wanigan's heavy wooden door in its groove. As soon as it was open we shoved the dogs inside, trying to ignore their pitiable attempts to encourage us to pet them and comfort them and stay with them.

Mom still waited at the floathouse door, the lamplight yellow behind her. Above her the aluminum roof reflected so much moonlight that it glowed eerily. Smoke from the chimney was almost transparent as it drifted silently. We were supposed to run back as soon as the dogs were safe inside the wanigan.

We gave a few hasty pets, slid the big door shut, and ran for safety. The wolves' howls grew louder the closer we got to the floathouse, speeding our frozen feet over the gravel, up the wooden ramp, along the deck, and into the warmth of the floathouse. We gained at least one victory over the wolves that night.

"They don't call me James Neilson for nothing." —Jamie

CHAPTER ELEVEN

WE LIVED in a pocket universe during those years when it was Mom and us kids, with Dad visiting from that other, almost mystical world on the outside, where movies and Hostess snacks proliferated.

I was eleven years old when we heard our parents talking about neighbors moving in. Robin and Chris were young enough not to remember what it was like to have people other than our family around us, so the concept of "neighbor" was entirely alien to them. Megan and I had only ever needed each other for companionship so we saw nothing of value in the idea and didn't know how to process the news.

Jamie, as usual, had it all figured out. He knew exactly what to make of it.

INVASION.

He immediately set about dealing with the issue by building a huge pile of arrows and a bow for each of us. When he was satisfied with the results of his labors, he began to instruct us in the ways of war.

This was no longer play warfare. This wasn't wooden sword fighting without real intent to commit harm and "crush your enemies, see them driven before you, and to hear the lamentations of their women," to quote one of Jamie's favorite movies, *Conan the Barbarian*. It was serious, and it was covert. Mom, Jamie told us, was under no circumstances to know of our battle plans for the Invaders.

As Jamie drilled us, he evoked the memory of listening to *War of the Worlds*. This was the Martian invasion all over again, fought this time on a remote Alaskan shore in front of our floathouse home. They would be coming by sea, by motor-powered boat. We'd hear them in time to take cover with our weapons.

That was the important thing. We had to be able to react immediately and with deadly force. "Show no mercy," he commanded. "Lethal force is the only thing that will protect our way of life. Strangers will never colonize our land. We will execute our duties with extreme prejudice. With our last breath we will spit at them," he decreed, borrowing indiscriminately from various favorite movies.

We practiced and practiced, following in a crouched run wherever Jamie led, shooting arrows with our bows until we were sore—especially Robin and Chris, who were so small you'd think they'd be exempted from active service. But no. In Jamie's guerilla army there were no exemptions.

We were the mercenaries in *Wild Geese*, the Rebel Force in *Star Wars*, and the winged warriors in *Flash Gordon*. Jamie was our merciless leader.

Zero hour arrived. Mom, sublimely unaware of this fact, ambled down the beach to greet the boat, named *Jaws*, which was towing a skiff piled high with furniture, boxes, and other invasion paraphernalia.

It was a quiet day, overcast, with a light drizzle obscuring the tops of the silent, forested mountains. The bay was mirror flat, reflecting the gray sky, and it was damp behind the cedar log that all five of us hunched behind. We eyed each other, hearts beating fast, ready for Jamie's signal that would trigger our scorched-earth strategy.

I remember the scent of cedar and salty seaweed, and the sand fleas hopping out of the wet beach gravel we'd dug ourselves into. The boat idled its way into the middle of our inlet as Mom approached the line of pilings that stairstepped down into the still water, mirroring themselves so that they seemed to climb back out of the bay.

The anchor dropped with a splash and running rattle that tightened our nerves. We heard enemy voices carrying across the water as a couple people shortened the towline and climbed into the skiff, one of them maneuvering around the pile of enemy trappings

Jamie, building weapons in the ruins, his favorite pastime.

to get to the outboard at the stern.

When the outboard engine roared to life, I looked at Jamie. His steely blue eyes were intent as he peered over the hairy bark on the log at the approaching hostiles.

"Now?" I asked. My legs had started to cramp and the boys were shifting awkwardly.

He shook his head, holding his hand up, palm out, without taking his eyes off the advance of the heavily loaded, low-riding skiff as it puttered toward shore. It was probably the most awkward and lame invasion of any shore in the history of Manifest Destiny.

When Jamie was satisfied that he'd accurately judged the distance, he dropped his hand with judgmental force. "Now!"

We sprang into form, pulling the fishing line back on our homemade hemlock bows, expertly nocking the cedar shake arrows with their sea gull feathers and sharpened stone heads.

"Fire!"

Arrows lanced the leaden sky, reaching the apex of their arcs, hanging there for a glorious moment, before gravity drew them down to destroy the invasion force. Before they struck we had already whipped our next arrows into place and fired again at Jamie's ruthless command.

Eric Johnson, the commercial fisherman who was so identified with his boat that he was known locally—like a Viking created by Steven Spielberg—as "Eric of the *Jaws*," had embraced Alaska's allowance of the personal use of marijuana to the full limits of the law, and then some. As he steered the skiff full of a friend's belongings to their new home, he looked up through a haze of marijuana smoke into a hail of arrows.

"Far out, man," he said to Mom who stood frozen in mortification on the shore. "Whoa. Are there Indians around here? Far. Out."

The arrows rained into the water. In the case of the boys, some of them never got beyond the beach. Megan and I managed to at least dent the bay with our projectiles. Only Jamie's arrows came anywhere near their target.

"No," Mom said to Eric, "those are just my kids."

She looked over at the log irately, but we were no longer there. We'd retreated into the woods to lick our psychological wounds.

• • •

I think all of us, except Jamie, were graciously willing to concede defeat and accept the neighbors. Jamie put a good face on it, especially since one of the neighbor boys, named Chris, turned out to be exactly his age. However, we should have all known that he'd get his revenge in subtle ways. Revenge, he had always let it be known, was a dish best served cold.

The neighbors were Dave and Sheila and Sheila's kids: Chris (since we called our Chris by the name of Mitmer at this time, it wasn't confusing), Dawn, Gabriel (Gabe), and Iolare (Lare). The two younger boys were my age and Megan's. Poor Dawn, at sixteen, was on her own. She was missing the tip of one thumb which she'd lopped off while chopping kindling. (I think of her probably more than any other person because I think of her whenever I cut kindling, a common, almost daily chore.) She was quiet and preferred to hole up by herself. She seemed sad to me, divorced from her family and the present.

The neighbors had moved into the only still-standing building on the cannery side, the one-room cabin (plus loft) situated across the creek from the ruins where Muriel and Maurice, and then Rand and Linda, had lived.

Dave, Sheila, and her kids were there for one summer, and Dad didn't see that much of them, not just because he was there only on weekends, but that summer he and Mom and Rory and Marion went on a weekend hiking and camping trip up to a lake on a nearby mountain.

While they were hiking, Megan and I stayed with our grandparents in Meyers Chuck with our little cousins LeAnn and JoDean (who everyone called GiGi).

This left Jamie and the boys at the cannery with the new neighbors. Dave decided not to feed them the groceries Mom had left with them. Hardcore hippies, Dave and Sheila had declared that they were dedicated vegetarians, subsisting mostly on figs and goat cheese.

Jamie wasn't about to forego his rightful meat. He took matters into his own hands by killing salmon in the creek, despite Dave's meat ban, and cooking it on the beach to feed himself and his brothers. Dave confronted him and said he was going to apply corporal punishment for disobeying him.

"Go ahead and hit me," Jamie told him, looking him straight in the eye. "And my dad will kill you."

Dad, with his wild beard, extreme capability, unbending will, and brooding Vietnam vet persona wasn't someone Dave was willing to cross. He backed down. It was Jamie's first triumph over the neighbors; it wouldn't be his last.

What none of the adults foresaw (or knew) was that Jamie swiftly adapted his desire of repelling the invaders to subjecting them to his martial rule. Among other cruel reprisals, he created a little pastime he liked to call "running the gauntlet." You had two choices—you could either challenge him to single gladiatorial combat (to the death, it was implied), or run the gauntlet. In our new neighbor Chris, Jamie found an able enforcer.

Everyone chose the gauntlet, which entailed all of the rest of us lining up on either side of a stretch of the forest where the remains of the cannery's old wire-wrapped wooden waterline was half-buried in moss. As the runner/victim ran the distance, dodging behind saplings and what other sparse cover he or she could find, we on the sidelines hurled pine cones, skunk cabbage cones, and whatever else came to hand.

I remember standing there halfheartedly hurling cones at Gabe as he weaved, winced, and ran, thinking, "Why are we going along with this?"

But no one wanted to challenge Jamie, not with Chris backing him up, so his decrees and gauntlets went unchallenged until the end of that summer. When the family moved on and we were once again alone in the ruins.

• • •

One fall day, a hunting group from Meyers Chuck got stranded by the weather. Since we had the only homestead around for miles, they took shelter with us. The floathouse, already bursting at the seams with the seven of us, was wall to wall with chattering people. Three women fit into Mom's tiny kitchen to cook, while the men all stayed outside as Dad, who happened to be home, took them on a tour.

In the morning when there was a break in the weather, the guys decided to chance going hunting and left their wives and kids behind with us. Mom was talked into putting her exercise tape on the stereo (Joanie Greggains exhorting her high-stepping listeners, "Don't forget to breathe," while "Let's Get Physical" by Olivia Newton-John played in the background). We girls stayed and exercised while the boys made themselves scarce. Megan and I, hardened by our daily athletic play, were baffled when all the ladies limped and winced afterward.

It was a bizarre event for us to have strangers in our outpost. But we were delighted with the all-you-can-eat crab and all the geese the women fried up.

Another day, this time in summer, we were surprised when almost all of Meyers Chuck showed up on our beach with their lawn furniture, beer, and food. We hadn't invited them and never found out what was behind their appearance, reminiscent of the mysterious way limpets suddenly covered the beaches at night.

Whatever the case, Mom immediately set to work flattening

TARA NEILSON

dozens of hamburgers from the ground beef the Meyers Chuck store owner had brought for Dad to barbecue on a firepit outside. There were packages of hot dogs for the kids and coolers full of ice, with cans of beer and sodas stuck in it.

We were flabbergasted. Our remote shores were suddenly populated with kids of all ages, from toddlers to teens, with women in swimsuits—who had no intention of getting in the water—working on their tans.

All the young local guys were at their beck and call, vying with each other to get the ladies' attention. One woman was sophisticated enough to have a cigarette holder, which she, with ostentatious leisureliness, drew out of her shoulder bag and had a fawning teenage boy light. "Thanks so much, daaahling," she drawled.

This strange infestation occurred when our neighbor Sheila and her kids were still living at the cannery. They were strict vegetarians when Dave was around, but they took advantage of his absence that day to stuff themselves with as many hamburgers and hot dogs they could tuck into.

Sheila settled right in, lying on an unfurled, tattered towel next to one of the alien-looking lawn chairs, chatting about her days as a Grateful Dead follower in California. She whipped off her shirt, deciding to go topless, and everyone acted like it was nothing out of the ordinary.

Sheila claimed that one time she'd been so stoned that she stared into the sun for too long and had holes in her eyes. I never saw them, but it creeped me out thinking about the holes in her eyes so much that I had a hard time looking anywhere near her face, while Megan was horrified by her topless stunt.

Everyone was gossiping, laughing, and skiffs were coming and going. We had, for one brief, bizarre day, become the Alaskan Riviera.

• • •

We didn't know about two other neighbors until one day, while playing on the beach like usual, a male and female, barely out of their teens, staggered out of the woods.

We had never experienced any shock quite like that before. Bears and wolves might emerge unexpectedly and unannounced from the woods that surrounded our home. But humans?

Impossible.

Where had they come from?

The dogs went crazy, of course, and we had our hands full stopping them from biting the mysterious strangers.

They looked terrible. Their clothes were shredded, their hair was wild, and they were ghostly pale, except for all the scratches that marred them with dark red lines. They swayed and could hardly speak.

We led them to the house for Mom to deal with. Mom was startled, but she got their story out of them pretty quickly.

They were two kids from New York City who had yearned for adventure, and the lonesome Alaskan wilderness had seemed just the ticket. In Ketchikan they met up with the Polish miner who lived by himself with his dog Rascal (who Moby hated with a passion) to the north of us. He'd taken them out to his place and then left to get more supplies. The problem was that whenever he went to town he tended to go on a bender, and apparently he completely forgot about the young couple from New York he'd left behind.

When they ran out of food and he still didn't return, they had no idea what to do. They knew about Meyers Chuck but had no idea how to reach it, since he'd taken the only skiff. They decided to walk the shoreline.

The shores between his place and ours were forest and rock bluffs, and the forest was unlike anything they'd ever had to deal with before. They were ripped and torn and shredded in no time. They were in such bad shape when they finally reached our place that I have no doubt if we hadn't been there, if they'd had to walk all the way to Meyers Chuck, they never would have made it. They would have been two of the two thousand people who disappear in Alaska every year.

They knew it too, how close they'd come to dying in the forest.

Mom gave them salve and Band-Aids for their wounds as they sat and stared like zombies, barely able to get their story out. With empathy and her love for the more civilized things in life, she knew exactly what else to give them that would help them the most.

Close-up of the floathouse when the tide is out,
with cannery pilings in the foreground.

They came back to life when she set before them steaming cups (using her good blue-and-white Dutch dishes that we were never allowed near) of her special treat, the tinned, sweetened powdered latte called Café Français.

It almost made them cry, they were so grateful to experience something civilized and even remotely similar to what they'd grown up with in NYC. They sipped it slowly, making it last as long as possible, holding the cups on their trembling knees and lifting them with scratched and quivering hands.

Dad gave them a ride to Meyers Chuck where they could catch a floatplane to Ketchikan and then back to New York, leaving the near-fatal Alaskan adventure behind them.

• • •

Years later we had someone else try to live an off-grid adventure out near us. A man brought his entire family (grandmother, wife, and two kids) with him and built a home on a granite outcropping about halfway between us and the Polish miner. They had lived Up North in the "true Alaska" as they made it known, and they refused to heed any advice about living out in Southeast Alaska's wilderness on a year-around basis.

"We've lived Out before, we know what we need to do," the man of the family said, rebuffing all suggestions about where to build based on local knowledge of the severity of storms from certain directions. He gave the same response to suggestions about stocking up on firewood and what kind was best.

Not surprisingly, things didn't go well for them.

At one point the grandmother was left alone with the kids in the middle of winter and became so desperate that she called us on the radio, begging for any kind of firewood that would warm the house. Our whole family went by skiff to help out and found her trying to dry rounds of dripping wood on the stove which had a tepidly smoldering fire in it. Dad rounded up some dry firewood for them and sawed and chopped it, and we kids and Mom hauled it.

Then, still winter, his wife was alone with the kids while he was away, and sent out a frantic Mayday call on the CB radio.

It was blowing a gale with hurricane-force winds and she was terrified that the house would be swept off into the bay, taking her and the kids with it, as the wind roared around her exposed home and monster seas crashed into the house's foundation pilings, splattering the windows, exactly what the locals had tried to warn them about building in that spot.

Mom was fit to be tied, furious that the woman had been left in such a position, apparently not seeing any similarities with her own situation. She was angrier when she and Dad realized they couldn't turn their backs on the cry of distress. He'd have to go out in the storm and bring them to our place.

"Have everything ready," Mom told the woman on the radio as the trees thrashed around the house. We could hear the waves booming against the rocks as Dad headed outside. "He'll be there in a few minutes."

"He can get the kids," the woman replied, "but I'm staying." She was apparently afraid of what her husband would say if she abandoned the place. "I'll go down with the house."

That was the final straw for Mom. "No, you won't. What will happen is once my husband risks his life to get your children and gets back here, you'll decide you don't want to die after all and you'll get on the radio demanding that my husband risk his life again. That's not going to be how it works. You're going to get in the skiff when he gets there!"

We all thought, but didn't say a word, about the night Rand went down.

Dad turned down all offers to go with him and headed out to the skiff. He told us later that when he finally got to their place, soaked from the seas he'd taken over the bow and sides as he steered into the waves, that they weren't in the wave-lashed house; they were huddled under a tarp behind the house.

Mom's furious words apparently got through to the woman because she clambered into the skiff and Dad managed to bring her and the kids safely to our place where they shivered and stared at us mutely, terrorized by their experience of a Southeast Alaskan winter storm.

She and the kids never returned, and the man was forced to sell.

Other than family visiting us or a school kid from Meyers Chuck once in a great while spending the weekend, these were our experiences with neighbors.

*"It was complete culture shock, but in a fascinating way.
I wanted more. I wanted to go to that world one day."*
—Megan, about the first time seeing *Miami Vice*

CHAPTER TWELVE

WHEN WE lived on the floathouse side of the cannery, our daily life was shaped by mail days, random adventures, music, movies, and eventually TV.

The mail arrived in Meyers Chuck by floatplane and the post mistress would hold ours there at the tiny store/post office until Dad was home. If the weather cooperated, he'd take Mom over to pick it up and they'd shop for groceries and fuel at the same time.

It was an all-day trip as Mom took the opportunity to get caught up with her family, and the adults sat around yakking all day.

One mail day, Mom and Dad didn't return even as it began to get dark. There was a special strangeness, we found, in being completely alone in the wilderness without adults around as evening fell. It felt like we had a forgotten and lost world to ourselves.

We played Fleetwood Mac on the outside speakers that Dad had made out of a few nailed-together boards and punched tin to keep the rain off the car stereo speakers that he'd placed inside and then wired to the car stereo inside the house.

Stevie Nicks's voice singing "Sara" wafted through the depths of the forest as we played on the beach. Jamie had some Jumping Jacks left over from the Fourth of July—the store in Meyers Chuck sold them every year—and he discovered that if he threw them in the water they'd still whiz around and glow brightly for a few seconds.

We also discovered that among Lady's many accomplishments, she could swim underwater. She dove right in, chasing the Jumping Jacks with her nose and head completely submerged. She got burned by the fireworks, but she didn't care. Every time Jamie lit another Jumping Jack, she wagged her stubby tail furiously and then dove in as it raced around underwater.

Mom and Dad made it home that night, but I wondered what would happen if the weather kicked up and they weren't able to make it back. Or what if the weather got bad while they were out in the skiff and they were lost?

The five of us kids would be completely alone in the wilderness with no nearby neighbors who we could ask for immediate help if there was an emergency. As it turned out, on one of the days when they went to get the mail it wasn't our parents who disappeared—it was our little brothers.

We checked everywhere, both sides of the cannery. There were lots of places to look for them... but it didn't matter. They were nowhere to be found. And some of the dogs were missing as well.

If it had been winter we might have thought the wolves had gotten them, but instead it was summer and bear season. The salmon were spawning in masses at the cannery's creek, and the bears—both black and brown—were busy gorging themselves. After looking for Robin and Chris everywhere, Jamie, Megan, and I had to wonder: what if the bears had gotten tired of a straight seafood diet and decided to spice it up with a surf-and-turf meal?

Robin told me later that two guys in a seine skiff were pulling on a net and holding it to the beach on the creek side of the cannery when he and Chris stepped out of unbroken forest with a few of the dogs.

The fishermen were astonished. They had approached the cannery in a way that had concealed our floathouse inlet, and believed they were in an uninhabited part of the Alaskan wilderness. And yet here were two ragged, barefoot children apparently living on their own in the woods with only the companionship of feral-looking dogs.

All that existed in this spot, as far as they knew, were the burned remnants of the old cannery. How could children have been transported to such a remote place?

The guys asked Robin and Chris how they came to be there and they responded, "We live here." The deckhands didn't buy that and got on their handheld radio to call the skipper of their purse seiner, the *Memento*, to ask what they should do.

The skipper, Captain Harvey Hanson, who must have been perplexed by the unusual problem in a routine day of fishing, said to bring the boys out to the boat with the net. They grabbed Robin and Chris and the dogs. The boys were far too interested in the new experience to protest. They willingly went out to watch the huge net, heavy with wriggling salmon, be hauled in.

The crew must have thought the boys had to be near starvation depending on how long they'd been alone in the wilderness. Once aboard the *Memento*, Robin and Chris were fed junk food in such quantity that it probably would have killed them had they really been starving: Coke, Doritos, Snickers bars, pig skins, etc. The boys, of course, were in heaven. And so were the dogs, who got treats too.

The captain and the crew probably discussed what they could do about the situation. Call the Coast Guard or the State Troopers and ask about a shipwreck where two young boys had been lost, possibly along with their family? It's possible Captain Hanson did exactly that, outside of the boys' hearing, but if he did then he would have come up empty for that location.

The crew figured the boys had to have been on their own far longer than anyone could have thought possible because of the condition of their feet. Children casually strolling around rugged, rocky Southeast Alaska barefooted? It seemed impossible. They tested how tough the urchins' feet were by poking, pinching, even rubbing jellyfish on them, and got zero reaction. The bottoms of their little feet were like leather from years of running on rocks and gravel.

Meanwhile, as the boys were living high off the hog, we three older kids were in dread of our parents' return, wondering what on earth we'd tell them, what sort of excuse we could give for the boys' disappearance. It was our job to look after them.

Once the net was hauled onto the *Memento* and the fish were dealt with, the deckhands who'd found them were told to take the boys back in the skiff and check around the corner of the rock bluff peninsula to make sure there weren't any others in the area. When they turned the blind corner, they saw the floathouse and knew the boys were telling the truth and they had a home to live in.

As they pulled out of the bight and headed back to the boat to inform their skipper, Mom and Dad arrived in the Whaler from Meyers Chuck.

Once Mom realized what was going on, that her two youngest kids had blithely gone aboard a boat and would happily have stayed there chowing down on junk food until they disappeared from our lives forever, she was appalled. For years to come she'd be haunted by the thought of how they could have disappeared and no one would have had a clue what had happened to them.

Robin reminisces, "When Mom got out of the skiff she was a little perturbed. 'What did I tell you about strangers?' she demanded. Me and Chris looked at each other and just mumbled. These were good strangers that fed us!"

To make up for Mom's distress, Captain Hanson threw a nice-sized king salmon into the Whaler and explained his and his crew's concerns about finding the boys apparently abandoned in the wilderness.

Mutual good feelings resulted and Mom allowed Robin to write to Captain Hanson, who wrote back several times. The next year the *Memento*'s crew picked up the boys, with parental permission this time, and fed them on junk food again. When they came home they were—to our envy—loaded down with candy bars, but what they treasured most was the lasting memories of the *Memento* and her crew.

• • •

The outdoor speakers on the floathouse provided us with a soundtrack for everything we did and accompanied innumerable unforgettable moments.

Mom told us about a day the rain fog hung low in the trees, turning the world black and white, the way some of us kids thought the world used to be back when black-and-white movies were made and historical photos were taken.

Stevie Nicks was on the stereo, this time her second solo album *The Wild Heart*. As Mom stood on the front deck soaking in the misty

RAISED IN RUINS

atmosphere, Nicks's haunting song "Beauty and the Beast" came on and a great blue heron swooped down and landed with delicate ungainliness on the shore. It picked its way into the mirror-still bay in awkwardly elegant slow motion, searching for sculpins and bullheads, its reflection pecking back at itself.

With the beautiful piano and sweeping chords of the song echoing in the mist, the moment etched itself onto Mom's heart, as if she'd become a part of a piece of living art.

On the other end of the spectrum, Dad liked upbeat, catchy music to come out of the outdoor speakers. After Dad had his sawmill set up on a deck he built above the tideline near the bigger garden, I watched him and a local fisherman chat and then haul freshly cut lumber to the fisherman's skiff, accompanied by Cyndi Lauper's song "Girls Just Want to Have Fun." Dad liked music with a jaunty beat to help him work, and Lauper's 1983 breakout album, *She's So Unusual*, fit the bill perfectly.

Dad was oblivious to the incongruity, though the fisherman had a grin on his face when he asked me about the choice in music. I couldn't help wondering how Lauper would react if she could see to what use her song about girl freedom was being put.

Every weekend, Casey Kasem counted down the American Top 40 hits. The Eighties songs boomed out from the speakers mounted on the exterior wall of the floathouse, and one time Megan and I gathered her Barbie Doll RV, red Barbie Camaro, and all of my model horses for an Oregon Trail–type migration. We arranged it on the trail Dad was building with sawdust from his sawmill. As Casey Kasem urged us to keep our feet on the ground and keep reaching for the stars, we set our caravan in motion.

The sunlight filtered down through the trees, glowing on the reddish orange sawdust with its fresh, carroty cedar scent as we had our Barbie and Ken dolls venture deep into the wilderness enjoying various adventures along the way, barely noticing when Prince won the top spot with "Raspberry Beret."

Actually, I had a bone to pick with Prince.

One day we were chasing each other over Dad's corral of floating logs, playing log tag. This was something Mom had forbidden us to do, telling us horror stories about kids falling between rolling logs

163

and drowning. As we tried to roll each other into the water, Casey Kasem counted down the hits, adding in little bits of trivia here and there. All at once, I heard something that stopped me in my tracks and nearly made me suffer the fate Mom had warned us about.

I jumped off the rolling logs and swam to shore and sat on a weathered drift log almost buried in tall beach grass above the outhaul. Overhead, puffy clouds trudged across a brilliant blue sky, intermittently crossing the sun and darkening the day, as if the sky had a giant dimmer switch someone was playing with. I sat there perfectly still, entranced as a man sang about dancing in the dark.

Thus began my obsession with Bruce Springsteen's music, and my deep disapproval of Prince who kept "Dancing in the Dark" out of the number one spot with "When Doves Cry."

One of the things I'd gotten, in one of Mom's epic Family Presents Day parties, was a Walkman. I loved it because it meant when Dad or Mom was playing whatever they wanted on the outside speakers, I could make up my own soundtrack on a cassette to listen to on headphones as I went on solitary rambles and hikes through the woods and ruins.

Bruce Springsteen was my constant companion on these wilderness explorations. I got every one of his albums up to *Born in the U.S.A.* and loved all of them, but my favorite was his *Darkness on the Edge of Town* LP that he recorded when I was seven years old. It was the one I listened to the most as I climbed the forested ridges and emerged out on the rocks to stare across the endless bay to where the sun set on the ocean at the distance-blued northern tip of Prince of Wales Island.

There was something about the album that fit with the always-present past. It made me think of all the stories that would never be told about all the men and women who had worked and lived at the cannery. Ordinary lives, full of ordinary emotions; people with everyday thoughts and experiences that were, nevertheless, unique and important to them.

I yearned to know those stories, to know those people who had roamed where I now roamed, and in a way it felt like Bruce Springsteen was singing those stories to me because he sang about humble, destined-to-be-forgotten working men and women.

• • •

Music was such a huge part of our childhood. Dad's favorite performers were Bertie Higgins, Neil Diamond, ABBA, and Blondie. Mom loved almost every kind of music there was and exposed us kids to all of it: Tchaikovsky and Beethoven, Gershwin, the classics, 1930s and 1940s music. We loved to sing "Stone Cold Dead in the Market," copying the Latin accent, or echo Cab Calloway as he belted out "Minnie the Moocher." We warbled along to "Old Rocking Chair's Got Me." Mom had a rocking chair and she'd laugh about it getting her one day.

We knew Sam Cooke's songs by heart because of her love for him. Dire Straits, Carole King, Rickie Lee Jones, and Van Morrison were there for when she was in an easy-listening mood. She was obsessed with Eric Clapton's "Layla," telling us it was one of the greatest rock songs of all time. Donovan, with his "Sunshine Superman," was there for her quirky moods. But her all-time favorite song was Ben E. King's "Stand by Me."

She bought all the modern hit albums, so we missed out on nothing of the Eighties as far as synthesizers, saxophones, and drum machine music were concerned. She also became infatuated with Herbie Hancock for a while.

Dad's tastes were mostly rock and pop hits from the 1950s onward, but he did like Tchaikovsky's *1812 Overture*. He had other unexpected likes too, and talked about buying the soundtrack to *My Fair Lady* when he was sixteen and how he played it repeatedly until he almost wore the record out.

• • •

Dad bought a Montgomery Wards VHS player and recorder for his house in Thorne Bay when he worked as a logger on Prince of Wales. He bought it to record movies off the TV, which he brought home to us on the weekends. We watched them once a week, on the Friday when he got home to run the generator to recharge the battery for the radios and stereo. Mom called it "Friday Night at the Movies."

Almost as much as the movies, we loved the HBO opening

where it zoomed in on some city's suburbs, which were alien to us. Everything came to Alaska late, no up-to-date movies, though there were some early CNN broadcasts (CNN's first broadcast was June 1, 1980, four months before we moved to the cannery), HBO concerts, Solid Gold Countdown, and Video Jukebox, a precursor to MTV.

A couple of young guys who worked as fish counters at a weir on the big salmon-spawning creek to the south of us, about midway to Meyers Chuck, made a habit of showing up for Friday Night at the Movies once they learned about it. After all, it was the only social event in the wilderness.

Dad set the living room up like a tiny stadium. In Montana he'd built a dining room table for his large family reminiscent of a picnic table, complete with benches. For movie night he set up the benches and table as bleachers. We all perched around the glowing box, for once ignoring the wolves when they howled outside, glued to the fictitious adventures taking place on the screen.

When Luke Skywalker stood on that sand dune, his Seventies long blond hair blowing in the hot wind, gazing at the dual suns setting, I was there. I was transported to that galaxy so far away, so long ago, completely forgetting the grease-stained brown paper bag Dad had filled full of buttery popcorn for us kids to dip into, or the hard bench I was perched on, or the faces around me lit by neon TV tubes.

The cannery ruins slumbered all around us in the darkness outside, the broad Alaskan bay lapping at the beach, but I was on Tatooine meeting Han Solo in the cantina and then on to the Death Star to rescue Princess Leia.

Whatever we watched, we immediately acted out. In the summertime when the days lasted forever, we'd have time to run outside right after the movie to play before bedtime. After watching *The Man from Snowy River*, we ran out and grabbed bull kelp to make bullwhips out of and then tried to round the dogs up like they were Australian brumbies.

After watching *The Dark Crystal*, we took up positions on the beach as the sun set and acted out the scene with the elders all deeply intoning, "Aaaaaaah." We tried to imitate the ululating cry of the Arabs in *Lion of the Desert*. A day didn't go by when a line from *The Wrath of Khan* or *McLintock!* or *My Fair Lady* or *The Ten Commandments* or

The Empire Strikes Back or *Coal Miner's Daughter* or *Mommie Dearest* or *Hawmps!* or *Seems Like Old Times* wasn't quoted.

One evening, after watching *Cannery Row* and laughing uproariously for the umpteenth time at the frog round-up scene, we stepped outside to find the beaches teeming with frogs. They were everywhere, a veritable plague of them, which was amazing considering how scarce they were ordinarily, let alone right after watching the round-up scene.

We always watched every movie to its last end credit and note of music. None of us wanted to leave our immersion in that other world's existence. Then Dad would head out into the Alaskan night. In the winter, the only lights outside were the stars and the yellow lampshine from our windows. The silence was always sudden and intense when he turned off the generator.

Everyone was allowed to have a Friday when they got to pick the movie. We all had to suffer through Mom picking *Sophie's Choice* (Stingo was from Jamie's favorite movie, *Dragonslayer*—later, we would meet Peter MacNicol on a school fieldtrip when he was with a touring company playing in *Tartuffe*). Mom's other choices were *Tess of the D'urbervilles*, *The Man Who Would Be King*, *Terms of Endearment*, *On Golden Pond*, *Chariots of Fire*, *The Far Pavilions*, *Camelot*, and other high-class fare that I was surprised Dad bothered to record. Although we did like some of her picks, like *Das Boot*. It was a gripping war movie for kids who were impacted by a veteran's trauma, just as impactful as *Big Red One* was. (With excellent acting by Mark Hamill: Luke Skywalker as a coward!)

It has to be said that we were in part delighted when *Das Boot* was chosen because Dad had recorded some *Looney Tunes* cartoons right after it and Mom and Dad always let us watch them, even if it meant letting the generator run a little longer than usual. Dad named one of the dogs after one of the cartoons, calling him "Hansel" and pronouncing it the way a double-taking Bugs Bunny does in *1,001 Rabbit Tales*.

These movies, concerts, cartoons and music videos were watched and rewatched, week in and week out, as the seasons changed. One of the Fridays when Dad didn't make it home, Jamie started the generator a little early and Mom allowed us to watch more TV than we would have been allowed to on Dad's more practical watch (he knew the limits to how much gasoline he could stock up).

Mom, who came of age in the tumultuous Sixties, was concerned that we knew nothing about race relations. She got her hands on documentaries and movies about desegregating schools in Little Rock, Arkansas. Having never been exposed to racism, we didn't understand what we were watching.

"What did the kids do wrong?" we asked Mom. You couldn't tell from the film why the kids were being yelled at and attacked. They were just trying to get to school. We were convinced the filmmakers had left out something important.

"They didn't do anything wrong," she said.

"Well, they had to have done something wrong to be treated like that!" we insisted.

"They're being treated like that because they're black."

We hooted at her, shouted her down, and pretty much let it be known that she obviously didn't know what she was talking about. Why would anyone care what their skin color was? We were used to Mom, off in her daydreams or books, not getting the real picture of what was going on around her, so it didn't surprise us that she'd come up with such a farfetched reason for what we were seeing.

On the other hand, we never were able to come up with an alternative, logical reason for why the kids were being attacked—and needed police escorts—for trying to go to school. It was a stranger world out there than even our vivid imaginations could conceive.

Later, Meyers Chuck got a huge satellite dish installed, ostensibly for the school's use, but the entire village was tuned in to the state-sponsored channel. It was memorably named RAT-Net, standing for Rural Alaska Television Network. I didn't know it was an acronym and, trying to make it make sense, thought it was some kind of tongue-in-cheek nickname for the rat race's entertainment offerings.

Someone mounted a repeater antenna on a tree high enough that we, way out in the wilderness, were able to sometimes, usually in the evenings, pick up a fuzzy black-and-white version. Mom would stay up all night watching whatever movies the programmers put on it. Earlier in the evening, we'd catch episodes of *Airwolf, Simon & Simon, Magnum P.I., Miami Vice* (many of the TV shows seemed to be about glamorized Vietnam vets), *Dynasty*, *The Facts of Life*, *The Cosby Show*, and many more.

When we stayed at our grandparents' home in Meyers Chuck, we saw the shows more clearly in all their color and vibrancy. *Miami Vice*, in particular, was riveting. The contrast between the bearded men in checked flannel and boiled wool and the sunny glamor of men in sunglasses and pastel Italian fashion in Miami's heat was striking and indelible. (The show made such an impression on Megan that as an adult she moved to Miami and lives there now.)

After the show, I'd step out of Grandma's house and hike over the rocks, my boots crunching on barnacles and making sticky seawater squirt out of the popweed. As the night deepened I'd walk out to the entrance marker on its concrete pad, listening to my *Miami Vice* soundtrack. I'd stand there looking out over the strait and soak in the wilderness scene as Jan Hammer played in my headphones.

We girls made occasional stabs at being modern, like the time Megan and I and one of the girls in Meyers Chuck bought red leather high-top sneakers similar to ones we saw someone on TV wearing. They were completely impractical: they dyed our socks and fell apart almost immediately from exposure to the saltwater all around us. But while we wore them we knew we were as cool as anyone else in the Eighties.

When it snowed, the uptilted giant saucer of the dish, its huge knob pointed toward outer space to receive signals at the speed of light, would fill with snow and we'd hear people in Meyers Chuck get on the CB radio and ask whose turn it was to head out into the night with a flashlight, get in their skiff, and cross the harbor to the school to sweep off the dish. It seemed like the school's long-time custodian, Terry Johnson, was the one to do it more often than anyone else.

What struck me was how modern these TV shows assumed the world to be. They took it for granted that people lived with basic modern conveniences. That outhouses, for instance, were a thing of the remote past, and that hot running water inevitably emerged from the tap.

I was fascinated by the divide between our reality and the TV's reality. There was a whole world out there in the 1980s while we watched them from what felt like the 1880s. Or, perhaps it's more accurate to say we were caught in a limbo between the two worlds, a place where time was different.

During a visit to town, on a school field trip, we saw *Star Trek IV: The Voyage Home* on the big screen. It felt like we'd come from the past to watch a movie set in the future, where the characters travel to their past that was our world's present (the Eighties)—it all seemed futuristic to us.

There was always a transition to be made between our world in the ruins and the world racing by outside.

• • •

In the long summer days, when the rest of my family watched life captured by film on movie night, I'd head outside. With them riveted to the screen, I had all of Union Bay, the cannery, the ruins, all of time, to myself.

While the generator rumbled in the background, I imagined the far greater mechanical sounds of the busy cannery. Back when the salmon ran in vaster numbers than they did in my present, the cannery workers would have worked long hours, late into the evening and early in the morning, laboring to turn what had been leaping in the bay hours before, into canned food.

All that activity was silent now, only hinted at in the twisted wreckage beneath scorched pilings, washed by sunset tides.

I was enamored of time. Its mystery, its fullness, its ability to be changeable and steadfast at exactly the same... time. I bonded with time in those long, lonesome walks I took by myself.

I wondered why it wasn't a subject covered in school. We learned quite a bit about space and its dimensions, and how things operated in space, but there was little about time. We were told there were three dimensions of space, but only one rather mundane, if useful, dimension of time.

That never made sense to me. Time was at least as rich and full and stacked with dimensions as space. I knew there were distinctly different kinds of time, such as the Moving Now of instant change, a sort of zero time that was constantly emerging and creating our experience of life.

I'm sitting on the rocks a few yards down from the red cabin,
watching the creek and thinking about Time.

The present time of childhood seemed to stretch forever. Those
days at the cannery—each day was a full year, and each season a
cosmos. Day by day, hour by hour, I experienced the sensual nature
of living in the present, where scents, sounds, colors, tastes, textures
were more vibrant, than any other dimension of time.

As for the future, I thought you had to be a little bit in the future to
truly appreciate and live in the present. Like athletes who were said to
be "in the zone"—I thought to myself that they were just that little bit
in the future which made everything around them slow down.

And of course there was the past all around me, making its
presence felt.

It was the zero time of the Moving Now that formed a bridge
between space and time that I was convinced allowed for all motion
and got rid of the scientific paradoxes I'd read about in our math and
science books. I didn't know how, I couldn't explain it, but I knew it.

One evening while my family was watching movies and I
was climbing the ridge toward the fire tree, listening to Bruce

Springsteen on my headphones, I suddenly stopped. Standing there, my heart beating fast, I heard something over the lyrics of "Racing in the Street." I pulled off my headphones.

Up on the mountain, I heard the wolves. They were in full hunting cry, coming down fast. On a dog-hunting raid. I ran down the ridge, finding the quickest way through a series of cliff-like drop-offs, jumping down from one to the next, judging the distance and making decisions blindly as I yelled for the dogs at the top of my voice, naming them one by one.

I had a visceral sense of the Moving Now, of the present being created moment by moment. Every decision I made had an outcome one way or the other. I was making decisions in time and when I acted on them, they became spatial—irreversible, with inevitable, concrete consequences following. If I didn't judge the drops and my landings perfectly, I would break my legs or my neck and no one would have known where to look for me. Except the wolves.

I and all the dogs ran to the floathouse. With the generator on and the movie blaring, no one else had heard the wolves, so they were all startled when I burst into the house, dragging and urging the dogs in after me.

Dad turned the TV off and we listened, but the wolves stayed away from the rumble of the generator. To be safe, we kept the dogs inside with us and watched the rest of the movie. It was *The Searchers*, in which actors, some of them dead or no longer the people they were on the screen, pretended to be people from another time.

Time, and our experience of it, I was convinced, had a lot more going on than science was willing to grant.

"During those summers in Alaska, Jamie was always more like a brother to me than a cousin." —Shawn

CHAPTER THIRTEEN

OUR COUSINS were more like siblings, however infrequently we got to see them.

Rand's son Shawn came up every summer to stay with Grandpa Frank and Grandma Pat in Meyers Chuck half of the time, and the rest of the time he spent with us. He came from the small Washington harbor town of Anacortes, where Jamie and I were born, and was our only regular contact with the urban present.

He brought with him city sensibilities and came from the world's Moving Now of ever-changing cultural trends. His life and interests revolved around girls, TV, and hard rock or heavy metal bands. He was picky about his hair and clothes—which we thought amusing—and finicky about what he ate, which made us think he was seriously wrong in the head. In our experience, if it was edible, you ate it and counted yourself royally favored. End of story.

Like many males of all ages in the mid-Eighties, he sought to emulate Don Johnson's *Miami Vice* cool in how he dressed, talked, and acted. Since he was blond and blue eyed and inherited his parents' good looks, he came closer to pulling it off than a lot of others. Bereft of the usual town distractions, he continually claimed to be bored, which was an alien concept to us kids, and we tended to give him a hard time about it.

But he soon adapted—or was corrupted, however you want to

look at it—to our way of entertaining ourselves in the wilderness. He even came up with a few refinements.

For instance, he considered a midnight snack a vital element of healthy living. The idea was a novel one to us since our food had to be carefully conserved and stretched over weeks and months. We couldn't imagine a world where you got up in the middle of the night and helped yourself freely to a snack.

Shawn was not to be deterred, however, and made do with what he could scrounge up. On one memorable occasion, all that he could find were some dill pickles, leftover boiled potatoes, and grape jam, which he combined for his snack.

Shawn discovered that Megan and I loved to make up stories and then act them out with our dolls and my model horses while we recorded them with my tape recorder.

He was fascinated by the stories of how Megan talked in her sleep. I was able to hold conversations with her which she never remembered in the morning. One time he suggested to me that we should stay up all night with the tape recorder handy and record whatever she muttered.

This was no particular hardship for me. Shawn and I had a habit of spending entire nights talking about everything under the sun, from music to TV to science to God. Much of the conversation circled back to his various love interests, unrequited crushes, and celebrity fantasies while I listened and offered sage advice founded largely on my Louis L'Amour and Barbara Cartland reading.

When I was twelve, after a major floathouse remodel that turned Mom and Dad's bedroom into the new kitchen, Mom and Dad moved into the back bedroom. They built a small room off the living room that became Jamie's bedroom. Megan and I were moved to a roll-out couch in the living room. There was another couch opposite it that Shawn slept on.

He and I whispered away as everyone else in the floathouse slept.

The wooden frame of the house creaked and settled on its raft as the endless Alaskan summer night never quite darkened the front room with its enormous, bullet-pocked bay window. Although his features weren't particularly visible, his blond hair shone even in that light as he sniffed (he seemed to be under the impression that sniffing added to his Eighties cool) and played with a rubber band.

He stiffened into alertness, breaking off mid-whisper, when Megan stirred. He stealthily pushed the record button. "This is Shawn Bifoss reporting from the Neilsons' floathouse in Union Bay, Alaska. We're here to observe the nighttime communications of the Neilsons' second youngest daughter, Megan, as she talks in her sleep. Let's listen in."

He held the tape recorder out next to her and its mechanical whirring broke through her sleep.

"Wha—at? What are you guys doing?" she mumbled. For the most part she and Shawn maintained a fractious relationship and most of the time they squabbled. But on this night, when we explained our plan and how disappointed we were that she'd woken up, she decided to join forces with him.

"Why don't we make up something?" I don't remember which one of us said it, but the other two approved.

Megan was not at all averse to exercising her impromptu acting skills. Especially since we hashed out how we'd convince ever-gullible Mom into believing it was real.

We didn't dare turn on a light to write anything down, but we tossed around some spooky suggestions and then let Megan wing it. Shawn pressed record and held it out as the three of us tried not to giggle.

Megan spoke in a far away, eerie voice. "It's coming… something terrible is coming. I can see the darkness of it coming through the forest… At the stroke of midnight it will come for you… Run, Tara. You have to run… before the clock strikes twelve… run…."

We hadn't planned it, but Mom had a Dutch wall clock weighted by heavy, solid brass spheres that chimed out the hour. As Megan was speaking and Shawn was recording, the clock whirred and chimed out a measured, portentous count.

We stared at each other in the darkness with our hands clapped over our mouths. It didn't get any better than that.

We could hardly wait until morning. Shawn made a great show of being astonished and agitated by what he'd recorded in the dead of night and insisted that Mom listen to it.

She listened with riveted attention and flinched when the clock chimed. She tried to pry out of Megan what terrible thing was going to happen and why Tara was supposed to run. Why Tara? Megan shook her head, wide-eyed, and said she had no idea. She didn't remember any of it, she claimed.

Mom was so spooked that for years afterward she'd tell the eerie story to other people and have them listen to the recording, and they were all amazed. Megan and I would snicker to ourselves, until one day we told her the truth. She was flabbergasted and chagrined, a state she would continue to have a recurring acquaintance with over the years.

While Shawn and I were close and could talk about anything for hours on end, Jamie and Shawn were inseparable. They were as close as Megan and I were. They would hole up in Jamie's castle fort perched on top of a giant red cedar stump that was accessible only by a trapdoor, with a ladder burrowed into the hollow part of the stump.

They'd sit up there hatching who knew what kind of terrible plans for world—or at least ruined cannery—domination. When Shawn was there, Jamie's boom box blared Pat Benatar. She often belted out "Hit Me with Your Best Shot" into the remote Alaskan woods. Megan and I battled back by blaring John Cougar (Mellencamp) bellowing, "Come on, baby, make it hurt so good," from the floathouse's outside speakers. Benatar was Shawn's one true love. He was obsessed with her and hated our habit of bequeathing nicknames on singers. To his disgust, we called her "Bennie."

Megan bore the brunt of Jamie's and Shawn's machinations. During one of my forest strolls I came across them, with Robin and Chris happily in tow, in the process of lynching her.

Jamie, naturally, had made it his business to teach himself the nearly lost art of noose-making. We would watch him in the bedroom at night by kerosene lamplight as he crafted noose after noose until he'd perfected the skill. We were uneasy, sure that he wouldn't be content until he'd tested a noose on one of us.

Megan had a quirk to her nature, and it was that she considered—perhaps justifiably—males as the absolute end. They were dirty, loud, and obnoxious with no refinements. I don't think she vocalized these convictions, but they knew. Her brothers and cousin took special delight in living up to her worst suspicions at every opportunity.

When I came across them, Jamie had a length of rope that terminated in a sterling example of one of his nooses thrown over the branch of a spruce tree. He was hoisting Megan by the waist a few inches at a time as the noose tightened.

Megan wasn't about to let the males think they had the upper hand with her as Jamie hand-over-handed the rope. Every time he pulled, the noose tightened around her waist, but pride sealed her lips against surrender.

"It doesn't hurt," she gasped disdainfully.

Jamie took this to mean he should try harder, and Shawn and the boys hooted at her, which made her all the more determined to give them no satisfaction.

"Still doesn't hurt," she managed to utter, her face turning red.

I arrived in time to spoil everyone's fun. "What do you think you're doing?"

"She asked for it," Jamie said.

"You could really hurt someone doing that," I said. "That rope is probably crushing her organs."

"She said it doesn't hurt," Robin piped up, smirking.

"Does it hurt, Megan?" Jamie taunted.

"I don't feel a thing," she retorted, trying not to grimace.

"See?" Shawn said. "She likes it."

"Just let her down," I said in my weary *Why don't you grow up?* tone of voice, the only one I'd found that Jamie responded to; and Shawn was civilized enough to be slightly uncomfortable. Megan maintained a stiff upper lip while she was lowered back onto her feet, waiting until Jamie and his snickering retinue disappeared into the woods before she doubled over and grabbed her side, groaning at the pain.

"Why didn't you tell them to stop?" I asked as I helped her hobble back home.

"I couldn't let them think they were better than me."

Since Mom was usually buried in a book, it often fell to me to be the mother figure and the ever-irksome voice of reason. Megan mostly backed me up, but occasionally she joined with the enemy to overthrow my boring rationality. Consorting with the enemy never went well for her.

Like the time she, Shawn and I were paddling around in Jamie's small aluminum skiff. Shawn suggested we tip the boat over. I didn't think it was such a good idea and said so. Megan, competitive to the core, couldn't resist the challenge, believing she could tip it over faster than Shawn. As I gripped the seat they ran from one side to the other.

The next thing we knew, the skiff rolled over and we were dropped, fully clothed, into the drink.

I swam to shore and seated myself on the floathouse's front deck to let my clothes dry on me in the sunshine. The sun was directly overhead, gleaming blindingly off the water and the floathouse's tin roof. It lit up the shaggy cedar, spruce, and hemlock that encircled the bay. Reflected waves rippled across their variegated green wall as bees hummed in the tall beach grass.

Many of those trees would have been there when the cannery was operational, and as I sat there wringing out my waist-length hair and my clothes, sticky with salt, I wondered what they had seen. Do trees have memories? Did they compare the activity of the long ago cannery laborers in their eternally fish-smelling clothes, with the shouts and laughter of the carefree children playing in the small inlet?

My teeth chattered lightly as my body transitioned from the shock of the Alaskan water to the summer sunshine. I sat on the edge of the front deck, my wet legs hanging over the front of the logs, the water dripping onto the gravel beach below. My arms rested on the weathered wood rail as the smell of sun-heated seaweed, beach grass, and evergreens spiced the air and I marveled at being alive in this place that seemed set aside from the world's version of time. Shawn, I thought, had an almost visible aura of differentness, from being formed by, and coming from, the world of the Moving Now.

I looked over and saw that he'd swum to shore as well, leaving Megan to deal with the overturned skiff.

"Get out here and help me tow it to shore," she yelled at Shawn. "You helped tip it over! You have to help."

Shawn laughed at her naiveté and sunned himself on the beach.

She struggled against the dead weight of the overturned skiff, slapping away the dive-bombing deer flies, ducking under the water to escape them. She made zero progress. Every time she came up she yelled at Shawn, getting madder and madder. It wasn't like she could let the rowing skiff float away. Jamie would not be happy about that. Though she almost never cried, she was on the point of frustrated tears so I jumped back in the water and helped her tow it to shore, and we slapped at the hungry deer flies the whole way.

Outside of books, music and movies, one of Mom's pastimes was photography and she loved to dress up any kids around and take pictures. The only way she could interest Jamie and Shawn in this was to make it Western dress-up. They decked themselves out in guns, wide-brimmed hats (Dad bought Australian-style ones and oiled them to keep the rain off), cowboy boots, and bandoliers full of cartridges. To their delight, Mom used eyeliner to pencil in mustaches on their youthful faces. They loved them so much that they wore them until they were eventually smudged off.

She dressed Megan and me as dance hall girls and posed us in front of the weathered boards of the wanigan. Megan struck a haughty pose while I tried to pull off a one-sided Princess Leia hairdo. Jamie and Shawn posed with the guns and pretended to cheat and fight at a poker game while Mom snapped pictures.

It was easy in our Western attire to feel that we had slipped back in time. Aside from Mom's modern camera, there was nothing to say we weren't living in the 1800s. As usual, the cannery gifted us with the ability to live in any time, and all times, at once.

Naturally, with everyone else having multiple puppies, Shawn had to choose his own and named one of the excess puppies, a sturdy black one, Little Ann. He had a logical fear of bears and hoped she'd grow up to be big enough to keep the bears at bay. Once, when we were all playing in the woods, Mom was interrupted in her reading by Shawn racing into the floathouse by himself.

He could barely speak. "Bear!" he finally got out. "Brown bear! A big one!"

Mom thought he was kidding, trying to get a rise out of her, until she saw how pale he was under his Down South tan. He'd tried to warn us but we'd been making so much noise that we didn't hear him.

She flung the door open and yelled, "Bear!" but we were still so busy making noise, hammering, sawing while we worked on a new fort, and shouting to each other, that we didn't hear. She grimly

Playing dress up, Old West style.
Left to right: Megan, Jamie, Shawn, and me (rocking a Princess Leia hairstyle).

grabbed the hated and feared gun and went to fetch us. To her horror she found the enormous bear prints not far from where we were playing.

We were herded back to the floathouse and made to complete the bear drill practically at gunpoint. But she couldn't keep us in the attic for too long, so we were cooped up in the floathouse's living room on a beautiful sunny day, peering out every window, waiting for the bear to make an appearance. We had that familiar "under siege" feeling, the same as when the wolves came down off the mountain.

We never did see Shawn's bear; it probably went back to the cannery side where the spawning salmon struggled upstream. Shawn was never free of the fear of bears, especially at night. But then, who of us didn't have nightmares about one of the largest land predators on earth?

Once, when Mom and Dad went to Meyers Chuck to get the mail, Megan and I had the idea of cleaning the house from top to bottom as a surprise for them. Megan locked the front door, telling me, "That way the boys won't get in and mess it up before Mom and Dad get back to see it."

"The boys aren't going to like that," I said. Mom had told us of the time she'd locked Jamie outside when he was seven, when we lived in Montana, to get him to respect her curfew. All it did was enrage him and he never forgave her or got over the psychological injury of being locked out of his own home.

"Too bad. They shouldn't be so messy," Megan retorted.

The first Jamie knew of it was when he and Shawn and the boys returned from whatever misadventures they'd been up to all day and tried to get inside. To his surprise, the knob resisted. The door was never locked—why would it be? He rattled it.

"Open the door."

Megan stood at the door and shook her head. "No way. You guys will come in here and make a big mess, and me and Tara spent all day cleaning it up for Mom."

"Open the door," Jamie ordered with an edge to his voice.

"Maybe you should let him in," I said uneasily.

"No. You can all stay out there until they get back home."

The knob rattled violently. Telling Jamie no, thwarting his will, was an excellent way to court death.

"Open. This. Door."

"After all our work? No way. I told you," Megan explained in the kind of voice designed to trigger a berserker rage, the kind Jamie was known to possess, "you'll mess everything up."

"You're just making him mad," I warned her.

"I don't care how mad he gets. They're not coming in."

Jamie snarled, "Open the door or I'll break it down!"

"You can't do that. You'll get in big trouble. Why don't you go somewhere and we'll let you in when—"

Ka-thunk!

Bare inches above her head, a sharpened welding rod stuck through the door. It was attached to Jamie's homemade spear. Megan stared from it to me wide-eyed. A few inches lower and it would have gone through her head.

"*Open the door!*" Jamie roared.

Megan jumped to obey, putting her hand on the knob.

"No, Megan, don't!" I exclaimed. "Are you crazy? Don't let him in now. He'll kill you!"

"I have to, he's really angry."

"Exactly! Don't open it."

She opened the door.

Jamie bowled into the house and grabbed her by the throat, lifting her off her feet. He was literally out of his mind with fury and choked her. Shawn and the boys followed him inside. Shawn laughed and seated himself on a stool, ready to be entertained, thinking it was more of the usual game of harassing Megan. But I could see Jamie had lost complete control of himself and Megan was in serious trouble.

"Oh, that's so clever, Jamie," I said. My first instinct was to grab his hands and pull them away from her throat, but I knew that would make him tighten his grip. I made my voice extremely dry and weary, using the tone that usually got through to him. "That's such a great example for the boys. Showing how you can't control your temper. Like you're a two-year-old, or something."

It worked. He let go of her and she fell to the side holding her throat, coughing and gasping.

Jamie turned and glared at me and I stared back.

"Why don't you try acting your age?" I said. He grabbed a book and threw it at me. I easily dodged it and picked it up. "Nice. A Bible study book. Real mature, Jamie. Real mature."

"Shut up, Tara!" He stormed off to his bedroom to nurse the aftermath of his bloodlust in private.

I'm sure he regretted his lost control. For one thing, as much as he liked toying with all of us, experimenting on us, and using us in his battle scenarios, he was actually very protective. The times when we went somewhere and some other kids thought they could pick on any of us, he'd step in and put a stop to it, intimidating anyone who tried to mess with us. And, despite having a big appetite as a boy who would grow to be over six feet tall as a teenager, he'd go without food to make sure the rest of us had enough when he felt it was necessary.

I always felt that his ever-ready rage was attached to his early frustrations with Dad, trying to get Dad to treat him as a father should. But Dad never really figured out how to be a father, especially with Jamie. Partly because he was oldest, and partly because Jamie was born thinking he was rightfully the center of the world, which didn't sit well with Dad who was under the impression he occupied that position.

Shawn, not surprisingly, had his own father issues. He was devastated by the loss of his father, and not seeing him when he came up to visit as he always had before was hard on him. He tried to keep anyone from seeing it, but occasionally he let his guard down and I tried to find words to comfort him, but I never managed to assimilate Rand's loss myself, so I didn't know how he possibly could.

Shawn held a special place in Mom's heart and she loved telling him stories about hers and Rand's childhood adventures. Every year she told him the same stories, but neither of them cared. They both loved the retellings. Our grandparents, to try to cheer him up when his parents had divorced, had named their commercial fishing boat the *Shawno*. (Grandma's CB handle was Shawno Base.)

Every summer, as the longest day approached, we got excited knowing Shawn, with his intriguing differentness, as an ambassador from the outside world, would be coming to stay.

• • •

The other two cousins we saw regularly were LeAnn and JoDean (GiGi), Rory and Marion's little girls. When we first moved to the cannery, JoDean was too young to stay with us—the one time we tried it, she didn't last the full night and Dad had to take her back home in the skiff.

LeAnn visited more frequently and stayed for weeks at a time. She was like a little sister to us, being two years younger than Chris. She fit right in and could give Mom a run for her money when it came to sheer gullibility.

LeAnn was adorable, like a life-sized doll, with glossy dark hair and green-flecked brown eyes (that Mom called "breen"), and freckles sprinkled across her nose. Megan and I soon had her obsessed with Barbie dolls, and when she went home she spread the contagion to her sister, who was equally adorable with her straight blonde bob.

LeAnn and Mom had a meeting of the minds, or rather of the imaginations—both of them loved to play pretend and dress-up.

Chris and LeAnn dressed up as pioneers.

Mom dressed LeAnn up as a pioneer woman, complete with bonnet, and dressed Chris as a mountain man trapper and took pictures. Then she dressed Robin up as a prince with an artfully created tinfoil crown and LeAnn as a princess and again took pictures, outside in the snow-reflected light against a snow-covered drift log. They looked like something out of a children's storybook.

Another time Mom had us all dress up as Snow White and the Seven Dwarves—or the few dwarves we could produce. Mom asked LeAnn if she wanted to be Snow White but LeAnn insisted that she wanted to be the witch—it was a much juicier role for a little girl whose favorite pastime with Robin and Chris was to play a *Dynasty*-like soap opera game they called "Kill and Marry."

However, when Mom whitened LeAnn's face, made black circles around her eyes and placed a big wart on her chin, LeAnn looked in the mirror and was so terrorized by her own appearance that she burst into tears. She couldn't be consoled until the witch was gone and her face was scrubbed clean of all trace of her. But only after Mom took her photos.

LeAnn brought the "pretend" out of us as we played in and

around the *Zippy*, a boat Lance owned that was tied to a tree beyond the wanigan. He'd painted bright, garish images from the comic strip *Zippy* on it. We loved to pretend we were steering it far away, to wind up castaways on a *Gilligan's Island*-type shore.

One day, Megan and I were playing with our little cousin on the Big Log, an enormous former tree that would one day provide most of the lumber for our six-bedroom home. As we sat there we heard eerie thumps far up the mountain, rhythmic and certain. "What's that?" LeAnn asked, wide eyed.

It sounded to Megan and I exactly like the natives in *Blue Lagoon* that the two characters in that teen movie called the boogeyman. Staring at each other, we said simultaneously, in hushed voices, "It's the boogeyman."

LeAnn was horrified and worried about what he would do. Megan and I, infected by her absolute belief in what we'd said, were just as worried. We would hear the drums in the distance at odd times and the hair would stand up on our necks. Today, looking back, I suspect what we heard was the rhythmic hooting of grouse distorted by the distance and the forest.

• • •

Before Rory and Marion lived in Meyers Chuck, close enough for us to have LeAnn visit us more regularly, they lived farther south on Prince of Wales Island in a tiny community called Saltery Cove, where Marion's parents and a couple of her five brothers lived. They once had Megan and me stay for Thanksgiving with them in the cabin the two of them had built.

They took us skating up on the lake, and Rory entertained us with a lively puppet show with Miss Piggy figuring prominently (he had her voice down perfectly). He had us rolling with laughter, partly out of surprise because he was always the quiet one in any gathering of adults. Though he did once climb the floathouse roof and drop some fireworks down the chimney while Mom was lighting a fire. When they blew up, *she* blew up, yelling at us kids until Rory sheepishly fessed up. She laughed at the sheer incongruity.

The night before Thanksgiving, which we would be attending

at a neighbor's house, Marion decided to do something special with our hair. "Why don't we put a nice ripple in it?" she suggested for me after she put big rollers in Megan's hair.

She wet my waist-length hair and started making about a hundred braids by kerosene light. It took so long that Megan and the girls went to bed and Marion's fingers began to give out. She had obviously underestimated how thick my hair was. She had to keep resting them and wondered aloud if she'd bitten off more than she could chew. But she was determined not to give up and finally finished the last braid.

The next day, before we set off for the neighbors with Marion's food contributions, she let my hair loose.

When she stepped back to consider her handiwork, I had a two-foot afro sticking out on either side of my face, much to her chagrin and amusement. I think everyone had a hard time keeping a straight face when they saw my hairdo. I tried to think of ways I could tame it down, but I thought any efforts I made would backfire and embarrass me more. So I sat on the couch, hyperaware of the strange, extra personal space my distended hair entitled me to while Marion took pictures before we headed out.

It wasn't any relief to me that Megan was also embarrassed by the way the fat curls Marion had given her were lopsided—fat on one side, limp on the other.

In our best clothes we trooped through the mud and seaweed and then a winding, narrow footpath to reach the neighbor's house up on a hill. Inside, it was warm and surprisingly plush, with floral upholstery and thick carpet, which was unusual in the bush. The woman of the house was delighted to have young girls around and pounced on Megan and me, assuming that we would share her passion for all things "Princess Di."

We'd never heard of such a person. This shocked and thrilled her. She wasted no time in piling glossy coffee table books and magazines into our laps, inundating us with images of the "Wedding of the Century." While Megan was deeply absorbed in the pomp and fashions, I kept sneaking interested glances at the buffet being spread out on the table. I was determined to get closer acquainted with the peas and pearl onions in cheese sauce.

The woman regaled us with how long the veil and train were, and a bunch of other details that didn't stick with me. Megan soaked it all up and would later adopt Princess Di's haircut, but there was only one thing that stuck out to me. That is, besides the complete incongruity of a seemingly pragmatic adult (unlike our completely impractical mom, who didn't surprise us with her interest in dead British Royalty, including her infatuation with Charles II) in a remote and rugged part of Alaska surrounded by sea, mountains and evergreens obsessing over modern British royalty.

The one thing that stuck with me was the information that Princess Di read and was related in some fashion to Barbara Cartland. Which—through the magic of the written word that could allow people existing in opposite stations of life experience the same emotions and story—made us related to Princess Diana.

• • •

Rory and Marion worked together as commercial fishermen on the *Velvet*, formerly her father Leroy's boat. They retained the black color he'd painted it, which set off the bunches of brilliantly colored buoys and gave it a piratical air. When LeAnn and JoDean were born, Rory and Marion kept the girls with them on the boat when the fishing wasn't too heavy. When they were under a tight timeline, they'd have the girls stay with us.

Despite the fun we always had when LeAnn stayed with us, for some reason she always seemed to attract injuries.

Like the rest of us, she loved swinging on the swing set Dad had built for us. He'd constructed it by topping three trees that formed an L. He then de-limbed the tops and laid them horizontally across the still-rooted trunks, fastened them in place, and hung homemade swings from steel eyes he'd screwed into the cross logs. No matter how hard we swung, high enough to put slack in the lines, gravity free for a thrilling moment before we were snapped back down— what we called "going to warp"—the huge, sturdy swing set never shook or budged. None of us ever got an injury playing on it, but LeAnn knocked out a baby tooth.

Another time, she got bitten by one of the dogs.

But once it was her sister who got hurt when she and JoDean stayed with us, when our neighbors—Sheila and her kids—still lived at the small cabin on the other side of the cannery. Sheila's boys had a BB gun and despite Mom's law that Robin and Chris not play with it, somehow it ended up in the backroom.

JoDean was a toddler and Mom had just laid her down for her nap when she heard an odd cry. A moment later LeAnn, only about four years old at the time, sauntered out and happily bragged: "I just shot my sister in the eye."

Mom couldn't believe her ears. It was obvious LeAnn had no idea that she'd done anything bad, so Mom rushed to the backroom to see what had happened. As it turned out, LeAnn had told the truth. She'd shot JoDean in the eye with the neighbors' BB gun.

To Mom's absolute horror, JoDean's eye was swollen and streaming blood and tears. Mom wasn't reassured when the boys told her that it had been loaded with popcorn kernels instead of BBs.

Mom couldn't see what the damage was, but she'd heard somewhere that it was important to protect a damaged eye from light so she taped a fresh diaper around JoDean's head. All her worst fears about being responsible for children in the wilderness had come true. And the worst part was it wasn't even her own child who'd been injured.

She was terrified that JoDean would lose her eye if she didn't get her to professional medical help as soon as possible. She got on the marine radio and an hour later a floatplane arrived. JoDean was so young that of course Mom had to go with her. She asked our neighbor Sheila to keep an eye on us, while we were left to wonder what the outcome would be.

The Coast Guard flew out to where the *Velvet* was fishing and airlifted Marion to the hospital in Ketchikan. When Mom saw her she was overcome and said, "I am so sorry. I am so sorry." Marion didn't say a word, just enveloped Mom in a hug.

Fortunately, JoDean's eye was okay and her vision unaffected. She did, though, grow up to have one blue eye and one green eye.

During one summer, instead of the girls staying with us, Rory and Marion took Megan and me with them on the *Velvet* for a trip to Ketchikan.

It was early in the morning when Dad skiffed us to Meyers Chuck. The *Velvet* was still tied up at the dock and Marion suggested we climb into the bunks in the foc's'le and sleep for the first part of the trip as LeAnn and JoDean were doing.

Megan was excited about the trip, but she had one major concern. She was prone to every kind of motion sickness there was, especially seasickness. We'd only been lying in the bunks as they vibrated to the rhythm of the engine for a little while, with the boat dipping heavily from one side to the other, when Megan groaned pathetically and said, "Tara, I don't think I'm going to make it if it's going to be like this the whole way. Check and see how far we've gone."

I got up and checked out the porthole window and my eyebrows shot up. I turned back to Megan.

"What?" She clutched her stomach, her face glowing palely in the shadowy fo'c'sle that smelled of diesel, coffee, and a hint of raw fish.

"Um," I said, trying to think of a way to break it to her gently, "we haven't left the dock yet."

The swaying of the boat was caused by Rory and Marion walking from one side to the other as they prepared the boat and untied it as the engine idled, warming up.

Megan was chagrined but decided that rather than climbing out and having Dad take her back home, she'd gut it out.

Fortunately, once we were underway the boat's motion eased, especially after the trolling poles were let down, and Megan was okay for the rest of the long trip. Rory and Marion trolled their way to town so as not to waste a day of fishing.

I remember sitting outside on the hatch, watching Alaska go by in its shades of blue. I was reading Louis L'Amour's *Sitka* and I loved that the characters in that book sailed right down the waters Rory and Marion fished.

We anchored up that night in a quiet, sunny spot—since it was summer the sun didn't set till way past bedtime—and Megan and I slept on the floor in sleeping bags up in the pilothouse that was lit by undulating water reflections.

The radio had been playing all day and Megan and I were falling asleep to Gary US Bonds when Marion appeared at the steps that led down to the fo'c'sle. "Sorry," she whispered. "I know you like listening to the music but I have to turn it off. I wish I could go to sleep to it, but I always end up listening to it and thinking about things and then can't get to sleep."

Marion was only eleven years older than Jamie, so in many ways she seemed to us more like an older sister than an aunt. She could transition between talking with us on our level to talking with Mom and Grandma about history, science, and religion, and then talking with the men and old-timers about their fishing, hunting, and trapping interests from the strength of her Alaskan experiences of building her own log cabin and fishing with her husband in often dangerous waters. We girls admired her, loved her, and wanted to be like her. And, when we married, we wanted to have a marriage like hers.

Rory and Marion were living the real romance, and everyone knew it. Marion was the only girl in a family with five boys so it's probably no surprise she turned out to be a bit of tomboy. But she was also a natural beauty, with long, rippling dark hair, dark eyes, and patrician features. All of the Alaskan guys were immediately smitten, but she chose Rory.

Rory, a self-sufficient six-footer, had his own admirers. Mom told us how, when her family lived Down South, teenage girls would try to make friends with her because she was Rory's sister in hopes that she would introduce them to him.

Rory and Marion were married in Meyers Chuck after Marion's mother, Joann, picked up a wedding dress in Ketchikan. Joann had arrived at the floatplane base with the wedding dress over one arm and a new firewood ax in her other hand.

The thing that always stuck out to anyone who met them was how perfect Rory and Marion were for each other. No one ever saw them argue, they were casually (as if it was common) at ease with each other, and while they didn't have exactly the same tastes in everything, they were able to share many of each other's enthusiasms. They had a harmony about them, something that always set them apart from other couples, that made everyone like and respect them and secretly—or not so secretly—wish they could have something similar.

When the *Velvet* arrived in Ketchikan, we weren't overwhelmed by the influx of people and speeding traffic as you might expect children from the wilderness to be. I think it was because Rory and Marion were so stable and of the time—they always lived in the current stream of culture in a low-key, mostly conventional way (adapted to a wilderness lifestyle). Since we were with them, we felt like we belonged.

After docking in Thomas Basin we strode past the rows of fishing boats and up past the fisherman's bar, the Potlatch, that stood on a street made of warped wooden planks. Everyone knew Rory and Marion and greeted them with delight.

"Our first stop is the Pink Store," Marion told us as we walked on the unfamiliar flatness and hardness of the sidewalk. "That's what the girls call the candy store," she explained.

It was a little building up the street painted a Pepto-Bismol pink. Inside, Megan and I were stunned by the lavish display of every kind of candy and treat there was. In fact, we were too stunned by the abundance to do more than stare. Meanwhile, LeAnn and JoDean immediately found their favorite treats.

Marion paid for them and for a few treats for Megan and me, and then we all headed for a long store set on an enormous pier that was attached to the street. Rory and Marion called it Tongass, an Alaska Native name that belonged to the narrows Ketchikan was built alongside, the highway that ran the full length of the city, and the millions of acres of rainforest that covered most of Southeast Alaska.

"Keep an eye on the girls while we buy fishing gear," Marion told Megan and me. The moment she was out of sight, the girls—hopped up on sugar—lost their usual good manners. While the downstairs area was devoted to fishing gear and hardware, the upstairs area was full of furniture. The girls chased each other around lamps, over chairs, and bounced on beds with Megan and me blushing and racing after them.

We lost them at one point until a store employee marched them up to us. "Are you responsible for these children?"

Megan and I were mortified.

But worse was to come. Rory and Marion had to unload and sell their fish to the cannery, so they dropped us off at the small library with totem poles in the parking lot and a salmon spawning creek running past it.

TARA NEILSON

Marion took us past the museum and down the stairs to the children's department, and made sure we were set up with some books. Megan and I would have been happy to immerse ourselves in the bookish atmosphere. I found an entire row of Nancy Drew books I hadn't read and wanted to delve into every one.

But the moment Marion left, LeAnn and JoDean turned into candy-fueled terrors again. The librarian kept giving us reproving looks and shushing us as the girls tore around, threw books, and jumped off the chairs onto bean bags.

By the time Rory and Marion picked us up, Megan and I were completely frazzled. But we perked up when they took us to Ben Franklin's store that smelled of popcorn and new rubber dolls and carried everything anyone could possibly want. While Marion chose bolts of cloth in the back, Megan and I cruised the Barbie Doll aisle. After that they took us to the Pizza Mill, a small diner-like restaurant that overlooked another boat harbor called City Float.

The strong afternoon light flooded through the front plate glass windows and lit up the modest room with its booths and bench seats smelling of pepperoni, cheese, Italian seasoning, and tomato sauce. Megan and I felt like normal, modern people for those few days in town with Rory and Marion.

I was glad to head back to the ruins of the cannery, but I think it was then that the yearning for a different life was planted in Megan's heart.

"When we lived in the old cabin across the bridge, I remember finding all the old treasures from the cannery... and Dad catching trout for breakfast out of the creek." —Chris

CHAPTER FOURTEEN

EVERYTHING CHANGED in 1983, the year I turned twelve, when Dad lost his logging job on Prince of Wales Island as a result of a strike. For the first time, he lived at the cannery with us fulltime. The problem was he had no way to make a living. The plan he and Mom came up with was for Dad to get a one-man mobile sawmill. He could cut and sell lumber, and also cut enough to build Mom's dream house.

To raise enough money to buy a sawmill they decided to sell the floathouse. They figured they'd fix it up as much as they could while all seven of us moved to the cannery side into the tiny red cabin, perched right on the edge of the creek, that our neighbors had stayed in. It was one open room, about 320 square feet, and had a small, kiosk-like front porch lined with shelves that Mom converted into a pantry. The front door was white, to match the trim, and had a glass window in it.

Dad set about getting the cabin in shape to take all of us. He'd already laid green roofing on top of the aged shingle roof, but now he punched out the front wall and put down a new section of floor that jutted over the creek where the salmon swam. After a heavy rainfall the creek level would rise until it came within inches of the floorboards. There was no glass around for windows, so he put opaque plastic (Visquine) up. It let fuzzy light in, but didn't let us see anything but blurry images outside.

There was one loft at the back of the house above the kitchen that all of us kids, except Jamie, would be stuffed into like canned sardines. We kept our belongings in cardboard boxes on shelves at the back of the loft and along the sides. Jamie would sleep on the couch in the middle of the cabin. On the other side of the couch, in the new section, was the large dining room table with the benches on either side for us kids.

Dad laid down new boards on the open rafters, above the part he'd added on at the front, for him and Mom to sleep in. The front of the house bumped up against an alder tree that had grown up since the cannery burned. When Mom lay in bed with the window open she could look through tree branches and easily imagine herself in a treehouse. (In fact, there was an actual treehouse next to the cabin that Dave and Sheila's kids had built.)

There was no indoor plumbing. Just an outhouse up on the hill several yards down from the cabin, and a sink without a faucet in the cabin that drained into a five-gallon bucket that had to be emptied. The counter was unpainted, raw wood.

Mom jazzed up the place as much as she could, despite having room for only the couch, a rocking chair, and the table with its benches. She added bookcases and shelves wherever she could squeeze them in. She hung curtains along the front of the rough counter to conceal the drain bucket and dishes and cardboard boxes that acted as drawers. Behind the round barrel stove next to the door, she put up a coat rack. But her most inspired idea was painting the entire floor of the cabin cannery red, like the exterior. When the sun filtered through the Visquine windows, the whole house filled with a rosy glow.

Dad's contribution to the décor was to add two large stereo speakers mounted to the slanting ceiling. As with every sound system he ever installed, he tested the speakers with Tchaikovsky's 1812 Overture. He cranked the volume up so loud that when the cannons boomed and the bells rang, the fragile walls of the old cabin shook and the Visquine windows wheezed.

Typically he was satisfied only when there was no distortion, but his time, no matter what he did, no matter how many times

All seven of us standing in front of the only intact cannery building,
the little red cabin, across the creek from the ruins.
Left to right: Jamie, Chris, Dad, Robin, me, Mom, and Megan.

the cannons boomed, he couldn't get the sound right. I couldn't
help wondering what the bears and the fish thought of the cannons
and bells.

The creek was anywhere from one hundred to two hundred feet
wide at the mouth, where it met the bay, depending on rains and
snowmelt. Up at the cabin it was boxed in by rock walls and was only
about thirty feet wide. It rumbled noisily through the cabin's thin
walls and plastic windows all day and night.

Black and brown bears hunting salmon passed within a few feet
of the front of the house. I remember watching a giant brown bear
plod purposefully past us as we sat at the table. Because there were
no details through the fuzzy plastic, it looked like a big brown hill had
detached itself from the forest to travel upstream. If it had wanted,
one sideswipe of its long claws would have granted it entrance to our
home.

There was no shelter on this side of the cannery from the gales,
so Dad kept the skiff on the floathouse side. Getting across the

creek to the trail that led to the other side of the cannery, jumping from slick, smooth rock to rock, was a hassle on a daily basis and impossible when there was a deluge that raised the creek level. So he built a thirty-foot-long, fifteen-foot-high bridge out of poles, planks, and cable that spanned the entire width of the creek, from a hill on the other side to rocks in front of the cabin, with steps down from it.

Our dogs and cats soon learned to cross over the creek on the bridge and got into stare-downs on it as they approached from opposite sides. The bears, on the other hand, were indifferent to the sudden advent of the bridge.

On the floathouse side where we rarely saw bears—mainly just saw evidence that they had been around—we'd been scared of them. On the cannery side, where we lived right on the creek with the salmon fins flashing in the sunlight from one side to the other for the entire length of the creek, bears roamed constantly.

They were focused on the salmon to the exclusion of everything else. Their attention was centered on eating their daily intake— which was prodigious. We found out how focused they were when the dogs ran at the bears. At first we were appalled, thinking it would be the wolves all over again. But the bears were oblivious to the snarling, snapping, barking dogs. Moby and Lady bit the huge, lumbering beasts all day long and the bears showed no reaction.

At least, they didn't react until late in the day, after they were gorged on salmon and became aware of their surroundings again. Without fail, and it was funny to see it, the bears would be startled by the dogs and crash into the creek, splashing madly to get away. Moby and Lady would tear after them, biting at their hind legs. It was absurd to see such frightening and deadly creatures running from a golden Cocker Spaniel and a Sheltie.

One morning when I let Lady outside I saw Megan heading for the outhouse. She had her head down and was watching where she stepped on the rocky bank of the creek. I was startled to see a burly black bear headed straight for her. He had his head down, sniffing the rocks as he trudged over them. In a few more moments they'd walk into each other.

"Megan!" I called. "Look out! Bear!"

She and the bear looked up, straight at each other.

It would be hard to say who was more horrified. They tore off in opposite directions in complete disarray and full-on panic.

Not all of our bear encounters were quite so comical, however. Once, while we were on the other side, getting the floathouse in shape to sell, Mom asked me to return to the cabin to pick up part of our lunch she'd forgotten to pack.

She would never have dreamed of doing that before, but being around the hyper-focused bears all the time had made us less concerned about them. I crossed the lonesome trail with its expansive moss clearings and finally reached the top of the bridge.

I loved it; the bridge was pure adventure, like something out of *Swiss Family Robinson*. It had rope railings and you could see the creek between the boards as you stepped. The lofty, panoramic view of the bay and the mountain ranges on Prince of Wales Island on the horizon couldn't be beat. I felt like I was living in a wilderness adventure movie every time I crossed the bridge.

Once in the cabin I grabbed the tinfoil-covered bowl of potato salad Mom had left on the counter and then headed back across the bridge. I was about a quarter of the way across the planks when something in the creek below caught my attention.

A massive brown bear stood there, the sunlight glinting off the fur that bristled on his hump.

Unlike all the other bears, he wasn't fishing. He was watching me.

The golden creek eddied around the pillars of his legs, creating whitewater rapids. The salmon swam all around him, their fins breaking the surface of the water. He ignored them, his black eyes fixed on me.

I froze. My heart thumped heavily in my ears, louder than the rumble of the creek. I didn't try to move, afraid to trigger any of his aggressive, predator instincts.

He wasn't fooled by my sudden lack of motion. With a smooth heave, he raised his enormous weight up onto his hind legs. The bridge remained above him, but I was stunned at how much his standing up narrowed the distance.

I stared at him and wondered what I could do if he decided to charge. Brown bears could knock over rooted trees. I didn't think the bridge could withstand a determined brown bear attack. I prayed he wouldn't charge, that he'd lose interest.

How long it would be before Mom wondered where I was with the food? Probably not long, because the boys would be bugging her for lunch. Maybe she'd send Dad after me and he'd have the gun. But would he get here in time to find that instead of getting lunch—I'd become lunch?

The only thing I had for protection was potato salad. Would throwing it at the big bruin distract him long enough for me to reach the cover of the woods? Out of his sight, I could run all the way to the other side. On the other hand, would he see the flying potato salad as an insult?

To my leg-weakening relief he dropped back down with a splash and slapped at a salmon, hooking it in his lengthy black claws. He munched on it, stripping the skin off its struggling, wriggling body.

I waited until my legs steadied and then eased over the boards, making for the other side. I'd only taken a couple steps when he stopped eating. He lifted his enormous head and pinned me with his weirdly prehistoric stare. I had the sense that I was being studied by something from the dinosaur age, from a predator line that had survived from long before man reached these salmon-rich shores.

When I remained still, he turned back to shredding the salmon.

I made it a few more steps. We kept up the back and forth, the halt and stare, eat and step, until I made it to the shade of the forest. I forced myself to continue to move slowly even after I was pretty sure I was out of his sight. Only when I'd passed the two-story steel fuel cylinder—one of the few things that had survived the cannery fire—and the rotten, collapsed structure that had been attached to it, did I run.

• • •

When Shawn stayed with us at the cabin, he was horrified by the bears right there on our doorstep. Riveted, he listened to my story of the face-off with the brown bear and then that night, as he was squeezed into the already full loft with the rest of us, he poked me and whispered, "Do you have anything I can use for a weapon in case the bears try to get in?"

I sleepily tried to think of something. "All I have is this Zane Grey hardback," I said.

He took it gratefully. *West of the Pecos* was better than nothing.

Another cousin named Darrell, whom we hadn't met before, came up to stay with us at the cabin. (Grandpa Frank had two daughters from a previous marriage, Shirley and Eileen. Darrell was Shirley's youngest child.) Darrell had inherited Grandpa's height and was well over six feet tall. He had sandy-colored hair and blue eyes and his father's slow, Southern accent. He was eighteen, which meant that we saw him neither as one of us kids nor as one of the adults. He was, to Jamie's speculative eyes, a fresh subject for torture.

To get away from us in the cabin, Darrell would sequester himself in the treehouse next to the cabin. It was accessible only through a rope and pulley system that went through a trapdoor. It was easy to keep us at bay... he thought.

After some calculation, Jamie decided that since Darrell had found a way to escape physical torment, he would be subjected to psychological torture instead. This turned out to be the repeated playing of the song "Snoopy vs. the Red Baron." As soon as Mom and Dad left to get mail in Meyers Chuck, leaving Darrell at our mercy—I mean, leaving him to watch us—the cassette with the song went in the stereo and the sound was cranked up and the door of the cabin left open.

It wasn't long before Darrell snapped. He yelled down from inside the treehouse for us to play something, anything, different. Naturally, this only made it inevitable that "Snoopy vs. the Red Baron" would fight their aerial dogfight again at a louder volume. Again and again. And... again.

Driven down from the treehouse, Darrell would slip and lurch over the rocks in his slick-bottomed cowboy boots to escape us. Whenever he returned, "Snoopy" would go back in the stereo.

At night, Mom and Dad inadvertently contributed to Darrell's unsettled state of mind by regaling him with bear stories. He slept on the couch (Jamie had to squish in with us in the loft), the most vulnerable place in the tiny cabin. His only comfort was that the .30-.30 rifle hung on nails pounded into the outer rafter of Mom and Dad's loft right above where he slept.

After the kerosene lamps were blown out—not counting the lantern, turned down low, up in our loft that had to be left on for Megan—everyone settled in for the night. One evening a wild, snarling, crashing commotion broke out.

Darrell leapt off the couch and snatched the .30-.30 off its nails and worked the lever action, pulling the trigger repeatedly.

Instead of a brown bear tearing through the half-rotten walls or thin Visquine, it turned out to be a dust-up between the dogs and the cats. Fortunately, no one got shot. Mainly because Mom didn't allow the .30-.30 to be loaded within reach of the boys. The rifle's ammunition was kept separate from it to prevent any accidents.

• • •

The summer we lived in the cabin was when we first truly interacted with the ruins on a daily basis, when they became an integral part of our lives.

Mom went with us kids on treasure hunts, digging up the past. In new-growth forest that had sprouted up thickly on the edge of the beach on the other side of the creek from the cabin, where the fire had torched the buildings, we discovered the remains of a cook shack.

Half buried in the dimly lit brush we stumbled upon a large rusty machine that was eight feet long with three racks. Dad told us it was the oven and that it would have been able to cook dozens of pies at once or several hundred cookies. We could only dream of such an amazing device.

We dug out stacks of steel plates, pots, pans—some of them in almost mint condition. There were scads of cutlery, some of it rusted together, but others perfectly okay and perfect for playing with. There were long, flat steel spatulas and mixing spoons, roasting forks, and also knives, which Mom wouldn't allow us to play with, but we kept some anyway.

From the debris we carefully pried out bits and pieces of pottery. Every now and then we found saucers and handleless cups that looked Asian. Mom kept the most whole and complete ones to display on a shelf. I looked at them all the time, trying to imagine who the last person was to handle them.

Megan (left) and I play with our dolls on the scorched wreckage
between the pilings that formerly held up the cannery wharf.

Down on the beach, where the cannery machines had fallen and
corroded, we played on and around them amidst giant piles of rusted
together lids and flattened, lidless cans. There was a satisfying
fascination in pulling them apart and crumbling them into red dust.

Megan and I played with our dolls on the twisted framework
of the machinery that had once rolled tin, to be cut into cans. Some
nameless worker had stood there for hours pushing long sheets onto
the rollers that our dolls sat on. Megan and I shepherded the dolls on
their adventures as we munched on Saltine crackers in the shadow
of the tall wharf pilings.

• • •

A couple hundred yards below the cabin, the rocks gave way to a
sandy beach that seemed to stretch forever on a minus tide. This
was uncommon in Southeast Alaska, which was nothing less than
an enormous drowned mountain range, its intricate maze of islands
the tops of mountains. The Inside Passage with the waterways

branching off from it contained a series of deep river valleys that the ocean had breached millions of years ago.

Most of the land of this vast archipelago was sheer rock bluffs. The mountains rose up from the water without a gradual buildup as in other parts of the world. The benefits of this was that in a skiff or boat it was possible (there were exceptions: occasional unexpected reefs and ancient rock mountain tops that didn't break the surface except on the lowest tides), to hug the shoreline so close you could practically reach out and pluck the buttercups growing in the cracks of rocks as you drove past. Humpback whales could glide right alongside the forest without fear of beaching themselves.

In such a sheer mountainous world, our fine sandy beach was a unique asset. When the Fourth of July rolled around while we were staying at the cabin that summer, family and friends in Meyers Chuck descended upon us with lashings of picnic supplies and lawn furniture to take advantage of the beach.

Dad built a firepit in the rocks above the sand for grilling burgers and hot dogs. Fortunately, that early in July it was before the salmon began to run so there were no bears around yet.

Rory and Marion with LeAnn and JoDean arrived with scads of goodies and so did Grandma, who arrived in Grandpa's fishing boat the *Shawno*, bringing its namesake with them to stay with us at the cabin. A girl from Meyers Chuck also came to play and go swimming with Megan and me. We couldn't stay out of the water with that inviting, softly gradual sandy beach to swim from. The creek ran right alongside it and its mountain-chilled water brought the saltwater temperature down and made it less buoyant than we were used to from swimming on the other side, but we adapted.

It was an all-day picnic so when the tide went back out, instead of mourning our lost swimming pool, we invented a game we called Circle Tag. We drew a huge circle in the sand with ragged and erratic lines inside it, branching off and connecting unexpectedly. Then we chased each other on the lines. Anyone who fell off a line was automatically "it." Dad, Rory, Marion, and Mom got involved and much shrieking and hilarity ensued.

• • •

Later in the summer, Rory and Dad went hunting over on the islands and Marion and the girls stayed with us at the cabin. When it rained and we were all cooped up inside the single room with two lofts, Mom and Marion had to come up with something to keep the kids occupied.

Marion cooked up a huge batch of maple bars from scratch. Her homemade rolls, that she was accustomed to cooking in an old-fashioned wood-burning cook stove, were something we kids would brag about to each other whenever we had a chance to eat them. Mom made the maple bar frosting. Afterward, when she went to wash her hands in the wash bowl, she got distracted by the ruckus we were making. She told us to settle down over her shoulder as she washed her hands and thought the consistency of the water was strange. When she looked down she found she was washing her hands in the frosting.

She almost fell over laughing, which set us kids and Marion off too.

The error of this maple bar distraction was only apparent after the sugar lit up our already over-energized systems. To stop us from bouncing off the walls and hanging from the lofts, Mom came up with the brilliant idea of a dance marathon. She told us that the flappers in the Twenties had made it a craze and that some people had died from exhaustion to win the record. She wondered aloud, how long could we go?

We embraced the idea. We pushed the table up against the front wall, pushed the couch into the kitchen, and moved the loft ladders out of the way. While we danced to Foreigner, Blondie, and Rick Springfield, Mom had the idea of putting makeup on her sister-in-law.

Marion had grown up out in the wilderness without access or much interest in more traditional feminine outlets, such as cosmetics. But she let Mom experiment on her.

We were all curious to see what would come of it, having never seen Marion wear anything except lip balm on her face. As we danced hour after hour on the red-painted floor while the rain drummed on the roof, and the music throbbed from the ceiling accompanied by the constant rumble of the creek, we watched Mom apply her brushes, eyelash curlers, powders, and lipstick to Marion's face next to the fuzzy light of the front Visquine windows. She gave Marion a professional hairstyling as well.

When Mom unveiled the finished result, we were all surprised. We'd seen Mom work her makeup tricks on all of us and the effect had always been memorable, even transformative.

Not this time.

As it turned out, Marion had such a natural, strong beauty that adding artificial dyes and colors made her less, not more, striking. Mom shook her head and summed it up as "painting the lily."

• • •

One day, when we went to step out of the cabin, we were surprised to see that the ground was no longer stable and firm. Every inch of it moved with a surreal, undulating motion. Closer inspection showed that ants had invaded.

It was a plague of ants, like the night the frogs came out on the other side. Just as we never saw many frogs, ants weren't all that common either. But now millions of them were crawling over every inch of ground.

They didn't cause us any problems, though trying to get to the outhouse and back, or across the bridge without stepping on any of them, was impossible. But I tried not to hurt any of them. We were in awe of the mass migration, having no idea why they were on the move or where they were headed. By the next day they were all gone.

Since we were all living on top of each other and Dad was home now, the boys couldn't harass Megan quite as much as they preferred. But in the tighter confines they got on her nerves more than usual, and one night she had something of a psychic break and went into a cleaning frenzy way past bedtime. We all hung over the loft's edge and watched her sweeping, dusting, rearranging knickknacks, putting books away, tidying the kitchen, and sweeping some more.

Mom called from hers and Dad's loft, "Megan, thank you for all your cleaning, but you can go to bed now, honey."

It was obvious to all of us that Megan had finally cracked.

Shortly afterward, Dad crossed the strait to pick up groceries and supplies. When he returned and we hauled everything up to the cabin, he pulled something out of the boxes and handed it to Megan.

It was an enormous art kit with everything a budding artist could want, with sketchpad, pencils, paints, and brushes in different sizes. It was amazing that a store as small as the one in Thorne Bay had such a specialty item, so he had to have gone deliberately looking to find it.

For the most part, we felt that Dad wasn't aware of us kids as anything more than an ever-present underfoot irritant that he had to work hard to support, or conversely an always on tap labor source. But every now and then we were surprised to learn that this wasn't true. That he did know each of us individually, and cared when we were hurting.

Robin remembers being teased incessantly by Jamie and Shawn when he was seven years old. Dad saw him after a teasing session and, much to Robin's surprise, noticed how unhappy he was. Dad said, "Let's take a walk."

They walked to the outhaul, but Dad passed it until they reached a weathered rootwad. Dad pulled a hatchet out of it. To Robin's amazement it was brand new, and not one of the cheap rubber-handled camping hatchets—it was a leather handle, one-piece Estwing hatchet. Dad handed it to him and said, "All I ask is you don't lose a finger. But you're man enough to have this." Robin never forgot it.

Chris was always more determined than the rest of us to be close to Dad. He'd follow him around and climb onto his lap, and Dad would let him. He remembers sitting on Dad's knee while out wood logging and Dad letting Chris help him steer the outboard when he was only five years old.

One time, in the floathouse, I became upset about something, but I almost never showed when I was unhappy in front of anyone. I retreated into the back room to cry over my paper dolls while everyone else was in the front of the house laughing and enjoying themselves. The next thing I knew, Dad appeared. He rarely came into the kids' domain. But he silently squatted down next to me and picked up one of the paper dolls, and awkwardly attempted to play with them with me.

Even Jamie had one of these moments when Dad, a couple years later, sacrificed his carefully hoarded fuel for Jamie's benefit.

• • •

In late summer it rained heavily for days, so heavily that the creek rose higher than we'd ever seen it. We watched as a downed alder tree from somewhere upstream washed down toward the bridge. It bumped into rocks and got wedged into place just upstream from the cabin and held there for a day.

Dad paced, muttering, willing the rain to cease. It didn't.

The alder, after holding against the pummeling creek, suddenly popped free and plunged down on the bridge. Shoved up lengthways against the bridge's supports, whitewater foamed over the tree.

The waiting was the worst. Feeling under siege by the deluge, holding our breaths, willing the bridge to hold. The creek swirled higher and higher under the floorboards beneath our feet.

With a crack that we heard over the rain and the thunder of the rushing water, the pole supports gave way. We ran outside and saw an entire section of the bridge torn loose, tumbling and splashing into the creek.

It was soon washed away along with the tree in the roaring water. We got it, then, why the cannery owners had built their bridge on massive concrete blocks that still remained, though their corners had been rounded off from decades of exposure.

As soon as the rain and the whitewater in the creek subsided, Dad rebuilt the bridge. This time he made sure that there were supports on either side of the creek, using one of the cannery's concrete blocks to anchor the cabin side of the bridge. It was the center of the bridge where the waters rushed the fiercest during heavy rainfall, so he supported it entirely on swifter cables. He didn't bother roping the railings—in fact, there weren't any railings with this version.

One other thing happened that summer. Because of Dad losing his job, for the first time the annual land lease payment to US Steel was late. It was a twenty-year renewable lease with option to buy, if US Steel ever wanted to sell, which they said they "wouldn't ever, in the foreseeable future."

Mom wrote to Mr. McKenzie and explained the situation, asking to be granted an extension, sharing with him the plan to sell the floathouse.

Jamie, Robin, and Chris on the bridge Dad built, holding puppies
and watching as Moby confronts the cat, Creosote Bill.

Mr. McKenzie wrote back, assuring her that she had nothing to
worry about, that we would never lose the lease due to a late payment.

• • •

Our brief time crammed into the cannery cabin stands out for
all of us as a pocket eternity of sun-drenched summer days. We
had managed to do that best of all things—go on vacation while
remaining at home.

It was an entire adventure on its own. We remember it as being
an entire year, a complete novel of events. It was our most favorite,
fullest time at the cannery. Perhaps because we were thrown so
much into each other's company.

If we hadn't already formed a bond that nothing in the years to
come could break, we formed it during those months in the cannery
cabin.

*"I don't think any other man did what he did to make sure
we all got our education. Four times a day in some of the
worst weather in the world, and I still graduated!"* —Robin

CHAPTER FIFTEEN

ONLY ONE person came out to look at the floathouse thinking to
buy. He flew out on a floatplane and asked whether the house was on
a sled so it could be slid off the float and onto shore. It wasn't. Plus,
he didn't think the size was right for the logging cook shack he had
in mind to use it for, so he passed on it.

With no other interest being shown, we gave up on the idea of
selling the floathouse. Instead, Dad thought that if we pooled our
Permanent Fund Dividends (Alaska's annual oil revenue dividend
for every resident) we'd have almost enough to buy the one-man
mobile sawmill he had his eye on, and he could borrow the rest.

They usually let us kids have a large part of our dividend to be
used in our yearly blow-out party, as well as for buying whatever
else we needed—everything from clothes to personal hygiene,
but mostly music related: Walkmans, headphones, boom boxes,
cassettes, batteries. Lots and lots of batteries.

We were still in the little red cabin when Mom and Dad sat the
five of us kids down at the long pine table Dad had built in Montana.
The creek rumbled by loudly, almost under our feet. The fuzzy light
through the Visquine plastic windows was enough to set the red
floor and white walls aglow.

They asked if we'd be willing to give up our dividend that year so
Dad could buy the sawmill. They set it all out, like we were investors

at a company board meeting, all the pros and cons, and then told us kids to take our time and think seriously about it.

Mom insisted that we'd get a percentage of the profits, but we all knew that wasn't likely to happen. Mainly because Dad would probably only make enough to keep us fed and alive, which meant our investment pretty much paid for itself. I personally thought they could have taken our dividends and used them without asking us, as any parent would have a right to do, if it meant the difference between being able to feed and clothe their kids or not.

At any rate, we didn't hesitate or need to talk about it. We all agreed.

We moved back into the floathouse, hauling skiff-loads of our belongings around the sheer bluff, forested peninsula that separated the two sides of the cannery and reassembled everything in the freshly renovated floathouse.

It now had a delightful, tiny kitchen with wrap-around counters. The side that faced the living room had been made into a bar with five stools for us kids to eat at. The shelves between us and the kitchen were open so we could watch Mom as she worked, cooking her fabulous Spanish rice or German potato salad, as if we were at a fast food diner. Dad had varnished the top with fiberglass resin, and we quickly discovered that you didn't want to put a hot paper plate on it—the resin leaked through the paper and into our food.

As Dad put the stereo speakers back in place, he heard a rattling inside one of them. When he dismantled it he finally discovered the reason why he'd never been able to achieve the proper, distortion-free cannon fire when booming out Tchaikovsky's 1812 Overture at the cabin. The speakers were full of Mom's rock jewelry. (Her maternal grandfather had been a rock hound in the Great Lakes area and had his own jewelry shop). For some reason, known only to themselves, the boys had stashed the beautifully cut and polished stones there.

One overcast day in the fall of 1983, while we kids were swimming on the floathouse side, Dad showed up towing Rory and Marion's thirteen-foot Boston Whaler, a twin of Dad's, both skiffs piled high with wooden crates. When he beached them and got out his beard was split by the biggest grin we'd ever seen.

Mom took pictures of him as he stood with his hands on

Dad at his happiest, the day he brought his one-man
mobile sawmill home to the cannery.

his waist, beaming with happiness and pride, in front of the
unassembled sawmill. I was deeply impressed. I hadn't known he
could be that joyful. And maybe it was the first time he'd felt that
way since Vietnam.

He was like a kid as he swiftly took the crates apart with a
crowbar and put the orange-painted sawmill together. We marveled
over the long, intricately braced track, the enormous circular saw
and its carriage with giant wheels. It was the only thing with wheels
in our life. The whole assemblage looked alien.

From then on the purr and shriek of the sawmill became the
background of our days, in combination with the music Dad liked to
boom from the floathouse's outside speakers to listen to in between
slicing off another board. We were commanded never to run or play
in front of the track when the sawmill was in operation because we
could get hit by flying debris.

After assembling the mill, the first thing Dad did was build a
platform for it with ways to haul logs up. Because the platform would
be underwater on the higher tides (making it easy to put the bigger

logs on it), he had to weight it.

As part of the design he built wooden boxes between the platform's supports that we filled with rocks. Jamie, Megan, and I hauled the bigger rocks while Robin and Chris filled in the cracks with smaller stones. It took a backbreaking amount of labor to do it, even with Dad helping out—he wanted to have a part in every bit, no matter how menial, of creating his sawmill operation—but we did a good job. The deck never budged even in the worst storms and biggest surges.

He had a logging winch which he anchored by running a cable around a deeply rooted tree and attaching it to the winch. In order to get the logs lined up where he needed them, he used gravity and the tide as his assistants, especially if the tide he needed was at night when he'd be sleeping.

He'd tie a line to a log and then throw the free end over a tree branch. He would then tie it to a five-gallon bucket full of rocks and tighten the line on the log end, lifting the bucket until it was several feet off the ground. As the tide rose, the weight of the bucket would pull the log up the beach. When he'd wake up the next morning it would be where he needed it.

For a long time, before the sawmill arrived in our lives, before we moved to the cannery, Dad had an insanely huge log that we all called "the Big Log." It was 110 feet long and 40 inches in diameter on the small end, and over 6 feet tall on the big end. It had been one of the logs in the sled under the massive donkey that lifted log bundles at the logging camp where Dad had worked. It was found to have rot on the top side and had to be discarded, so Dad promptly spoke up, asking if he could have it and those in charge agreed.

It had always been the plan that one day our wilderness home would come out of that log.

But in the meantime he needed to make a living by selling lumber to the locals, as well as hiring himself out for his carpentry skills. Some fine wood came out of his mill because he loved every moment of it and took great pride in figuring out how to get the best product out of a log.

He didn't charge nearly as much as his labor was worth—in addition to sawing the lumber, he'd also make bundles of it and then tow it to whoever had bought it, undo the bundle, carry it up the beach, and stack it. We sometimes helped in all of this, but most of the time he did it while we were in school.

He was hired to use the lumber he milled to replace rotten wood in people's homes, replace their decking or build new decks, docks, and entire houses. There was hardly a household in the area that didn't have some of his lumber and/or labor in it.

Our days soon became dedicated to beachcombing for saw logs. The whole family participated, putting our shoulders to logs and rolling them down rocky beaches to the water. When Dad saw a log he wanted, he'd beach the skiff and climb up with his chainsaw and "buck off" whatever section he didn't want, such as when it was a "rootwad," a log that still had a portion of the roots attached.

He would stand in dangerous places, sometimes on top of the log as he ran the saw, and I'd cringe, waiting for some horrible accident to happen. But, like in everything mechanical, he had complete mastery over the saw and understood the forces in play. He never had an accident with it. Though, every now and then, he had problems with a saw not working.

His always on tap war rage could be counted on to be triggered by frustration. Once, when a balky saw absolutely refused to cooperate, no matter what he tried, he swore at it and flung it into the bay. Satisfied that he'd made his point, he waded out and fished it out of the water. Then he dismantled it on a log, cleaned all of its parts, put it back together, and to no one's surprise the chastened saw did its job.

The scariest part of logging with Dad was his "hack the mission" focus. He lost complete awareness of the human element in his equations and calculations. Once when he was pulling a log off the beach with the skiff, the line went tight against Mom, who sat next to him on the back seat by the outboard.

All his attention was on the log and he didn't notice or hear her attempts to get his attention as he revved the outboard. The more he pulled on the log, the more the line pressed against her, pushing her until she almost went over head first into the water. Our yells finally clued him in, and he slacked up the line before Mom went overboard.

We learned to keep a sharp eye out for ourselves and be ready for anything that came our way. Snapped lines were what I was always tensely anticipating. They could whiplash back and strike you if you weren't careful. Or you could fall off your seat when the outboard was revved up high against the weight of a log, only to shoot forward when a line snapped. Over time, Dad's reflexes became so honed that he could instantly turn the throttle down so that we only lurched when a line snapped.

If a log fell into a cradle of rocks, we'd all clamber back out and Dad would pack the heavy Peavey, a logging tool made of thick steel pipe with a pointed end and a big, hinged hook, up to the log. And while bald eagles stared piercingly from the tops of a spruce tree at the only humans in their domain, and humpback whales blew streamers of steam into the air out on the bay, Dad would hook the log and use the pipe as a lever to roll it up out of the rocks.

We kids would be quick to hold the log with drift poles, the weight digging into our shoulders as we breathed in deep the seaweed and musky mink scents of the beach, so Dad could sink another bite into it. We'd do it again if necessary until it was freed, despite the fact that all of us, except Jamie, were not yet teenagers.

When Dad was logging he'd get so deep into the logistics that I don't think he saw us as human, or even alive. We were tools, mechanical parts: handy, mobile extensions to be used by his engineering brain as needed. (He'd loosen up once the logs were under tow and let Chris—who was too small to have much part in any of the action—sit on his leg and steer the outboard.)

He also had logging jacks that came with the sawmill, and we'd use those on the beaches to liberate the logs he had his heart set on. I always dreaded having to be the one who worked the pipe, afraid I'd do something that would knock the jack over and drop the log on someone. But Dad, again, always knew exactly what he was doing and no one ever got hurt.

Like most things in our wilderness life, logging was heavy, sweaty labor.

· · ·

A sawmill, we soon learned, generates a tremendous amount of sawdust. At first Dad shoveled the sawdust into a deep, wooden wheelbarrow that he'd built himself, complete with a wooden wheel, and dumped it in a wide circle in a cleared part of the forest above the sawmill platform. (It was right next to the quarry of broken rock and core samples that US Steel had left behind after they surveyed the cannery for profitable ore. The stacks of five-foot-long aluminum and steel core sample holders were what we used in constructing our forts.)

When a big tide threatened, Dad would put the mill on its wheeled carriage and drag it up to the sawdust clearing and park it under some trees with a tarp over it to protect the engine from the elements. The sawdust kept coming, however, so he decided that we'd make a trail with it to connect both sides of the property.

The cannery managers had done that before us, with a wide, raised boardwalk set on pilings. It was mostly rotten and caved in when we got there, with rusty nails sticking out of it, so Mom told us never to play around it.

I liked to roam alongside it and wonder who had strolled the boardwalk back when the cannery boomed. What had they thought about under the cooling dimness of the forest canopy way up overhead? Where had they come from? Once they went home to their part of the world, did they long to return to the mystery and beauty of the Alaskan rainforest next to the sea?

Mom suggested that Jamie and Shawn be paid to tear the wreckage of the old boardwalk down. So all of one summer they dragged the heavy, crumbling boards aside. Jamie, of course, had to get some fun out of it and swung his homemade machete at it, hacking and chopping an imaginary enemy with many a "hi-yah" and *Conan the Barbarian*–type grunts. Shawn followed suit with either the ax or sledgehammer. They got their entertainment's worth out of the destruction, and got paid in the bargain.

Dad did a lot of the sawdust hauling, pushing a heaped wheelbarrow to dump where the boardwalk had been, but so did Megan and I. Sometimes we had to do it late into the day, when the shadows gathered in dark density under the trees, in order to get the sawdust off the deck before the tide came in.

Mom was still worried about the bears and also the wolves later in the year, so Megan and I had to pack Dad's .44 revolver in its hip holster, the belt heavy with cartridges as we shoveled sawdust into the wheelbarrow and then pushed it up the hill and down the first part of the trail to dump it and then stamp it down.

Megan, with her night terrors and fear of the dark, did not count these among her favorite moments, though with my love of Westerns I liked the frontier adventure of it, emphasized by the presence of the gun.

Robin and Chris, inspired by watching one of their favorite movies, Disney's *Swiss Family Robinson*, decided to dig a "tiger pit" like the boys in that movie did, in the sawdust trail. Their plan was for either Megan or me to push the wheelbarrow into it while they chortled on the sidelines. They laid live hemlock branches over the hole, interweaving them so that the sawdust would stay on top of them and look like a solid part of the trail.

Then they hunkered down out of sight and waited, exchanging anticipatory glances and readying their high fives.

However, when the person pushing the wheelbarrow hove into view, they saw it was Dad. They froze, forgetting to breathe as they watched him push the load of sawdust with his usual fast, impatient stride along the already built trail. All at once the wheelbarrow dropped into the hole and he crashed into it.

They ducked down, staring at each other with their hands over their mouths as Dad roared curses and threats of what he'd do to whoever had pulled that trick. They found that retreat was the better part of valor and scrambled away as silently as possible. Dad probably had his suspicions about who did it, but since he couldn't prove it all he could do was brood and glare and make it clear that if it ever happened again, life wouldn't be worth living for any of us.

• • •

We didn't have much opportunity to enjoy the changes to the floathouse. That fall Mom realized that the boys were not taking their schoolwork seriously enough with her as their teacher, and she was afraid they'd fall too far behind to ever catch up.

She and Dad talked it over and the upshot was that Mom, Robin, Chris, Megan, and I would move back to Meyers Chuck so we kids could attend the school there while living in the wanigan. Jamie would stay with Dad to keep the place going in Union Bay, doing his correspondence lessons like usual.

Mom fixed up the tiny wanigan and Dad towed it to the Chuck with us aboard, including Lady, who had separation anxiety whenever she was apart from me. He towed us into the Back Chuck (the small lagoon behind the front harbor), where our floathouse used to be before we moved to the cannery.

We were delighted to find that Linda would once again be our next-door neighbor. She and her husband Art had built a floathouse of their own and it was moored in the Back Chuck. They'd had a baby, a happy, friendly little guy named Noah.

The brand-new state-built school in Meyers Chuck had won an award for its architectural design and had been built with half a million in oil-revenue dollars. It was a startlingly modern structure in a roadless, tiny fishing village. It had its own generator and, alien to us, a furnace room that provided central heating. Even more alien were the boys and girls restrooms, including a modern shower. The entire front of the school was made of windows and it had a lofty cathedral ceiling.

Every aspect of the school was impractical, but it did manage to create a kind of bridge between the modern world and our rustic lives. Especially with its Apple computers (on which we happily played *The Oregon Trail* and *Where in the World is Carmen Sandiego?* for hours on end) and gigantic TV dish.

It was strange being around other people again, but it helped that many of them were related to us—by then Rory and Marion had returned to the Chuck from Saltery Cove and were building a log cabin. We also got to see a lot more of our grandparents, especially Grandma Pat, who was the teacher's aide. With four of her grandchildren calling her Grandma, it wasn't long before all the other school kids, and the teacher too, wound up calling her Grandma too.

The school district got state money for every kid they had in one of their schools, so once the school year was over and we moved back to the cannery, they offered to buy Dad a new outboard motor and pay for his fuel if he'd agree to skiff all five of us kids to school every day. Dad agreed.

This meant that he had to make the trip on open, mercurial waters four times a day—taking us over and then going back to the cannery to work with the sawmill, then back to the Chuck to pick us up and take us home. Including crossing the strait every weekend in the thirteen-foot Boston Whaler for two years, he logged an impressive amount of hours in an open skiff.

One of the first things Dad did was build a sturdy, sixteen-foot wooden skiff, the design of which impressed the local men. The little Whaler was getting too small to ferry five growing kids on unpredictable waters. He'd previously built a shallow, twelve-foot dory. This time he built the frame of the skiff much deeper. He didn't put any seats in, since he planned to use it for hauling freight and lumber. We sat on the duck boards and leaned against the sides.

When we got in rough weather, a fairly common occurrence since we had to round one of the most treacherous points in Alaska to get to school, the skiff would take water over the bow and cascade down on us. We didn't have raingear, so Mom cut holes in fifty-gallon garbage bags and we put them on over our lifejackets. Our backpacks got drenched and we had water-stained, swollen textbooks and smeared homework.

There were days when it blew so hard that we couldn't go to school at all, so the teacher called us on the CB radio and gave us our lessons that way. For math she'd give us the answer key for the even-numbered problems and we'd have to show our work for the odd-numbered problems. I wound up figuring out algebra on my own by trial and error; it was an amazing epiphany when it all came together.

Dad listened to the forecast every night and we got in the habit of choosing to do our homework or not according to what the weatherman reported. If he said it was going to blow, I'd put my homework aside in favor of reading a Western.

To our dismay, we learned that the weatherman was not to be trusted. Sometimes we'd wake up to not the forecasted storm but a gloriously calm day, and Dad would skiff us to school without our homework done. This constant betrayal bred in me a deep and abiding distrust for all weather forecasters.

We missed almost as many days of school we made. Which the teachers hated, so it's surprising that Jamie and I were allowed to

Dad skiffing us to school in the wooden skiff he built himself to haul lumber.

take a month off to work Grandpa's trapline in Bear Creek, about two miles from the cannery.

I was fourteen, Jamie was sixteen, and we were completely on our own in the wilderness. (Grandpa later wrote an article about our experience, interviewing each of us. He wrote of me: "At fourteen, Tara is a tall girl, with loose blonde hair; her luminous blue eyes darken when she is serious, but usually sparkle with gaiety. They have a trick of looking directly into yours, not boldly, but with assurance and self-possession. She has a wide mouth grin that illuminates her whole face and a sharp mind that made it easy for her to become an 'A' student.")

We had to promise Mom that we'd take the walkie-talkie with us wherever we went and call in every night. We loved being on our own, cooking our own meals, reading books in our bunks in the cozy cabin, playing cards, and rhyming entire conversations. The only part I didn't like was the actual trapline. Jamie knew my softheartedness and, without mocking me for it, allowed me to go off while he dispatched the animals.

(In the same article by Grandpa, Jamie was also described: "Jamie, at sixteen is a six-footer with large hands and feet that seem to promise he will be a big man when he fills out. He too has a quick mind… he could survey the options and quickly decide where to make a set.")

When I was away from the cabin for a few days to allow an infected finger to heal, Jamie shot a wolf when a pack came down off the mountain and prowled on the creek bank opposite him. He was quietly proud of overcoming his fears and later sold the hide during a school fieldtrip.

One night we woke up to hear a low growl. We shot up in our bunks, listening hard, asking each other if it was a bear. To our horror we realized it was something a lot worse. It was Dad in the skiff.

It struck us both at the same time—we'd forgotten to call in!

Dad was coming to see if we were alive in the middle of the night. He wouldn't have been able to get to us until the tide came in, and at night the trip up the winding creek with unpredictable sand bars on all sides would have been treacherous and stressful.

We looked at each other, imagining what Dad's state of mind would be. Jamie suggested we take off for the hills and live off the land for the rest of our lives. But when Dad got there and found out we'd forgotten to call in and we were okay, he didn't say all that much. Apparently he was glad to find us alive.

• • •

The wolves were still a part of our lives.

And one year, the inevitable happened. They got Lady.

Mom was on a brief trip with Linda to San Francisco, one of the few times Mom got to get away from the wilderness. While she was away I spent hours trimming all the burrs and cutting out the matted fur Lady managed to accumulate with her super-fine, Cocker Spaniel hair. I wanted to impress Mom with how cleaned up I'd gotten Lady.

The day after I gave her dog show grooming, she disappeared.

We spent hours calling and looking. Dad took me down the beach in the skiff, letting me get out and call Lady's name for hours. I kept calling and looking, but I knew she was gone. I knew the wolves had gotten her.

Mom: *Did you feel that the ruins at the cannery were alive, that they welcomed us? I mean, did you ever think about the workers who used to live there?*
Dad: *No. I just thought about needing to clear all the rusty junk out of the way so I could build.*

CHAPTER SIXTEEN

CLEARING THE land for the two gardens was as nothing compared to the job of clearing Mom's chosen site for the New House, as we called it. Four years earlier, on our reconnaissance trip to the cannery, she'd picked out where she wanted her dream house to be, right next to the creek, set back in the woods a short way from the beach.

She couldn't be dissuaded despite the fact that the spot was overgrown with new growth after the fire and the brush was so thick you couldn't walk through it. We knew bunkhouses had been there previously because the brush and saplings had grown right up through twisted and burned steel beds—dozens of them. Many of the beds had become welded together from the intense heat, creating strange, abstract shapes.

Dad brooded about it, inspecting the seemingly insurmountable challenge for a while. Then he got his chainsaw and went to work. The five of us kids and Mom hauled small trees down to the beach (spruce trees and their limbs were the worst because they were so prickly and dripped sap), slapping at the swarm of bloodthirsty bugs as we worked. We hauled for hours, tossing the brush onto a crackling bonfire. I thought how strange it was that the brush we hauled down had been born from fire and was being returned to fire.

Dad chopped through the twisted metal with a sharp ax and we hauled it down to the beach as well, to let it make the acquaintance of its cannery brethren, already washed by decades of tides. Mom had insisted that all of us get tetanus booster shots from a district nurse who flew out to the Chuck every year, which was probably a good idea.

As we trudged repeatedly down the trail Dad had blazed, dragging brush and metal behind us, the creek rumbled. The bears ambled through the golden water amidst the steady fins. Sea gulls shrieked and fought over spawned corpses and pecked the eyes out of the living salmon. The stench made us glad to breathe in the fresh, sharp scent of burning hemlock and crackling spruce branches. The bugs weren't as bad down by the roaring bonfire either.

Every day we cleared. There were times when I inspected my sap-covered, scratched hands that I thought we'd never get it done. We were beat, but Dad was relentless. Like always, when he had a goal he was like a machine, a Terminator that nothing could stop. Quitting was not an option for any of us. That lesson helped us get through a lot of things later in life.

It wasn't all drudgery. There were high spots, like when we uncovered the remains of what Mom delightedly said was a Japanese garden. Although it had become wildly overgrown like everything else, it had escaped the fire and as we cleared it, the harmonious design became clear. Mom said that one day we'd route water from the creek to it and put a pond in to fill with fish. She wondered if it had originally been that way. I wondered who the imaginative person was who had designed the ornamental garden in the middle of the wilderness.

We also found another grave, and a low, square concrete pad with a raised lip which even Dad found puzzling.

Finally the cutting and hauling and burning was done. The cleared area was impressively large, but Dad didn't stand around admiring it. The next thing we knew he was digging innumerable holes and putting in foundation pilings. He anchored one part of the house on the concrete pad.

Mom's design for the New House was spectacularly impractical, considering Dad would have to mill every board for it and the only labor available were two adults and five kids, most of them not in their teens yet.

The house was to be two full stories high and two different buildings arranged perpendicular to each other, but under one joined roof. The side of the house that ran parallel to the creek would be about the size of our grandparents' house in Meyers Chuck, but with a much higher ceiling. The loft would have the master bedroom, while beneath and in front of it would be a single vast living room, with a soaring cathedral ceiling and huge windows stacked up on the front facing the beach, and a bay window with a view of the creek.

The other side of the house, accessible by a door at the bottom of the master bedroom's stairs, would have an entry hall with stairs to five second-floor bedrooms and a landing. Below, a commodious kitchen with an attached walk-in pantry would be built. On the side of these rooms there'd be a room lined with windows that faced the forest and ridge where access to the bridge was. It was a long rectangle of a room that Mom called the game room. Mom completely forgot to design bathrooms, so one had to be added later in the living room.

The house was designed to encompass nearly 3,000 square feet. In short, it was a wilderness mansion. How it would get from Mom's fantasy design on paper and take three-dimensional shape in our brutally real world was a mystery. As it turned out, Dad's engineering brain and sheer inability to admit defeat contained the necessary alchemy to effect the miracle. Oh, and our labor. Lots of labor.

The real work began when Dad stacked and bound bundles of lumber he'd milled from the Big Log and towed them over to the cannery side. We kids and Mom hauled board after board up the beach, skirting the giant cannery retort door half buried in rust-colored rocks, past some lonesome, outlying pilings, and into the shade of the woods using the trail we'd blazed while clearing brush.

It felt like we were passing the ghosts of our former selves, the innocent kids who'd thought the hard part would be over once they lugged the prickly branches down to the fire. I felt like saluting that naïve child as we sweated over the heavy, ungainly boards. Even with two kids to a board we couldn't keep up with Dad's impatient strides. He lifted several boards at once onto a shoulder and passed us like we were standing still.

When that bundle was neatly stacked near the Japanese garden, stickered and covered with a tarp to dry, he returned to the sawmill

Dad standing at one end of the Big Log that would one day build the New House.

to create another bundle and repeat the process—again and again and again.

There were also the long, massive beams that would be necessary to support the second story, and one beam that Mom had thrown in for purely decorative purposes. Dad slid short pieces of rope with loops at either end under these beams, stuck a two-by-two through the loops, and we kids were arranged on either side with our hands on the two-by-twos while Mom and Dad each took an end. With burning muscles and much halting, jerking, and dropping, we managed to get the heavy beams to where Dad wanted them.

Slowly but surely the house began to take shape. First, the fifty-four-by-thirty-four-foot foundation floor that the two sides of the house would sit on was laid out, with Dad sawing and nailing every board into place.

Then the first-floor walls went up. Dad needed us kids to lift and then hold the walls in place while he nailed them together where they joined at the corners. Next he put the stairs in. We loved the stairs and we would race up and down them all day long and then sit on the framing, or chase each other across the tops of it when Mom wasn't looking. The dogs loved the stairs too and chased us, yipping, as we ran up and down them. Sometimes we'd just sit on the stairs staring out at the bay from our unusually high vantage point.

One time Rory and Marion arrived, showing us a soccer ball that they'd found floating in the bay. We all, kids and adults, promptly played a game of kickball, dodging in and out of the wall framing and bouncing the ball off rolls of tarpaper.

It was a sad day when Dad put down the second-story floor and made it more of a house than a jungle gym. Then came the logistics of pulling the second floor's end wall into place. It spanned the entire width of the house and had a high, peaked top. We pulled it into place using rope and tackle with Mom and us kids straining on the ropes while Dad maneuvered it into place. We held on, sweating and scared we'd let go and it would fall. Dad squared it up, and nailed it in place.

Eleanor Agnew, in the book *Back to the Land*, described how the entire community she was a part of banded together to help raise walls for a modest home under construction. She said that about a dozen friends showed up and discussed strategy. Then a row of men and women pushed the wall up from inside while another row of men and women pulled on ropes from the outside. Agnew wrote: "Voices groaned… as the wall frame rose high and strong, among curses and yells. Sweat dripped and arms trembled as the wall at last stood upright."

It was a good thing we never knew that a dozen full-grown adults found wall raisings taxing.

But the wall raising was nothing compared to the six-by-twelve-inch beam, twenty feet long, that had to be raised above the living room floor to complete Mom's open beam design. (Dad put up the slightly smaller beams on the other side of the house that supported the second-story floor by himself while we were at school.)

Mom later wrote to a friend: "The huge living room beams went up as a joint effort, the kids and I pulling the rope as Gary maneuvered them into place. I recall on the biggest beam, we were all in a row, stair stepping oldest to youngest and all straining like crazy pulling that rope, pulling that huge beam up, inch by inch and we were all screaming "Dad!" "Gary!" "She's not gonna hold!"

"Hurry!" "We're losing her!" We were almost laid back flat pulling that beam! With block and tackle of course. But she went up. You can imagine that we'd have cheered had we energy."

As we worked alongside Dad, hauling boards and bringing him nails, we mordantly sang the Wilderness Family's song that, in the first movie, played over a montage of them gaily building their cabin: "We work together, cut, trim, nail those boards / We'll build a home forevermore / This is the life that loves and keeps us free / That's why we are a wilderness family."

Dad worked on the house with or without us kids all year round: during winter when snow covered the floors and after he skiffed us to school, and during the heat of summer in between milling lumber and hauling it to Meyers Chuck to pay the bills and buy more building supplies.

In addition, while he was building the house, he'd acquired a thirty-two-foot boat that needed extensive repairs. He took turns building the house, building other people's structures, helping put in a community waterline in the Chuck, and working on the boat. After building a cradle for it, he stripped the boat right down to the hull, replacing rotten boards and building a new deck and cabin on it.

Out of respect for Megan's artistic talent, Dad asked her to paint the hull blue, and she did so with her boom box playing Billy Idol's *Whiplash Smile* album on repeat (the stereo had been removed from the floathouse, with its outdoor speakers, over to the New House). Mom and I chipped in by painting the cabin white.

He named it the *Sea Cucumber* as a salute to the memorable night when Rand had prodded him into pranking Meyers Chuck on the CB radio with the account of a hundred-foot boat named the *Sea Cucumber* needing space at the state dock.

• • •

We moved into the New House before it was finished, when I fourteen. There was a roof on it (Dad hated the dormers Mom had designed but put them up anyway, using up additional roofing that had to be skiffed over from Thorne Bay and then packed up the beach like everything else), but all of the windows had Visquine in them,

The New House with old cannery pilings out front.

except the huge floor-to-ceiling ones that lined the game room wall.

They were sliding glass doors and it was a massive, swearing production under Dad's direction to get them up from the beach. He dismantled them and then used the separate pieces of glass to slot in place, all without breaking any of them. The front door had Visquine in it and the walls had the silver backing of insulation showing. We hauled the new wood-burning Earth Stove into the game room below my room. It was huge and heavy but we used the tried-and-true method we'd used to haul the living room beams up to move it.

Guarding the front door was a massive old alder tree we named Duke which came to feel like a part of the family, though Dad probably disliked leaving it standing where it could drop its branches (something alders were known to do) on the house, which he'd then have to repair. But despite his practical concerns, he let the tree stand when we all voted unanimously to keep Duke.

In addition to building a workshop on one of the concrete foundation blocks that sat on the edge of the beach, Dad also built a generator shed, a woodshed, and a 150-foot-long boardwalk that led up from the beach to the back door, where the game room was.

He also built an antenna platform thirty feet up a tree. He had us help him haul a forty-foot pole up to the platform. I climbed the tree to stand with him on the platform and help him fasten it in place. Attached to the pole were three antennas—TV, CB, and VHF. Unfortunately, though it should have been high enough to pick up a signal from Meyers Chuck, we never were able to get television on the cannery side.

The size of the pantry fascinated us kids. You could walk in there and be surrounded on all sides by shelves and barrels and buckets of food. It proved an irresistible temptation to the boys. They would sneak in and molest the food supply every chance they got, despite Mom explaining to them that there was no way to replace the food quickly and we had to make it last. It got so that Dad had to put a chain and padlock on the louvered doors he'd built for it. But the boys still got in, infiltrating under cover of darkness, slipping through the cracks in the stairs that ran alongside the pantry. Dad boarded up the backs of the stairs.

But they still got in. "How are they doing it?" Dad muttered in frustration.

Chris was the one who had figured it out. One day he saw Dad look at a line of DIY books in the game room. They had numbers on their spines and he noticed that once Dad looked at them, he went and unlocked the pantry to let Mom get out what she needed for dinner.

Lightbulb! Chris told Robin that all they had to do was look at the books Dad had looked at and the numbers on them would be the numbers on the combination lock. It proved to be true, and they were able to open every box in the case of Frosted Flakes cereal and dig out the prize—a package of M&Ms. Little did they care at the time that the entire case of cereal went stale because of their depredations.

For the first time in our lives, all five of us kids had our own bedrooms, and Mom and Dad had their own as well, over the living room, in the section alongside the creek that was like a separate house.

It was, perhaps, a little too much space for all of us after living in the cramped floathouse and the small cabin across the creek.

Chris pretty much moved in with Robin (though his bedroom was the only one that had paneling—gorgeous red cedar—since it was the smallest and took the least amount of lumber and work to plane and sand it). And Megan, for a while, stayed in my room

TARA NEILSON

until a second mattress could be found for her. She had a stack of cottonwood paneling that Dad had milled from a drift log which took up most of the space in her room, so she spent a lot of her time in my room even after she slept in her own. In fact, my room wound up being the happening place to be, probably because I'd worked hard to decorate it.

From our home school on the floathouse side, I laboriously packed a desk, chair, and the filing cabinet across the beach. Then I piled them in the wheelbarrow and pushed them over the long sawdust trail. When I reached the end of it, I hauled them across the beach on the cannery side and up to the house. In my bedroom, I arranged a writing area for myself, complete with kerosene lamp and an old manual typewriter that Grandma had bought for me from a Meyers Chuck resident.

I put a shelf up in the long window along the back wall to put my knickknacks on and pinned up sketches of horses I'd drawn and pages of heartthrobs with high-coiffed hair from a variety of teen magazines, like any Eighties girl. I devoted much space to Bruce Springsteen.

I didn't have a crush on him (Megan, to my disgust, kissed a photo of him seated on the side of a car—we both later got T-shirts with that photo on it), but I felt he was my alter ego and understood how I saw the world. I talked about him so much that my family came to think of him as a member of the family.

I also asked Mom for the blue-and-gold tapestry rug that had been in the floathouse. When I rolled it out with Megan's help, it covered nearly all the tarpaper flooring in my room.

My room was also the only bedroom, other than Mom and Dad's, that wound up having a door. Dad built it out of a slab of beachcombed redwood that he'd milled, though he used the best pieces from it for a redwood worktable Mom designed for the kitchen. I thumbtacked to my new door a long poster of Bruce with a guitar striding in front of stage lights.

From behind my desk I acted as a radio DJ, recording at BUB (Boomin' Union Bay) Studio all the latest local hits—my own favorites—Whitesnake, Baltimora, Don Johnson, Crowded House, Cory Hart, Cyndi Lauper, Heart, Tom Petty, John Mellencamp, and

Bruce Springsteen and more Springsteen (taking from his entire available catalog) played in between interviews with my brothers and sister about the latest goings-on in their spheres of influence. Usually with puppies barking in the background.

When Springsteen's remake of "War" was released, the family gathered in the game room to listen to American Top 40 to hear where his powerful version of the anti-war anthem would place, rooting for it to reach the top ten.

We lived primarily in the kitchen and game room. One day Chris recorded a typical conversation as we all sat around the table playing cards. On it, all seven voices are talking at once, telling their stories, what they'd seen and done, dogs barking in the background.

Dad talks about "running into the bear on the way down to the beach." Megan "found a neat old bottle with an inscription no one's ever heard of." Mom says "Dad got a new job, building a deck and we can all get new socks!" I'm "writing a new story." Robin's "fed up with crab, can't we have hamburgers?" and Jamie wants to "go off alone on my own trapline." In the background The Eurythmics are playing and Chris wants to know if they're "singing about cannibals." Then he yells at me for stealing his pickle.

Somehow, though we're all talking at once over each other, we hear and understand what everyone else says to be able to comment.

• • •

Jamie's room was the least finished and didn't have a window—it was supposed to have either a skylight or a window into the living room, but neither had been put in yet. It was in the middle of the house between Megan's room and the stairs. When he didn't have his lamp burning in his room, it was hard to tell if he was in there or not.

The boys used to creep past Jamie's room, crouched like they were a Special Ops team on a dangerous mission. Their fears were realized when, with a low growl, Jamie's hand would lunge out, snag one of them, and drag them screaming, kicking, and clawing into his dark lair. They always lived to sneak past his room another day.

Besides his books, Jamie became obsessed with video games. Instead of a movie when it was his turn to pick on movie night, he'd choose to play a couple hours of *The Legend of Zelda*. The music from it became the soundtrack to the Westerns I wrote by lamplight in my room right above the game room where the TV was situated.

It took him months, but he finally made it to the final level.

"Tara, get down here!" I heard everyone calling up to me. Usually they didn't bother to try to talk me into watching movies with them; they knew I preferred books. "Jamie's on the final level!" they yelled excitedly.

I felt compelled to join them, to share in bearing witness to this significant moment. The problem was Jamie only got partway through the level when it became time for the generator to be turned off. Dad was miserly with movie night's gas allowance and a stickler for not going over the allotted time, since it was so hard to rebuild our gas supply.

We all groaned, knowing Jamie was going to be hugely disappointed to have to leave the game so close to the end. To our surprise, Dad gave in and said Jamie could keep going—he let the generator run late into the night. Finally, Jamie conquered the game, accompanied by much jubilation from all of us, and won the quest.

It was the winter after we moved into the New House that we nearly lost Jamie. He'd worked the previous summer fishing on Rory's boat and with his earnings wound up with a brand-new, fourteen-foot riveted aluminum skiff called a Lund. He and a friend from Meyers Chuck named Bret (he was my age but was the only boy around close to Jamie's age) took it out one crisply cold day and tried to haul a crab pot. The pot turned out to be too heavy and it pulled the side of the skiff underwater. In minutes the skiff was swamped and sank under their feet, leaving them a long way from shore in fatally cold waters.

Bret later told me that he thought he was dead, there was no way they'd make it. He said Jamie saved his life because Jamie refused to give up. They had a buoy to hang onto and kicked off their rubber boots when they filled with icy water and tried to drag them down. In fact, Jamie and Bret had to ditch all their heavy, water-soaked outerwear. They kicked and kicked, and when Bret got tired and said he was done, Jamie told him to hang on because they were going to keep on kicking until they either made it or died.

When they reached shore they were still a long way from home and hypothermic. They knew, from classes taught in school about water survival, that they didn't have a chance of surviving if they didn't get their body temperature back up. They pulled brush out of the woods and lay down under it until their combined body heat warmed them enough for them to get moving.

They were barefoot and in skimpy, wet clothing, shivering and stumbling over the rocks. They had to stagger along some of Alaska's most remote and rugged shoreline without any hope of being saved—they had to save themselves. It must have seemed like an impossible feat to Bret, but Jamie grew up around Dad who didn't have that word in his vocabulary.

When they finally limped into the warm house, they told Mom what had happened.

"Yeah, sure," she said, used to them pranking her every time they opened their mouths.

She didn't believe them until Jamie showed her Bret's feet. Jamie's were fine because all of us kids spent half the year running around barefoot. Bret's were raw and bloody.

We didn't get to have Jamie with us in the New House for long. He became severely ill one winter and got so far behind in school that he decided not to graduate, taking his GED instead and leaving home to go fishing when he was sixteen. He wrote us occasional, long letters about what his life was like in Sitka and other places where he fished.

It was the six of us now, living in the ruins.

"All of our kids are very independent. And they all feel self-sufficient. Each of them has said that they feel capable of dealing with anything. That they know they can survive. Because they have." —Mom, in a letter to a friend

CHAPTER SEVENTEEN

AFTER JAMIE left Dad continued to skiff us to school until I turned sixteen. He handed over skiffing-to-school duties to me so that he could get more work done, especially in cutting the lumber that paid the bills.

It was nearly a half-hour ride and I sat on an overturned five-gallon bucket to steer. My left arm would grow tired gripping the ridged throttle on the tiller arm. The heavy wood skiff wanted to veer left and I'd have to pull it towards myself without letting up, until my arm, wrist, and fingers cramped. I had to grip the side of the skiff with my right hand to anchor myself against the pull of the outboard.

Megan, Robin, and Chris sat on the duck boards, leaning against the sides of the skiff. Dad hadn't put any seats in because he'd built it to be a work skiff to haul lumber in.

When I was one of the kids sitting down on the duckboards with the others, I'd look back at Dad steering with his farseeing stare, looking for drift and which way the waves were coming, and I'd feel safe. Through every kind of weather—rain, wind, hail, snow, high-latitude sunshine—coming and going, he faced into it while we could duck our faces into the hot-breath comfort of our lifejackets.

His beard would freeze in winter from the salt spray and Megan and I would grimace at each other, wondering if our faces would stay

When I was sixteen I took over the job of steering my brothers and sister to school.

that way. On the return trip we'd all race to get to the house to stick our numb hands in the canner full of hot water on the wood stove to thaw them out. On the way to school our hands would get so cold that when we got there we couldn't grip a pencil. I'd go into the girl's bathroom and run hot water over them to loosen them up.

It was far worse when I was the one steering. Dad gave me all kinds of pointers, telling me exactly where to steer, how to respond to different types of waves, how to look not at what's right in front of the bow but beyond it so you had time to plan your response. He told me where every rock and reef was, and how much of them appeared at what tides.

But he didn't tell me, perhaps because he took it for granted, what a heavy burden it was to feel you were responsible for the lives of three other people, two of them little kids. What it felt like to turn the corner of the long peninsula that separated us from Meyers Chuck and face a wall of whitewater.

When icy waves crashed over the bow and dumped gallons on my sister and brothers, there was nothing I could do about it except pray, even when the boys were scared and always-smiling-and-singing Chris would cry. Megan would meet my eye and say nothing, just start bailing the water out of the bilge.

It was up to me to remember everything Dad had told me. If I forgot something or did it wrong, if I panicked, I'd sink the skiff and dump my siblings in bone-chilling, heavy seas, the only shore steep, harsh rock. I had constant nightmares about the skiff swamping and being the only one to survive.

There was no escaping the knowledge of what these waters could do. Every day we skiffed over where Rand went down. My legs were often so shaky I could barely walk from adrenaline overload when we got to the dock. I felt like I was in shock for the first part of the school day, but finally my stomach would settle down and I'd be able to concentrate.

On the nice days there was nothing more delightful than feeling the power of the outboard's throttle in my left hand, the wind in my face, and the way the skiff skimmed the water as bald eagles wheeled overhead and porpoises joyfully played alongside us. I'd slow down so the porpoises could keep up and they'd mischievously drench us when they dived under the bow. We would all laugh together then and love being in an open skiff on our way to school.

Dad took us to school on the days when the forecast was marginal, or when we could see the bay was choppy. We'd have to get up extra early because he'd take us in the *Sea Cucumber*, which could handle heavier weather than the skiff, but took longer.

He'd skiff us to the dark little cove completely ringed with black rocks and towering trees where he'd securely anchored a log to moor the boat to. We'd climb onto the deck with our heavy backpacks full of seawater-exploded textbooks while he started the engine and warmed it up. We'd try to avoid the puff of black soot that always shot out of the stack when the engine was started with its familiar, chesty grumble.

Once he had the diesel boat stove going we got to climb into the warmth of the little cabin, which felt like an absolute luxury. We took turns sitting in the shotgun seat across from Dad's in front of the steering wheel. It had the only good view over the bow.

The *Sea Cucumber*, the boat Dad rebuilt, loaded with groceries,
fuel, and an entire pallet of fifty-pound bags of dog food.

Dad had, of course, installed a car stereo, complete with
outdoor speakers, and we listened to The Eurythmics, or the *Conan
the Barbarian* soundtrack, or Katrina and the Waves. And on one
memorable occasion, Fleetwood Mac saved our lives.

We got into some bad seas and even with the stabies out (anchors
attached to lowered trolling poles to stabilize the motion of the boat),
we got hammered.

The seas were so confused, coming from every direction with
a tidal current swirling beneath them, that Dad couldn't find a way
to counter or navigate through them. We got tossed around, futilely
trying to brace our legs and backs wherever we could, but the motion
of the boat was so severe that we got knocked loose repeatedly and
had to scramble for purchase.

We could hear things crashing throughout the length of the boat.
Every other moment we were suspended, weightless, with an alien
sense of zero gravity, before we smashed down into the trough and
slid askew with Dad reefing on the wheel one way and then the other.
Wind screamed through the rigging and wave after wave engulfed

the bow and slammed the windows.

Dad had pegged the side windows shut, but water managed to squeeze through and stain the walls. I'm sure we all felt the same sick, shivery fear in our stomachs. I wondered how long before one or more of the windows gave way to the relentless onslaught and how long the boat would stay afloat if we took water right into the cabin.

When Dad started swearing, we all knew it wasn't good. I couldn't help wondering if war flashbacks were being triggered, as I assumed happened when he was in life-or-death situations. Especially when he was responsible for other lives. I had no idea if he'd lose control and what would happen if he did, and I didn't want to find out.

There was only one thing I could think of to do that would help: I put Fleetwood Mac into the stereo. At the first note, hundreds of hours of warm memories flooded over us. Fleetwood Mac had always been the soundtrack to our lives.

I could feel the tension in everyone's muscles relax. The kids looked less scared and Dad quit swearing. He paid closer attention to the waves in a more clinical, calculating way, and soon the boat was riding less wildly. We were still taking constant whitewater over the bow as the wind howled through the stays, but we weren't laying over as hard.

We made it through safely that day, and I always carried a cassette of Fleetwood Mac's music with me after that, wherever I went.

• • •

Megan was the next to follow Jamie's exit. Although she could live the wilderness life and could more than keep up in our games of tree tag (chasing each other from branch to branch twenty feet up) and other bush pastimes, she'd always longed for wider pastures for her art and other talents than the wilderness could provide.

She was a phenomenal runner, but she had few opportunities to exploit her abilities. The few times she did participate in an island district meet, she blew past the competition in startling ways. (Chris, too—he'd later break a state record.)

When Rory and Marion moved to the city of Ketchikan, they

Me (seated) and Megan in front of the New House
down at the creek, the year Megan left.

offered to allow Megan to stay with them. The year she turned fifteen she accepted the offer. It was hard on Mom having to let her kids go at such young ages, but she and Dad had brought us up to be independent and know our own minds, so she had little choice in letting first Jamie and then Megan leave.

It was the first time I'd been without Megan's companionship for any serious length of time since she was born.

We only ever got into one fight, and that was when we were teenagers. Mom was so horrified that she went to extreme measures to nip it in the bud. She said, "If you two want to fight, then fight like Robin and Chris. Megan, hit Tara." Megan looked at me and her frown turned into tears. She shook her head. "I don't want to." Mom turned to me, "Tara, hit Megan." The idea was so appalling, I teared up too. We were never again tempted to fight about anything.

Before Megan left we'd started writing a book together about a private investigator named Liam McCall. We alternated chapters and had a blast seeing what the other one had written, trying to outdo each other in absurd details and humorous dialogue. After she left, I didn't have the heart to continue it.

I had recently finished my first full-length book, a Western, and she and I taped our reading the entire book. I read the narration and she read the dialogue, donning a Texan accent for every character. It took us many hours, much laughter, and many takes and retakes to finish it on four cassettes. (We had learned that batteries could be resurrected if you allowed them to sit for a little while. We also used pencils to fast forward and rewind cassettes to save our batteries.)

Writing an entire book took a lot of effort and we had ideas for so many that we took to writing just back cover blurbs and then drawing and coloring the covers, complete with one-sentence hooks: *He gambled her away and had to win her back!*

Every day we'd share with each other what had happened in the books we were reading, each of us suffering through the other's details while waiting impatiently for our turn. At school we put together a dance routine that employed moves from the HBO music videos we'd watched on movie nights going back to the floathouse years.

We no longer played with our Barbie dolls, but we did love to set up dioramas with them on a section of my floor. One time Mom came up and was horrified by one of the dioramas. In it, one doll with a platinum ponytail was casually steering her red Camaro, blowing a huge pink ball of bubble gum. On the hood of her sports car was Ken's head. To the side of the car was a high-stepping Palomino. Beneath its upraised hoof, a swaddled baby lay defenselessly while equestrian Barbie smiled fixedly astride the horse. Elsewhere in the scene, two Barbies had their hands on each other's throats.

Nihilism Barbie for the win.

Megan and I went to a junior prom together, with a brother and sister our age from the village (and Mom coming along to do our makeup and hair and act as chaperone), in the logging community where Dad used to work and commute from. The day after the prom, still wearing our finery, we attended the wedding of Marion's youngest brother Ray, who was more like a cousin than an uncle-by-marriage since he was Jamie's age, to Liz Donahue.

They seemed incredibly young to be getting married, but both of them had already lived more deep experiences than people twice their age. They had both lost brothers in the same fishing boat sinking that Ray barely escaped from when he was sixteen.

It was shortly after the wedding that Rory and Marion sold up and moved to Ketchikan to give their daughters the experience of a city life that Marion had never had. She didn't want her daughters to grow up feeling as socially insecure as many bush kids did when they approached the wider world as adults. Megan joined them in December.

• • •

One day when the boys were driving me crazy with their constant tussling and I was missing Megan, I wandered up the sawdust trail crying. I rarely cried or bothered feeling sorry for myself, but that day life felt particularly tough. It seemed that no one noticed or cared what it was like for me to lose my closest companion from as far back as I could remember.

Something made me look up and I saw Dad up ahead of me, facing me. I hastily wiped my tears away and continued walking because it would have been too awkward to do anything else.

When I got close I looked into his bearded face and tried to think of something casual to say.

He opened his arms.

I walked into them, smelling engine oil and sawdust, and he hugged me.

"I love you, Dad," I said, crying again. How was it that he was the only one who understood what I was going through? A man who was so emotionally shut down after Vietnam that he rarely showed affection, or even acted as if he was aware that the children surrounding him were his own.

He hugged me back. "I love you, too," he whispered.

• • •

Despite the drastically depleted labor force of Dad, Mom, me, and the boys, Mom continued to think up highly impractical, amazing house designs. One day when we were out in the skiff she saw the remains of the cannery fish trap high up on a beach buried in drift and beach grass. Her imagination was sparked and she immediately designed a kitchen nook implementing the massive twelve-by-twelve-inch timbers from the old trap.

So one day we all went down to the fish trap and after we cleared away some drift and brush, Dad measured the huge timbers and cut out what he needed to be able to follow Mom's design, which required two vertical beams and a lintel on top of them, a bit like Stonehenge, which was what we promptly named it.

I was writing a paper about the cannery for a school assignment, so the old trap interested me. I balanced along its huge timbers below the skirts of the forest and wondered about the men who had worked on it.

Had they been in league with the fish pirates who liked to plunder cannery traps? Or had they fought off the local fishermen who came under cover of darkness—blasting a shotgun into the dark to warn them away? Had Pinkerton agents walked these same timbers I stood upon as I paused to look out at the broad bay?

Once Dad had sawed what he needed, he shackled a chain, attached to his jerkline that he pulled logs off the beach with, around the largest timber and dragged first it and then the next heavy timbers down into the water and we towed them home.

Then came the tough slog of getting them to the house. Dad constructed a cradle of ropes with two-by-two-inch handles the length of each beam, like he had with the living room beams and the Earth Stove, and then assigned each of us to a side. With many pauses for breathers, our arms feeling like they were going to be pulled out of their sockets and knees about to give, we finally got all three timbers into the kitchen.

We managed to get the two end pieces vertically into position where Mom directed, and Dad secured them to the wall. But then came the question of how we were going to get the longest and heaviest piece on top of them to form the lintel. The ceiling wasn't high enough for us to rig a rope and tackle the way we'd done for the rafters in the living room. Maybe it couldn't be done?

Of course it could be done. Hadn't the builders of Stonehenge, with nothing more than the same tools we had—our muscles and brains—done the same thing with actual stones, much heavier than these wooden beams?

Dad heaved each end in turn onto one of the table benches. Then onto the table that we'd pressed up against the vertical beams. We kids and Mom then put the bench onto the table and Dad lifted the lintel, one end at a time, onto it, up next to the two uprights. As we got near the tops of them we had to use blocks of wood, sliding them under first one end and then the other until finally Dad could slide the massive beam onto the two uprights.

And we had our very own Stonehenge, Southeast Alaska–style, in our kitchen. I liked to sit at the table across from it and think about what the men who had worked at the cannery would say if they could see it.

• • •

With Megan gone, I buried myself in my writing. I found that I could write, by hand, an entire Western novel in two to three weeks by staying up late and scratching it on paper by lamplight.

Decades before I was born, Mom's grandfather had picked up a faded daybook from an old store building in the ghost town of Garnet in Montana. I used it for research for the books I was writing. I was amazed at the items and their prices that were listed in its old, yellowed pages. I loved to touch it and hold it and feel its connection to the Old West.

The teacher in Meyers Chuck, a dynamic, humorous woman named Patti MacDonald (along with her husband, Paul Mercer, who taught the younger grades) supported and encouraged my writing, arranging for me to run a school newspaper all about the village doings. She also contacted a newspaper in Ketchikan to try to get me a job as a columnist for their weekly supplement.

Knowing my love of reading, Patti arranged for me to anchor our school in the Battle of the Books competition. Bundled up in warm clothes, we had to tramp down the narrow forest trail to reach the village phone near the post office and store. Our breaths hung visibly in the air as we spoke the answers into the receiver.

Patti also set me up with a library account through Juneau's rural mail services department so that I could thoroughly research the cannery for the term paper she'd assigned. She helped me locate an old fisherman who had sold his fish to the cannery and I loved receiving letters from him, hearing about the early days.

He told me that the workers had been primarily Asian—Chinese, Japanese, and Filipino—but there had been men from European nations as well, particularly from Norway. He got a little coy when I asked him if he'd ever pirated the cannery's fish traps and I figured that meant he probably had. With or without the cannery watchman's collusion.

Through the library and the tirelessly helpful mail services librarians, I tried to research when US Steel bought the property but couldn't nail it down. They'd bought it for its possible mineral resources but never developed it. US Steel had been formed by JP Morgan and Elbert H. Gary in 1901 and was, at one time, the largest corporation in the world.

I was fascinated to read that JP Morgan owned the White Star Line, which had built the *Titanic*. In his personal suite aboard the ship he had his own private promenade deck and a bath equipped with specially designed cigar holders. He was reportedly booked on the ship's maiden voyage, but for some reason canceled the trip at the last minute.

Conspiracy theories immediately arose that he arranged for the ship to sink in order to eliminate any threat to his banking empire. Aboard the ship were some of the wealthiest men in the world, including John Jacob Astor IV, Benjamin Guggenheim, and Isidor Straus who were said to be opposed to Morgan's support of creating a Federal Reserve Bank.

As I continued to research, I found that US Steel had eventually tumbled from its lofty position until in 1980, when we moved to the cannery, it began shutting down its steel mills in city after city. I realized that Bruce Springsteen's song "My Hometown" was about this phenomenon—and it gave me a surprising link to him.

• • •

Without Megan there, I spent a lot of my time wandering the cannery by myself. At the end of the sawdust trail, on the cannery side, when I stepped from the shade of the forest into the light, I was immediately confronted by a blackened set of steps. They clung to the skeletal foundations of a missing building.

They fascinated me, those steps that led nowhere. I always made a point of climbing them and standing on the top one, feeling sure that if I only had the key to the invisible door in front of me I could step into Time itself.

I could almost see the shape of it. Was it a circle, where if you start with the past it followed clockwise into the present into the Moving Now, into the future and back again into the past as an endless cycle? Or maybe it was a spiral where the future circled one level above the past.

Time, to me, was like one of the video games Jamie and the boys played. God had designed the broad outlines of our future as we acted in the Moving Now. Every decision, every choice we made, shaped the next part, took us to the next level. The future was ahead of us, already set in its broad outlines, but we could affect how it affected us by our decisions and actions, our free will.

Our choices and the actions we took turned the limitless possibilities, the either/or, into the concrete present. It was an elusive concreteness though, because once the present became the past it began to dissolve, however slowly, like the rusty remains of the fire-scorched cannery ruins.

I thought about déjà vu as I stood on the top step that led to air. That feeling of having a memory of a place you'd never been but you felt like you had lived it. Was déjà vu memories of the future? We obviously had to live a little bit in the future to be able to form our present, a present edited according to our own biases. The Moving Now was a zero bridge between the present and the future. Maybe déjà vu was when our brain lifted the curtain on when we crossed the bridge and for a moment we experienced the raw, pure future as it happened before we edited it.

Every day, rain or shine, I'd climb the steps and wonder about the past when others had lived here. I'd wonder about the present when I stepped on the footsteps of those who had gone before and built these blackened foundations, and I'd wonder about the future... my future. Where would I be one day? Where did these steps lead me?

Sometimes I wandered over to the floathouse side and I'd push against the floathouse's front door that stuck, swollen from the dampness of not having regular heat in it. I'd stand in the silent living room and look out the huge, bullet-pocked window with its sweeping view of the wild bay and remember when it was just Mom and us kids.

I'd go up to the school and look at the clay people still arranged in front of the plexiglass windows. Our last homeschool lesson remained on the chalkboard in Mom's handwriting. Then I'd go and sit on one of the swings in the monumental swing set Dad had made for us out of rooted trees. I'd sit and twist the lines and look around at the forest and think of those immensely free childhood days when we played in the water and built forts all hours of the day, not seeing any other humans, just whales, bears, eagles and wolves.

On the cannery side, I climbed the rocks out at the point where the gigantic steel fuel drum sat on huge timbers and concrete. It was the only thing that remained intact of the cannery, aside from the little cabin across the creek and the other fuel drum behind our house.

I felt dwarfed next to it. With the bay spread out endlessly in front of me, I'd dance on the concrete pad as the sun set in brilliant glowing colors to the music in my Walkman.

*"Nobody believes my stories! It's fiction to everyone.
I have one old Native Alaskan logger friend at work
who whenever I tell stories he tells everyone else to
'shut up and listen. Everything Robin tells you
happened and you had better believe it!'"* —Robin

CHAPTER EIGHTEEN

FOR YEARS my address was FP Union Bay. The FP was an inside joke—we called the ruins Fool's Paradise because only a fool would work so hard to live somewhere and still call it paradise.

After living in the New House for three years we found out that we were, indeed, living in Fool's Paradise.

The catastrophic downturn US Steel experienced in the 1980s forced them not only to sell their steel mills but their undeveloped, remote properties as well. Mr. McKenzie had retired and the new man who dealt with our lease had no history with us and felt no stake in our homesteading difficulties and triumphs.

The lease was a twenty-year lease with option to buy if they ever wanted to sell. Included in the terms was a paragraph that said that if US Steel did decide to sell, whoever bought it had to give us "fair market price" for our "home and improvements." At that point we had a six-bedroom house, shop, trails, boardwalk, bridge, etc., and we'd renovated the little guest cabin across the creek.

Two potential buyers came out from town—the property had been advertised far and wide. One of the buyers was from somewhere in the Lower 48; and the other was from Ketchikan.

It was a shock to us and it happened incredibly fast. One minute we were living our frontier life in the ruins, the next perfect strangers were striding around our home, checking it out with speculative eyes, with a view to buying it.

Although we had the option to buy, we were barely scraping a living as it was. There was no way we could offer what it was worth. But at least, Mom tried to comfort us, we'd be paid for all the work we'd put into the place. It would give us enough to start over somewhere else.

The Lower 48 buyer absolutely loved the place and marveled over all that we'd accomplished, hugely impressed by Dad and his abilities. He wanted to figure out a way where we could continue to live there and help him build his own place using Dad's know-how and lumber-making skills. He told us that he offered the realtor $80,000.

The other man, the local, had come out with the realtor who was handling the deal. According to the realtor they were old friends and school chums. The realtor was impressed with the house, saying that Dad had done a "fantastic job" and that it would make "a wonderful lodge" or "anything!"

The Ketchikan buyer remained noncommittal. The place sold to him, for $60,000, or so we heard from the Lower 48 man who called us, upset about it. But there was nothing he or we could do.

• • •

Before the place sold, in the months when the cannery was being haggled over, I was living in Ketchikan. The previous summer when Megan was home, she talked about how much fun the two of us could have if I went in and stayed with her at Rory and Marion's house in town.

The teacher in the village, Patti, thought it was a good idea for me to get a taste of city school before I went on to college and she pressed the case with Mom. I saw the logic in it and also wanted to be with Megan again—it would be our last chance before we went our separate ways as adults.

Rory and Marion opened their home to me with the ready, hospitable generosity they were known for by everyone in their lives. Living with them was the easiest part of moving to town because wherever they lived had always been our home away from home.

They were the only part of living in town that I felt comfortable with, as it turned out. Megan had formed other friends in her grade and we had almost no classes together so I didn't see that much of her, except when we were back at Rory and Marion's.

I went into it thinking it would be a new adventure, but the city school experience alienated me. First there was the bus ride. I watched as kids boarded at each stop and then were disgorged at school, only to be returned to their spot later in the day. It looked coldly mechanical to me, like Fisher-Price toys being run through a factory on conveyor belts.

Then there were the school bells. I never got accustomed to kids being herded from one class to the next at the strident command of bells. They left one class at the ring of a bell, went to their lockers to switch out books, slammed and locked them, and moved onto the next class. Again and again, throughout the day, every day of their lives.

I'd put my Walkman on, playing Australian Crawl, and escape when the bells rang to wander the deserted ball field until I felt able to return.

The one thing I really enjoyed at school was the day my English teacher gave us our term paper assignment. I perked up and didn't hesitate when asked to write down what my chosen topic would be.

I wrote: Time.

Losing myself in the library in stacks of books, researching all the different takes on time, down through history—for the first time I felt like I belonged; I felt like I was home.

I realized, as I researched my subject, that Town was a spatially dominant world, whereas I'd grown up in a temporally dominant setting.

Town, and the social culture at large, had been shaped according to the limits of current science which dictated that there were three dimensions of space and one, the most obvious and easily graphed one, of time. There was no temporal depth in this world. Each second wasn't lived so much as skated on as if people were afraid—or at least, untrained—to dip deeply into the rich temporal current that our ever-moving existence depends on.

Instead, time had become a social construct, almost an illusion, that only worked and seemed real because everyone agreed to it for convenience's sake. Like the painted lines on the road. The reason

When an artist visited Meyers Chuck School and taught us to make masks, we were asked to make one according to a theme. I chose Time.

they worked was because everyone agreed to abide by what they represented. But if everyone had decided to ignore them and drive anywhere they pleased, they would have ceased to have any meaning, they would have just been paint splashed on the road.

I was a temporal refugee, being told on all sides that I needed to adapt to town life and town ways, that it was simple culture shock. But it wasn't that. I was starving for time in a world populated and formed by temporally malnourished citizens, a world suffering from temporal anorexia.

After graduating from high school (somehow as an honor student, despite my tendency to escape the strident bells and skip classes) I worked at the *Ketchikan Daily Newspaper* as a proofreader. It had odd hours, starting at three in the afternoon and stopping late in the evening. I didn't drive, so I walked home at night, skirting all the downtown bars with the drunks spilling out and propositioning me.

Because Rory and Marion lived so far out, at the end of the road, it had been difficult for Megan and me to attend the many school events that were sometimes required for a grade. Megan decided to ask if she could live with Lance, who lived right in town.

He agreed, and I wound up living there too. Megan had one of the bedrooms and Jamie stayed in the backroom when he was home from fishing. Lance's trailer home was soon overflowing with young people.

He lived on a hill at the opposite end of town from the newspaper so it was a long, thirty-minute walk at night on unfamiliar pavement, breathing in traffic exhaust. On the way I'd stop and buy a burrito at the mini mart and nuke it in their microwave for dinner, or I'd stop in at McDonald's and eat a burger and fries, sitting alone under industrial lighting with the dark city rolling by outside.

One day I decided that living in this time-choked and temporally deficient environment wasn't working for me. I couldn't do it.

I called Mom and Dad and told them I was coming home.

But the truth was, there was no home to go back to.

• • •

Dad offered the Ketchikan buyer the house and the improvements we'd done over the years for $20,000.

The buyer said, "No thanks."

He knew he had it all anyway, and for free. US Steel, under the new manager of remote properties, claimed that because Dad and Mom had been late on a payment they'd broken their lease. The new manager said he didn't have to abide by what Mr. McKenzie had said when he'd assured us that it wouldn't matter.

Once payment for the cannery went through, the buyer gave Dad and Mom a few weeks to clear out, so they worked their butts off. Their only option was to move back into the floathouse. It was in bad repair after sitting for three years without heat in that damp climate.

They needed beams and they needed lumber to refloor the living room and repanel the bathroom, but Dad didn't have time to mill it all. In fact, he had to pack up the sawmill. So he wrote and told the new owner that he'd either sell him the lumber and beams in the house for $3,000 (which, with roofing and everything else, if he'd bought it from a dealer, he'd have had to pay at least ten times that much for it).

If he didn't buy it, Dad said, he'd take what he needed from the house. The guy apparently thought Dad was bluffing and that he wouldn't go to all that work.

The buyer said, "No dice."

He probably thought he was going to get a huge, six-bedroom house for free that, as his realtor friend had said, could be turned into a lodge. But that's not how it worked out.

Dad took from the New House whatever he needed. He took up flooring. He took down the paneling in Chris's room, the louvered doors from the pantry, the bookcases in the game room. He stripped the house of anything usable.

And then he went in with a chainsaw and took those big beams down. He needed them for support under the workshop he had to build to put his tools and sawmill in, and at the same time he was remodeling the floathouse.

He wrote and told the guy, "Beware of the house, its support structure and beams are all gone, it'll cave in under the first heavy snow-load."

He didn't dismantle it in anger and didn't want anyone getting hurt. He was, at that point, sunk deep into a depression at losing the cannery and all he'd put into it. It was a depression that he wouldn't come out of for many years to come. Mom was just as devastated at losing her dream.

People told us later that the new owner put it out that we were squatters who had to be evicted from his property. This was interesting since for years afterward my parents continued to be billed for the lease until the twenty years were up.

Aside from a house that would cave in, the new owner had acquired trails and boardwalk, bridge, clearings, shop, guest cabin, etc. for which he'd have paid a fortune, way out there, to have had built. Every nail, board, and material and workers would have had to be barged or flown in. Yet the new owner was, we were told by locals, perturbed that we'd left the place in a mess.

Our forts throughout the woods might have been considered junk, I suppose. And with the short amount of time he gave for us to clear out, we didn't have time to tidy up our withdrawal. But we were told that what so disturbed him were all the twisted bedsteads and cannery equipment, the rusty machinery that littered the beaches, woods, and wherever we had not yet gotten cleared.

If he'd seen a burned-down salmon cannery the way we first saw it, odds were good he'd never have thought of buying it.

It took a Romi Neilson, with her limitless imagination, to see the potential for one family to bring it to life; and it took a Gary Neilson, with his limitless ability, to think, "I can do this," and then do it. And it took an entire family of seven giving their all to accomplish it.

• • •

When I got there, they had the floathouse ready to move into. They'd even put in a new hearth using cannery bricks. The boys and I helped ferry everything from the New House to the other side, including the heavy Earth Stove.

In the few weeks they had, besides getting the floathouse in shape, Dad also finished building his floating workshop.

I needed a place of my own, so Dad took the chainsaw and cut down the swing set in front of the school, and he put together yet another float and positioned it below the school. With poles leading to the float, he used his logging winch to pull the building onto the float logs.

I watched in disbelief as the school shook and shuddered, sure that there was no way he was going to get it squarely on the float. I winced, waiting for it to fall off either side of the poles. But, like usual, he knew exactly what he was doing, and the school settled perfectly into place.

The filing cabinet and desk that I'd carried across the trail four years before to put in my bedroom, I transferred back into the school. I used some of the steel core sample holders for a heat shield behind my stove. Megan's cottonwood paneling I put up on the school's bare two-by-four framed walls, and I sanded the floor and painted it cannery red, like the floor in the little cabin across the creek.

Finally, we were ready to set sail.

But there was one last thing I had to do. I spent one entire day walking all over the property, saying goodbye to every fort, every piece of cannery debris half buried in the moss in the quiet, familiar forest.

In a way the cannery was saying goodbye to us, too, saying goodbye to being lived in again since it was now owned as an investment, not a home, to be sold from one buyer to the next. Absentee owners would from then on take the place of year-around family, of constant life and motion in the ruins. It would sleep again in the shadow of the mountain.

I visited the grave markers on the point. I stepped inside the fire tree, touched the ancient burn. I crossed the sun-dappled sawdust trail that Megan and I had helped build while wearing a gun to ward off bears and wolves. I walked the boardwalk to the house one last time, but didn't go inside. It was too dangerous without its supports. I crossed the creek and looked in the little cabin where we'd spent our most memorable summer.

Back across the golden creek, below the remains of the bridge Dad had built, I laid my hand on the huge concrete block standing firm against time and current, remembering all the times we'd climbed and played around it.

I wandered through the pilings one last time, touched the twisted machinery we'd played with our dolls on, and crumbled a stack of concretized canning lids. And then I knelt and with a Mason jar I scooped up some of the rusty red pebbles and put them in the jar. I screwed a lid on and promised myself that I'd never open it. That I'd keep the air of the ruins, our home, forever inside it.

I walked back to the steps attached to the skeletal foundation of a ghost building. I climbed them slowly, climbed where I'd climbed a hundred times before, and when I got to the top I looked out at the bay. It stretched to Prince of Wales Island and beyond it to the largest ocean on our water planet. Behind me the forest reached up to the mountain that stared into space where galaxies swam in a current of time.

I thought about the house behind me, how it would collapse in the first big snowfall. It, with all our memories, all our work, my bedroom, Stonehenge… in time it would all be swallowed by the forest and our ruins would meld with the cannery ruins forever. Our childish shouts, the barking dogs, the memory of us would be united with the memory of the workers who had gone before.

No matter where we went or what was taken from us, those children would always be here, running free.

I stood at the top of the steps, one last time, and wondered where the future would take me.

THREE UNION BAY
CANNERY WORKERS

*"Gunboat interrupted, thinking that the old man was talking about
the Biblical hell, saying hell was but an imaginary place used as
a contrast for another imaginary place called heaven, and that
the whole thing was but so much mythology handed to us by our
ancestors. Bert and the Hindu soon joined us in the debate and the
rest of the day was spent in spirited outbursts of oratory... Anyway,
we solved the riddle of the Universe and that's something."*
—cannery worker Louis Evan, in a letter home sharing what life
was like and the sorts of conversations held at the cannery
(from *Three Salmon Summers: Working in Alaska Canneries 1909,
1937, 1939*, edited by Lucinda Hill Hogarty)

· · ·

WHEN I was growing up in the ruins, I spent a lot of time thinking
about the unknown cannery workers who had lived and worked
at the Union Bay cannery. I imagined who they were, what their
activities and conversations involved, and what sort of lives they
returned to when they left the cannery.

It wasn't until I was an adult and had access to the Internet that I
was able to find the stories of three workers. Amazingly, two of them
later became internationally known; but I think it was the third

man's story that touched me the most.

During a recent phone call with the grandson of one of the cannery workers, I kept marveling to myself that I was speaking to a relative of someone who'd worked at the cannery. When I disconnected I wished I could join my younger self as she wandered the ruins and tell her all about it.

Of all the debris that intrigued me as I wandered the ruins, one drew me the most: the giant circular door of the cannery's retort, through which millions of cans of caught and cubed salmon had gone to their rest. It had served as a sort of travel portal for the fish. They'd spent their life in the underworld wilderness of the ocean, to be raised into the light and sent, in cans, to that distant, noisy world of constant motion.

I was fascinated by the portal, and I'd walk on its ring as it lay partially buried in the gravel. It seemed like an ancient device of mystery. I almost believed I could step through it and walk out into the other present of when the cannery had been alive. As if it, fittingly circular, was the zero bridge between space and time.

And I'd finally get to meet the real, living people who had worked and lived there before I was born.

• • •

LI GONGPU
July–September 1928

For ten hours straight, he stood feeding sheets of tin into the can-making machine. His shoulders and knees burned with pain and he almost suffocated in the heat and the incredible stench of rotting fish entrails which combined with sewage and seaweed and surged endlessly under the foundation pilings of the cannery buildings.

The stench impregnated everything—clothes, wood, food, even the steel of the machines—and was impossible to escape. Likewise the constant, rhythmic thumping of the piles being driven at all hours for the fish trap.

He, who was more accustomed to reading, debating, and writing, was wryly impressed that he was able to withstand the long hours. None of his academic friends would believe it. Thankfully, as soon as the fish run began to dwindle, so did his hours standing and feeding the sheets into the can-maker. But day after day, he continued at the job of cutting out circular pieces of tin that would be made into cans, and soon enough a curious thing happened.

As he repeated the same movements again and again, hour after hour, his tender hands—more accustomed to holding a pen—toughened with calluses, and he became a part of the automated machinery.

Four- to five-thousand three-foot-long salmon were gutted, cleaned, canned, cooked, labeled, and packed in a matter of hours. And he was just another smooth working piece of rumbling gears and cogs in the busy cannery perched at the edge of a great waterway, surrounded by a vast wilderness of temperate rain forest, completely cut off from the civilized world and the academia he came from.

Li Gongpu (sometimes spelled Gongbu), born in 1902, was twenty-six years old and studying at Reed College in Portland, Oregon, when he first hatched the idea of going undercover as a common laborer to document the experience of cannery workers in remote Alaska.

He was part of a large movement of well-off young Chinese who, because of the lack of opportunities for higher education in their native homeland, invested in a university education in America during the 1920s. In the process, these young intellectuals absorbed the patterns of American higher education and brought back ideas for change in their home country.

Li was already a well-known progressive thinker who wrote for the Shanghai magazine *Life* (*Shenhuo*) when he decided to become an undercover cannery worker, but he was confident that no one at the remote cannery in Union Bay, Alaska, would recognize him. He was right.

The year before Li's arrival at the cannery, Chinese contractors had provided most of the workers for the cannery. Until then it had been common for Chinese contractors to exploit and cheat the workmen, serving them cheap rice, tea, and scrap fish from the cannery while they pocketed a significant proportion of the money the company paid for provisions.

In desperation, the Chinese hands—who weren't paid until

Academic Li Gongpu went under cover at the
Union Bay cannery in 1928. (Public Domain)

the end of the season (if then)—supplemented their meager diets
by keeping gardens and gathering plants and shellfish, bartering
for anything extra (for example, the feet and gall bladders of bears,
which was used as folk medicine) with local Alaska Natives. To keep
the overworked, hungry laborers from protesting, the contractors
supplied them with opium. A stoned worker was a happy worker.
The year before Li's arrival, the cannery owners fired the Chinese
contractors for mismanagement and gave the contract to the Japanese.

Once Li adapted to the work, the pain lessened, and he was able
to concentrate on his mission. He noted in his journal the instances
of prejudice that he and his intellectual friends had expected to find.
He was surprised by how many nationalities were represented at the
cannery, describing them in his diary as a "mini United Nations."

"Even though the cannery hires only about 100 workers," he
wrote, "this place is like a mini world, with people of many colors
and nationalities. For instance, Americans are the obvious white,
Japanese and Chinese are the obvious yellow. There are also several
tens of native Americans who I can call reds, Filipinos are brown,
those originally from Africa are black. These people come from
China, Japan, Korea, the Philippines, Mexico, Italy, Switzerland and

even some undocumented workers from other places."

The way they arranged themselves by color into separate areas and hierarchies did not surprise him at all. He wrote that the laborers "work, eat, and sleep in separate masses according to their ethnic affiliations. White people are a group; Japanese, Chinese, and Koreans another group; Filipinos belong to yet another. Blacks and Alaskan Indians sleep and eat as a group since they are mostly involved in fishing."

It amused him when undereducated European immigrants and Americans assumed they knew more than he, and how they trusted that they were more deserving of better treatment because of their naturally privileged position in the world. Little did they know that they had a mole from the ivory towers of academia spying on them.

Finding somewhere lonesome to concentrate on his conclusions, such as on a rock overlooking the bay where bald eagles rode the thermals above it and humpback whales spouted, he would muse in his diary: "By observing the interaction among workers, one can discern their psychology formed by the perceived status of their own countries in the world. The white workers come from probably more than 30 different countries. But about half of them were not educated. They speak rudimentary English but see themselves as the most civilized people of the world. Japanese workers are very polite to the white people but very arrogant to people of other nationalities. Filipinos appear self-important in front of the reds and blacks. The few Chinese, though with similar 'yellow' skin color and look as Japanese, do not get treated as courteously as the Japanese workers, probably because of China's relatively low international political status…"

Despite his best intentions, he found himself drawn away from his intended scathing exposé as he was seduced by the scenery and breathtaking sunsets of the cannery's location.

The Union Bay cannery faced an enormous open bay, with a peninsula to the south. Looking westward, far across the changeable waters, were the snow-capped blue mountains of a nation-sized island. The sun sank behind it every evening and on sunny days it colored the sky and the sea with swaths of color, so intense it defied description.

On overcast days when the mists drifted down from the

mountain, Li inhaled the forest-fresh air and wandered the shady boardwalk. It led through towering, old-growth evergreens, and as his boots clumped over the boards he made notes about the stream that emptied into the small bay at the other end of the boardwalk where the superintendent's house stood.

The building was separated from the stench of the cannery and its polluted creek full of spawned, rotting salmon that the sea gulls shrieked over and the bears shredded with their long claws. The smaller, clean stream provided the cannery's drinking water and the water used for cleaning and processing the fish, he wrote.

While the other workers entertained themselves during their free time playing chess and cards, gambling, debating, sleeping, swimming, playing music, and dancing with the Native girls down on the beach when the tide was out, Li liked to find a quiet place away from the stink and noise of the cannery, and during the long, northern summer days he'd soak in the birdsong and rustling of the breeze slipping through the underbrush while he caught up on his reading.

When he returned to the cannery, he particularly enjoyed listening to the Native girls sharing their songs. Their language was incomprehensible to him, but the sound of their singing fell sweetly on ears starved for the social refinements of life, especially after a working day full of raised male voices in a multitude of languages and the unending uproar of the processing machines, and the hiss and bang of the huge retort doors after stacks of cans were slid inside to be sealed.

The only contact with the broader world was through the mail boat that brought supplies and letters every two to three weeks. Li mailed off his diary entries to his editor at *Life* magazine in faraway Shanghai, a city that was suffering from severe political agitation. Earlier that spring the Shanghai massacre occurred when the Communist Party of China was violently suppressed by the military forces of Chiang Kai-shek and conservative factions in the Kuomintang (Nationalist Party). In city after city, more violent Communist purges took place all that summer while Li worked at the cannery.

Li was passionately opposed to violence and war. He wasn't surprised that the world at large, with its prejudices and segregation based on arbitrary privilege, couldn't find its way to a lasting peace, but despite the upheaval in his native country, he believed that a people of one race and one nation should find common ground and peace.

As his summer outside of time progressed, his favorite moments were the solitary hours spent late in the evenings going fishing. His boots crunched on shells and the musky scent of pop weed filled the air as the golden creek tumbled over rounded rocks glinting in the brilliant and extreme light just before the sun set.

He had time, as he fished amongst the teeming fins in the shade of rustling alder trees, to absorb this eternal moment. Behind him, the red-painted, white-trim buildings resting on concrete blocks and pilings, glowed in the trenchant sunshine. He cast his line and wondered about his future, the future of China, and where humanity was headed.

Li Gongpu became a high-profile anti-war protestor and university professor after his return to China. He was beaten up by government agents for his objections to the Chinese Civil War, but he was not intimidated. In 1946, one year before the Union Bay cannery burned, secret agents of the Kuomintang assassinated Li Gongpu in Kunming as he left a theater with his wife.

The famous scholar, poet, and popular literature professor Wen Yiduo, who was a close friend, gave Li's funeral oration despite being warned by friends that it was too dangerous. After standing up to give an inspiring oration on behalf of Li and the beliefs they both shared, Wen Yiduo was gunned down.

US President Harry Truman sent a personal letter protesting the assassinations to Chinese President Chiang Kai-shek on August 10, 1946. He wrote that the assassination of such distinguished Chinese liberals would not be ignored and that resorting to force and military or secret police rather than democratic processes to settle major social issues revealed a lack of understanding about the liberal trend of the times. "The people of the United States view with violent repugnance this state of affairs," Truman concluded.

Fei Xiantong, one of China's leading social scientists, wrote that "Li Gongpu's blood marks a new turning point in the history of the Chinese people's struggle for democracy."

Today there exists a beautifully cared for Li Gongpu Tomb on the grounds of Kunming Normal University in China.

Historians believe that Li Gongpu's written experiences at the Union Bay cannery are the only firsthand Chinese accounts of Alaskan cannery work before World War II.

• • •

GEORGE TSUTAKAWA
Summers 1930–1935

George Tsutakawa, born in Seattle, Washington, in 1910, was an artist whose belief that man is a part of nature allowed him to conceptualize and create sublime fountain sculptures that earned him worldwide recognition.

Tsutakawa, a second-generation Japanese American, was named for the first president of the United States, George Washington. His father, Shozo Tsutakawa, was a successful businessman whose export-import business forged connections between Seattle and the Japanese ports of Kobe, Osaka, and Tokyo. The Tsutakawas lived in a fashionable part of Seattle in a spacious house complete with servants, including a governess.

However, in 1924, the Alien Land Law (intended to limit the ability of Asian and other so-called "non-desirable" immigrants to own land and property and thus discourage them from settling permanently in the US) forced Shozo to give up his home, but his business continued to prosper.

Due to worsening attitudes and legalities, Tsutakawa and his siblings were sent to Japan to live with their grandmother, Mutsu Naito, in Fukuyama. She took Tsutakawa and his brother to the theater and sent them to study with a Zen master, who taught them philosophy, pottery making, and the tea ceremony. She had a samurai warrior's suit of armor that had been in their family for four hundred years and Tsutakawa was, on special occasions, allowed to wear it. They continued to live with her when their mother died of the Spanish Influenza and Shozo remarried.

Tsutakawa recalled that Fukuyama was "a very, very old town with a castle in the middle, a beautiful picturesque old city... there was a small group of painters, who had studied in Tokyo, and they were telling us about Picasso, Matisse, and showing reproductions of their works." There and then, he decided to become an artist.

This resulted in his being sent back to Seattle when he was sixteen and no longer retained any of his English. While he worked at the family business, he also attended high school and college, determined to become an American art student. His focus narrowed onto printmaking and sculpture. Like any modern teenager or college student, he bought a radio and record player, and as many albums of music (he preferred the classics) as he could afford.

In order to pay for his own tuition, Tsutakawa headed north to work in the Alaskan canneries. He ended up in the small, isolated cannery located in Union Bay, thirty-five miles north of Ketchikan, accessible only by water or air. One summer's pay amounted to $150, which, during the Depression, was enough to pay for his tuition, his books, streetcar fare, and hot lunches. "It paid for just about everything," he later said.

Cannery conditions had improved considerably from the time he was born, when the hell ships bore unwilling Japanese workers to labor unceasingly for little pay and almost no food at the "slime line," but it was a far cry from the civility of his grandmother's home, or his early home in Seattle. Tsutakawa didn't let that get in the way of his desire to be an artist, regardless of the work he had to do in order to achieve his dreams.

He soon discovered that the work was strenuous, monotonous, and unending. Fishing boats, or cannery barges (scows), would arrive at high tide at the cannery pier and the salmon—sockeye, coho, and pinks—were pitched into an elevator that lifted them and slid them into the cannery.

Tsutakawa's day typically started at 6 a.m. and ended at 6 p.m., but when the salmon were running he and the others would work well into the night, when the high-latitude sun barely set, to get the fish processed and canned before it spoiled.

Japanese workers stood for endless hours with their hands immersed in cold running water, scooping the viscera out of innumerable fish cavities. This was the job of "slimers." In earlier times, down the line, other nationalities (cannery work was arranged

George Tsutakawa painting on the beach. He worked at the Union Bay cannery and painted scenes of it in the 1930s. (Courtesy of Kizamu Tsutakawa)

by nationality) would have cubed the fish which were tapped into cans with a pinch of salt by the "table men." The cans, weighed and topped at the "patching table," were subject to the "crimpers" who used pliers to close the cans and then soldered the lids. But all of that work was now done by a machine, the "Iron Chink." In fact, most of the work was now done by machines and conveyor belts, but they had to be manned, directed, inspected, and guided by men.

The sealed cans, stacked in towering squares, were wheeled into the retorts (immense, barrel-like pressure cookers) to steam for an hour. Then the hot cans were vented, checked for leaks (resealed, if necessary), and returned for a second cooking. Afterward, they were sent to the cooling shed where an unmusical cacophony of lids pinging and popping as they cooled would ring out all day, every day.

The finished cans were slapped with the company label, stacked in boxes—they and the cans were made by cannery workers—and stored in the warehouse until the end of the season.

Despite the long hours and hard work, Tsutakawa's interest in art remained at the forefront of his mind. In his downtime he took the opportunity to visit the nearby native village and study the carvings on ceremonial buildings. He was interested in the totem poles, not only as intriguing pieces of art, but also as marvels of engineering: they were able to withstand many years of hurricane force winds. He made a point of talking to the Tlingit carvers about their art.

And he pursued his own art. Whenever he had the time he used watercolors to paint the cannery buildings with their white-trimmed, twelve-paned windows as they lined the pier, creating a lonely wooden alley that was littered with wood-stave barrels, a spool of line, fishing dories, stacks of canned salmon, and a long-handled flatbed cart to move them.

His artist's eye was caught by the colors and contrasts. He set up his canvas and paints on the bridge that spanned the creek to capture the frontier feel of the cannery with its red-with-white-trim buildings surrounded by the evergreen forest and embraced by berry bushes. Boardwalks wound between the buildings as they jutted out on pilings into the bay. In the distance Lemesurier Point was visible at the tip of Cleveland Peninsula. On the other side of that point was the fishing community of Meyers Chuck with a post office, barbershop, bakery, and bar.

His paintings are curiously absent of people and when he painted the huge fuel drum on the rock bluffs, with its attached shack and a boardwalk leading to it, and a pier out in front for boats to moor at when they took on fuel, it looks abandoned. Perhaps he subconsciously wished to have the cannery to himself without the distraction of bustling, shouting humans cluttering up the scenery.

When he returned to Washington, Tsutakawa created linocuts of fish, fishermen, fishing boats, the cannery, and Alaska. He created a self-portrait in one of the linocuts that captures a sense of lonesome tranquility. It shows him in a surprisingly civilized cannery bunkhouse seated in front of a writing table reading a book below an eight-paned window, adorned with drapes. On the wall behind him is a framed picture and beside the desk a bookcase bulging with weighty tomes.

Out the open door he recreated one of the most identifiable landmarks in the Clarence Strait–Union Bay area, Castle Mountain on Prince of Wales Island, with its three distinct turrets, the middle one larger than the two flanking peaks.

A linocut titled "Inspiration" shows a man standing on a

smooth mound overlooking a wide expanse of what could be water, reminiscent of the large, smooth rock at the entrance to the superintendent's inlet on the other side of the peninsula from the noisy cannery. The man is standing with arms akimbo amidst rays of sunshine or rain, or a combination of the two—what Southeast Alaskans call liquid sunshine—soaking up the rawness and expansiveness of Alaska's dramatic landscape. It's easy to imagine a man with an artistic imagination exulting in the mind-expanding breadth of the scene.

Other linocuts reveal Union Bay cannery at its busiest, a hive of industry, an outpost of busy civilization in the wild hinterlands. In "Longshore, Union Bay" he depicts a scene inside the cannery warehouse with its barn-like doors open onto the pier. On the right a ship dwarfs the cannery pier and its buildings as it winches aboard crates of canned salmon while in the foreground men haul boxes to large flatbed trolleys, maneuvered by a long handle. The ship is so out of proportion to the tiny workers and even the cannery that it gives a sense of the vast outside world suddenly intruding on the isolated post.

Another linocut, "'Iron Chink' or 'Slimer' (Union Bay Cannery, Alaska)," shows two men dressed in slickers and rubber boots and hats working by the light of a bare lightbulb in front of a giant machine complete with belts and wheels. They stand on planks stretched across two wooden boxes at a table heaped with salmon, eviscerating them and feeding them to the machine. There is a sense that the men, though standing side by side, are immersed in their own thoughts, isolated inside their own minds by the racket around them. Beyond the machine neat rows of cans are conveyed upward out of sight. It's an unsettling *Brave New World* scene, encapsulating the strangeness of how efficiently and matter-of-factly man can turn what was once a wild and free, living creature into a product.

Most remarkably, Tsutakawa made his most detailed linocut of the cannery itself, imagining it from a birds-eye point of view far above the creek. The tall pier on its multitude of pilings stretches far out into the bay, with a building on the end that must have been coated in sea spray and in danger of being blown away in the powerful northerlies that strike that unprotected shore. More buildings (the cannery, warehouse, commissary, and so on) crowd between the pier, the forest, and the creek. The radio shack sits next to what is most likely the power plant (where one day a fire would start and burn down the cannery), the antenna post towering above the trees.

It is a compact, tight-knit community, surrounded by the unlimited reach of bay, sweeping sky, and distant, faded mountains, iconoclastic and quaint in its 1930s enterprise.

With his cannery summers behind him, Tsutakawa found his art student days giving way to World War II. Japanese Americans, with the bombing of Pearl Harbor, had their property confiscated and were incarcerated by the tens of thousands in internment camps. The Tsutakawa family business was no exception, and neither were Tsutakawa's uncles who operated it while his father was in Japan. Tsutakawa volunteered for the US Army, where he was commissioned by officers to paint their portraits.

After the war Tsutakawa married Ayame Kyotani, a woman who had been forced to live in one of the internment camps, whose brother was killed at Hiroshima. They began a family, eventually having four children (who would later establish themselves in the fields of art and music). Tsutakawa was recruited to a faculty position at the University of Washington after receiving his MFA. A popular and generous teacher, he taught design courses in the School of Architecture, and later taught in the School of Art.

In his lifetime, he managed to try his hand at an astonishing diversity of art forms, media, and styles. In 1960 he "developed the fountain sculpture of fabricated bronze and completed seventy-five major commissions in the United State, Canada and Japan" (Mayumi Tsutakawa, *They Painted from Their Hearts: Pioneer Asian American Artists*, University of Washington: 1994). These fountains would bring him worldwide fame.

They were not typical jetting, or squirting fountains, but instead were created so that water would fall naturally over his sculpted shapes. "My fountain sculptures are an attempt to unify water—the life force of the universe that flows in an elusive cyclical course throughout eternity—with an immutable metal sculpture," he wrote in 1982.

In recognition of his contributions to art and culture, George

Tsutakawa received two honorary doctorate degrees, as well as achievement awards from the Emperor of Japan and the National Japanese American Citizen's League. He died in 1997 at the age of eighty-seven.

Tsutakawa appears to be the only Southeast Alaskan cannery worker, while a resident, to have captured in paint a pre-WWII Alaskan cannery.

• • •

INGEBRIGT (EDWARD) SINNES
1930S–1940S

The Southeast Alaskan city of Petersburg, not too far north of the Union Bay cannery, was founded by a Norwegian by the name of Peter Buschmann at the turn of the twentieth century. Today, this fishing town is known as Little Norway and has the tidy, colorful appearance reminiscent of the land of Buschmann's birth.

Peter's son, Eigil Buschmann, started the Nakat Packing Corporation with a partner named Haakon Friele, and together they eventually owned and operated six canneries in Southeast Alaska with 800 employees, producing an average 250,000–300,000 cases of salmon annually, 650,000 cases in peak years.

One of the six canneries was in Union Bay where a Norwegian by the name of Ingebrigt Sinnes worked.

Norway was well represented in the Alaskan fishing and cannery scene for good reason. In the late nineteenth century and early twentieth centuries, Norway lost as many citizens to American immigration as had comprised her total population in 1800. Many of them settled in the Midwest but were drawn toward the West Coast, feeling a familiarity with the land and lifestyle that was in many ways similar to their homeland.

Simple chain migration followed, as the immigrants sent letters and prepaid tickets home urging family to follow them. In addition, there were the snake oil promotional efforts by steamship and railroad agents who traveled around the country, telling fairytales about America in order to sell more tickets. Many of these Norwegian immigrants (but not all) just missed being on the *Titanic*.

Sinnes was exposed to all this talk, letters others sent home, and the stories his father told of being in America a few years earlier, so it's not surprising that he became infected by "American fever," as so many of his countrymen had been before him.

In photos he appears to be of average height with lean good looks (complete with a cleft chin) that bring to mind such film legends as Gary Cooper, Gregory Peck, and Cary Grant. He gazes directly into the camera with a slight smile and an air of easy, good nature. While the others with him look of their time, he looks like he could step through the camera into the present and fit right in.

Ingebrigt Johansen Sinnes was born in 1898 in Hemne, Norway, about twenty-five miles from the town where Peter Buschmann, the founder of Petersburg (and, as noted, father to one of the future owners of the Union Bay cannery), came from.

Sinnes was fourth out of six siblings in a working-class family. He found, as he came of age, that times were hard with no work to be found. The stories about America called to him, though by the time he was twenty-five and ready to make the journey there was now a quota system, restricting the number of immigrants that the US government permitted annually from any one country. He and a friend managed to make it into the quota for 1923.

Sinnes traveled with his friend Torger Stolsmo aboard the ship MS *Stavangerfjord* to Ellis Island, just outside of a modern New York City lit by electricity and kept up to date by telephone, at a time when "bootleggers and prohibition agents were killing each other in pitched battles on city streets and country roads, and occasionally killing an innocent bystander" (Mark Sullivan, *Our Times: The United States 1900–1925, VI The Twenties*, Charles Scribner's Sons: New York, 1935). At the same time, young people were dropping dead of overexertion from the popular stunt of "Marathon dancing." Exposure to the mad pace of NYC life must have been a shock to their Old World sensibilities, and apparently they reacted differently to it.

Working as loggers to pay their way, they traveled on to Minnesota where Stolsmo had family already established. At the same time, President Warren G. Harding was in the news for deciding to cross the continent by presidential train to vacation in Alaska. Was that when Sinnes first got the idea of heading for Alaska himself?

Left to right: Norwegians Ingebrigt (Ed) Sinnes, his friend Torger Stolsmo, and Stolsmo's uncle when Sinnes first arrived in America in 1923.
(Courtesy of Ove Korsnes)

In the photos, his friend Stolsmo resists the camera and appears nowhere near as forward looking or open natured as Sinnes. Stolsmo looks less committed to or certain of the adventure they've embarked on, possibly alienated by what he'd seen of America so far. In one picture, he has his back to Sinnes, turned unmistakably toward the comfort of his already established uncle. Sinnes looks unaware of his friend's ambivalence. He looks straight ahead, clearly ready and willing to experience whatever America has to offer him.

They parted ways. Sinnes, who had decided to Americanize his first name to Edward (Ed for short), was ready to follow this adventure all the way across the continent while Stolsmo was content to stay behind in the more established Midwest Scandinavian strongholds that had been settled for nearly seventy-five years at that point and still practiced the ways and language of the homeland.

Sinnes was apparently undeterred from following in the President's tracks to head for Alaska, even when the newspapers revealed that Alaska had been none too good for Harding's health. The trip had to be cut short and on the way back President Harding died of pneumonia complicated by a heart condition.

Before he reached Alaska, Sinnes worked as a logger (a faller) in the 1930s in Northern Washington. As Europe plunged into a conflict that would escalate into WWII, Sinnes arrived in Ketchikan, Alaska. It was the territory's largest city and first port of call for the fishing fleets, where totem poles could be seen in front yards alongside wooden streets and stairs that climbed verdant hillsides. Many of the downtown buildings and streets were built on pilings over the water, which had made it easy for Prohibition rum runners, with easily obtained Canadian liquor, to bring their boats in at low tide under the city and lift their illegal cargo through the trapdoors in the red-light district.

Sinnes apparently couldn't find work in the Ketchikan canneries, so he looked further afield—or perhaps he was drawn to the wilderness from the start. In any event, he wound up working at the isolated Union Bay cannery. (In 1942, Sinnes took a brief break from the cannery to work as a logger on Prince of Wales Island, building rafts of high-grade spruce to send to the mills in Anacortes, Washington. There the spruce would be peeled for plywood for use in constructing British bombers.)

Sinnes wasn't much of a letter writer, but he dutifully scratched out letters to his parents in Norway. These missives were so sketchy as to frustrate his loved ones who, understandably, wanted to hear all the details of his new life in America. Over the years they became more difficult to read as his Norwegian became more and more Americanized.

In one he writes of the difficulties of getting paid on time and how difficult it was to get or send mail at the Union Bay cannery. (The nearest post office was in Meyers Chuck, only seven miles by water away, but the journey could only be made on a weather-permitting basis.) He marvels at how he's lost track of time, especially when he hears that his younger brother, who was a little boy when he left, had gotten married. He also writes about getting ready to build a "big house" at the cannery, but doesn't say for what purpose.

In one letter home, Sinnes tells his parents that he doesn't think he'll ever marry because his way of life has nothing to offer a bride. He left out the problem of scarcity: Norwegian men outnumbered Norwegian women in the Pacific Northwest, and particularly the Territory of Alaska, by a good margin. Nevertheless, Sinnes managed to snag the attention of and marry, on December 21, 1941, a clear-eyed, direct, and unaffected young Norwegian woman fifteen years his junior named Signe.

They were unable to have children and at the beginning of World War II, when Sinnes was working as watchman* for the Union Bay cannery, he suffered a catastrophic injury. A steel cable used to brail fish from the boats snapped and struck him in the back of the legs, cutting them severely.

"The thing I feared worst," one cannery worker is reported to have said, "was that there were no doctors or medical facilities." The Union Bay cannery was unapproachable by anything but boat or seaplane, weather permitting. It is unknown how long it was before Sinnes was seen by a medical professional, but by the time he was, it was too late. A bad infection had set in and the doctors were forced to amputate both legs.

He and Signe moved south to Seattle, where she worked as a waitress and he worked in a toy store. Ingebrigt "Ed" Sinnes's Alaskan adventure and cannery days were over, but he had a lifetime of exciting memories to look back on. He died in 1958 at the age of sixty.

---

* I'm curious about the fact that Sinnes worked as a watchman brailing fish. The main watchman job was a winter/off-season caretaker job which didn't involve fish, since there were no winter salmon runs.

There was another watchman job. It involved pile-and-net fish traps, which local fishermen hated for the way they rapidly depleted the fish stock. Much pirating of them occurred, and these fish pirates soon became local heroes, but scoundrels to the cannery owners. The canneries hired a round-the-clock watchman for each trap, but often he sided with the fishermen and under cover of darkness, for a fee, would allow the pirates to loot the traps. They promptly sold these pilfered fish back to the cannery. In frustration the owners replaced the watchmen with Pinkertons (professional detectives).

If Ed Sinnes was one of these watchmen, he would have been there when the fish were brailed aboard boats to be taken fresh to the cannery. He could have been both a caretaker and a trap watchman, since in his letters he speaks of working at the cannery in winter. In that case, he would have lived at the cannery year around and experienced it the way we did. If he was a trap watchman, he didn't live to see them outlawed. A year after Ed Sinnes died, when Alaska attained statehood, fish traps were banned.

ACKNOWLEDGEMENTS

I HAVE been amazingly fortunate in having found out so much about three men who worked in such a small Southeast Alaskan cannery. While quite a bit is known about the actual workings of Alaska's historical canneries, the individual workers and their stories have all too often been lost and forgotten.

Thankfully, Li Gongpu, George Tsutakawa, and Ingebrigt Sinnes will not be forgotten. It has been a privilege getting to know these men, as well as their ideas, beliefs, art, and their families.

My deep gratitude goes to Ove Korsenes of Norway for sharing the story of his grand uncle's life. In addition to many emails, he sent me photos and translated Ed Sinnes's letters for my benefit. George Tsutakawa's family, especially Gerald and Kizamu Tsutakawa, have been generous with their time in emails and phone calls and, most wonderfully, in sharing watercolor paintings of the cannery that George Tsutakawa painted while he worked there. It was beyond thrilling to see the cannery through his eyes, as it was in its heyday.

The librarians working in the rural/mail services department at the Juneau Public Library have been assisting me in my writing career since I was fifteen, and have not slacked off in helping me during the writing of this memoir, with special thanks to Julie Coghill and Maggie Thompson-Johnston.

Lucinda Hogarty shared letters of family members who worked

at Alaskan canneries during the time the Union Bay cannery operated in her book *Three Salmon Summers*. It gave me a lot of insight into everyday cannery life, and I'd like to thank her for kindly giving permission to quote from the book.

Terry Levin of Chicago has been unfailingly supportive, and kindly sent me the movie *The Silver Horde* (1930) which was filmed on location at a working cannery only thirty miles south of the Union Bay cannery. Many times when I was stuck during the writing of this memoir, I'd put this movie in and be re-inspired.

I would like to thank Bjorn Dihle, author of *Haunted Inside Passage* and *Never Cry Halibut*, for encouraging me to write this memoir in the first place and giving me the name of his editor to help make publishing it a reality.

The entire team at West Margin Press has been enthusiastic and adaptable, taking in their stride my remote location which caused occasional hiccups in preparing and marketing this book. Publisher Jen Newens walked me patiently through contract negotiations, editor Olivia Ngai helped refine my manuscript, marketing manager Angela Zbornik never ran out of exciting ideas to promote *Raised in Ruins*, and Rachel Metzger came up with the fabulous cover and design of the book. I am sure there are more people behind the scenes whose names I don't know who have worked hard getting this book out there and I thank them too.

Family and friends have been amazing throughout the writing of this book, with special thanks to my uncle Rory and my aunt Marion, my uncle Lance Bifoss, my cousins Shawn Bifoss and Darrell Lee, and close family friend Linda Forbes who all contributed their memories to this book.

I'm especially grateful to my siblings, Jamie Neilson, Megan Duncanson, Robin Neilson, and Chris Neilson; they all helped me in writing this book by sharing their memories, and in other ways.

Megan helped me in ways too numerous to list, everything from always providing a listening ear, to reminiscing for hours, to doing online work when my signal was too weak for me to do it, and more. Chris recorded our lives while we lived at the cannery on cassette and listening to it brought it all back. Robin's independent research introduced me to Li Gongpu and George Tsutakawa. Jamie brought up details I'd forgotten.

Most of all, I would not have had this adventure and this life to write about if it hadn't been for Gary and Romi Neilson embracing the idea of bringing up their children in the remote ruins of a burned cannery. I will always be grateful to my parents for giving me Alaska. They've supported me through every stage of this book.

I thank my dad for teaching me to never quit (and for helping me map the cannery), and my mom for teaching me that if it can be imagined, it can be made real (and for her amazing photos, including the cover).

And finally, I'd like to thank my younger self for obsessively writing down everything that happened in my remote Alaskan childhood in journals and crumpled notebooks. They were a treasure trove that provided me with entire conversations and details I'd long since forgotten.

I wish I could tell her this book would one day be written.

Most of all, I thank my Creator for giving me the ongoing adventure of life and time.